In the Chair

In the Chair

Barrington-Ward of *The Times*,
1927-1948

DONALD McLACHLAN

WEIDENFELD AND NICOLSON
5 WINSLEY STREET LONDON W1

SBN 297 00305 4

Printed in Great Britain by
Willmer Brothers Limited, Birkenhead

I dedicate this book to the Warden
and Fellows of Nuffield College, Oxford,
whose hospitality and friendship I enjoyed
for eight memorable years.

Contents

CONTENTS

Illustrations List

PUBLISHER'S NOTE
The death of Donald McLachlan occurred
on 10 January, 1971, shortly after he had
passed *In the Chair* for press.

Preface

For some years while I was in Fleet Street there was in my mind a half-formed plan to write a memoir of Robin Barrington-Ward of *The Times*, for whom I had worked first when he was deputy editor of the paper and later when he was Editor. I felt very strongly that the last volume of the *History of The Times*, published in 1952 only four years after his death, had passed on him a premature and perfunctory verdict. Rather less strongly I felt that Geoffrey Dawson, too, had been unjustly treated and that this envious judgement, largely made by the late Stanley Morison, must not be allowed to stand as the last word on either man. I discovered that virtually none of the members of the staff of my generation (I joined the paper in 1933 at the age of twenty-five) had been consulted by Morison and that some of my former colleagues – though not all – shared my disagreement with his verdict.

When I found myself free to write, I realized for the first time the full scope of the Barrington-Ward diaries, fairly detailed daily records of office and family life over twenty-one years. These gave the most intimate account I had ever read of a newspaper editor at work. It seemed desirable to his widow and sons – one of them himself an editor – that the cream of these diaries should be available to the public. Not only do they reveal much that is interesting and important about the public life of the thirties and forties but they also present an engrossing picture of a man worth knowing for his own sake.* So the memoir swelled into a biography.

*About himself as diarist B-W wrote on 27 December 1946: 'A good diary requires (a) the diarist's indefinable gift (which I do not possess), something quite apart from ordinary literacy; (b) leisure for writing (ditto) and (c) opportunity to get things recorded at once while all the detail is fresh (ditto).' He overlooked a fourth quality, which these diaries undoubtedly have, contact with important events and interesting people. Elsewhere he explains that his father

The difficulty that then arose was to prevent the book becoming overwhelmingly polemical. Having supported 'appeasement' myself from 1937 onwards (although opposed to it between 1933 and 1937) I realized that some of the most damaging charges made against these two editors might be refuted in the course of my narrative. The desire to do so I have tried to keep within bounds. It would be undesirable, for example, to devote much of Barrington-Ward's biography to defending Geoffrey Dawson. That task has still to be performed in the light of all that is now known about the motives of British foreign policy and the limitations of British power. None the less, some explanation of *The Times*'s policy in the thirties is offered in the course of describing Barrington-Ward's work as deputy editor and frequent writer after 1935 on European affairs. As an individual he has more responsibility than Dawson had for the way in which the argument in favour of agreement with Germany was conducted.

The temptation to polemics was no less strong when I reached the period of his own editorship (1941–8). For then *The Times* was often at loggerheads with Winston Churchill, E. H. Carr was writing the principal leading articles and politically the paper was moving – in the view of most readers – to the left of centre. Again, I have refrained from making a detailed defence, this time against critics from the right, for whom Barrington-Ward's appeasement of post-war Russia was as objectionable and outrageous as was the appeasement of pre-war Germany to men and women of the left.

Polemics apart, the central purpose of the book remains to give a picture of a remarkably conscientious, intelligent, kind and brave man editing a great newspaper, living his official and family social life, undergoing a typical Edwardian preparation for the heaviest responsibilities, a militant lover of peace who survived one war determined to do all in his power to avert another, but who died too young to show what he could achieve with a full-sized paper and a staff chosen by himself.

---

had kept a diary continuously for over sixty years. After his death 'it seemed to me that the least I could do was to take it up where he had left it off and carry it on.' If allowed his three score years and ten, there would then be in existence a day-to-day record of one century of family life. It was only gradually that the family chronicle gave way to the *aide-mémoire* of the journalist – and then never entirely.

I have not resisted the temptation to play here and there the role of guide round Printing House Square, Blackfriars, the old office in the shadow of St Paul's Cathedral – now vanished – in which even my generation could feel the spirit of the great Victorians, with its 'companionship' of writers who were at once so aloof from and yet so much part of the Fleet Street a few hundred yards away. I was also influenced by the wish that politicians, historians and others interested in the conduct of public affairs should understand under what pressures the publishing of news and views was and still is done.

Because the biography of Stanley Morison is being written by Mr Nicholas Barker and because I did not wish to overload and unbalance the treatment of Barrington-Ward, I have made no detailed criticism of the last volume of the *History of The Times*. Its bias is clear – even though Morison himself supported appeasement at the time – and reference to the files of the paper will show how selective is its choice of quotations. It is most charitably regarded as a premature attempt to defend the paper against much ill-informed and malicious criticism and as a source hardly comparable in value with the excellent earlier volumes of the *History*. It was written under the influence of passions which are now spent or subsiding. Moreover, in its concentration on foreign policy (the account of the abdication episode is the only notable exception) the chapters give a misleading picture of how a newspaper is conducted.

If the impression is often given that the handling of news or comment in *The Times* had a decisive effect on the course of events, it is not because I believe that to have been so in each particular situation, but because there was a conviction in the office that it would be so. The tradition was that its paramount influence had been and must be kept decisive. In the Editor, leader-writers, correspondents and sub-editors alike – a few cynics apart – there was a sense of deep responsibility, of undisputed eminence, and of participation in the running of the country inherited from the great Victorians. How strong this was is most vividly shown in the change which came over a strong and critical personality like Stanley Morison. From being a critical, even mocking collaborator with the paper, he became so much its ardent defender that he found it necessary when writing the last part of the fourth volume of his

History, to attack Dawson and Barrington-Ward as men in order to defend *The Times* as an institution.

I have had the rare privilege of access to the archives of *The Times*, granted by the present Editor, Mr William Rees-Mogg, shortly after he succeeded Sir William Haley. My debt to Mrs Adele Barrington-Ward and her children, and also to other relatives, is obvious not only in the copious quotations I have been allowed to use but in many personal anecdotes. Sir Michael Barrington-Ward, the only surviving brother, and his sisters have been most helpful with advice and corrections. Likewise his niece Mrs Sylvia Crabtree, whose family connections with Westminster School and Balliol College give her a special understanding of her uncle, and his cousin Sir John Ward. Sir Harold Hartley, as a relative by marriage, a Fellow of Balliol and a Director of *The Times*, gave me a unique *vue d'ensemble*.

I am much indebted too to my old colleagues, the archivists of *The Times*: first to John Maywood, who was head of the Intelligence Department when I joined the paper as a sub-editor in 1933 and who retired in 1970 at the age of eighty-two, and then to his colleague Reginald Easthope.

Old colleagues of Printing House Square who have spent much time helping me are Sir Colin Coote, leader-writer there throughout the thirties and later Managing Editor of the *Daily Telegraph;* Iverach McDonald, now Associate Editor of the paper, who worked continuously with Barrington-Ward as a foreign affairs specialist from 1936 to his death in 1948; Donald Tyerman, formerly Deputy Editor and afterwards Editor of *The Economist;* Edward Hallett Carr, Fellow of Trinity College, Cambridge, leader-writer and Assistant Editor from 1941 to 1946; Arthur Crook, present Editor of *The Times Literary Supplement;* Oliver Woods, J. L. Garvin's stepson, who knew Barrington-Ward as friend and editor, Assistant Editor 1951 to 1966; H. C. Dent, former Editor of *The Times Educational Supplement;* G. L. Pearson, Chief Foreign Sub-editor in the thirties and forties; Dermot Morrah, leader-writer in the same period; James Holburn, former Editor of the *Glasgow Herald*, who was sub-editor, leader-writer and Berlin Correspondent in the thirties; Arthur Barker, later News Editor of the BBC, who was Diplomatic Correspondent at that time; Douglas Woodruff, who later became Editor of the *Tablet;*

Derek Hudson helped specially on the Editor's day and handling of letters.* Friends of Barrington-Ward's Westminster and Balliol days who have helped me include Lord Adrian, Sir G. G. Williams, D. M. Low, Sir. G. N. Clark, Sir Adrian Boult, Mr Norman Knight and Dr Lawrence Tanner.

I have also to thank Sir Edward and Lady Ford for access to the late Lord Brand's papers and Lord Reith and Sir Campbell Stuart for much advice and information. I was fortunate to have the help of the late Sir Basil Liddel Hart, who unfortunately did not live to read the finished M.S.

References to sources will be found at the back of the book with the following abbreviations:

P.D.   The private, unpublished diaries of R. M. Barrington-Ward.

T.T.A.   The Archives of *The Times* at Printing House Square.

B.W.L.   The collection of letters to and from R. M. Barrington-Ward in the possession of his family.

G.D.P.   Papers of Geoffrey Dawson.

*From 1933–6 the author worked at Printing House Square or abroad as sub-editor and foreign correspondent, with three periods of a few months each in Berlin; from 1936–8 as outside contributor of special investigations; from 1939–40 as Editor of the *Educational Supplement*, and after the war as leader-writer, assistant to Stanley Morison and temporary diplomatic correspondent (1946–7).

Introduction

That low man seeks a little thing to do,
  Sees it and does it:
This high man, with a great thing to pursue,
  Dies ere he knows it.
  Robert Browning: A Grammarian's Funeral

Like Banquo's role in *Macbeth,* the part played by the Editor of *The Times* in the drama of State and Empire between the two world wars was both crucial and subordinate. If his power over events has been exaggerated, his influence on people has probably been underrated. Because he had made it his business to know so much of public affairs, and to be known by so many in public life, Geoffrey Dawson was consulted on terms of intimacy by statesmen, officials, politicians and churchmen. Indeed, they were as near to equality as a journalist, whose business it is to disclose, can expect to be with persons of power, whose interest it is to conceal. Because his newspaper was still in many respects the gazette of the British ruling class – announcing (for a fee) their births and betrothals, their weddings and social engagements, while marking with solemn prose (gratis) their promotions and their deaths – its goodwill was sought, its help solicited. Claiming their custom by such services, the power of *The Times* over its readers lay in its ability to project day by day in news and comment what the Establishment in its various groups was wanting, thinking and saying. It also took great care to be the journal of record *par excellence.** Its reward for the pains taken was a privileged position in many capitals for its representatives and access to confidences and advice which were more often than not denied to rivals. To 'write a letter to *The Times* about it' was, people

---

**The Times says of itself in its *History*: 'To him [Northcliffe] the paper owes its being as a national daily newspaper and register, the epitome of the world for the information of the whole range of executive, professional and political men and women, who by their calling, intelligence and education, rank as the most influential constituency in Great Britain.'

believed, to be admitted to a platform of unrivalled influence – almost like making a public broadcast. In the eyes of its readers, perhaps three-quarters of a million strong, the Editor whose correspondence secretary they pleaded with on the telephone was a sort of Ombudsman – though they did not yet know the word.

In the power and status enjoyed by Dawson during his second spell as Editor his deputy could not help sharing, even if he had been a man of less ability and character than Robin Barrington-Ward.* For a hundred times a year, or more, he was 'in the chair' at night; for the rest he would be carrying out a host of duties inside and outside the office which the Editor readily delegated to him. He had been appointed in 1927 as someone having already, through his social and political circle, status and influence. If B-W, son of an HM Inspector of Schools, of Winton House, Westminster School and Balliol, had not quite the *cachet* of Dawson, the bank manager's son educated at Aysgarth, Eton College, Magdalen and All Souls, he had for three years (1915–18) shared with distinction the ordeal of his generation in the trenches, winning the MC, DSO and his majority. Then he had served for eight years as assistant to that remarkable and creative editor, J. L. Garvin of the *Observer*. If his academic record was less distinguished, he had none the less been a Scholar of his college and a good President of the Oxford Union.

Many contemporaries judged B-W's ability as first-class. John Reith, preparing to leave Broadcasting House in 1938, was convinced that here was the right man to succeed him as Director-General of the BBC. The Labour Minister, Herbert Morrison, used to praise B-W to the paper's Parliamentary Correspondent as someone who 'would make a fine judge'. Churchill respected and liked him, despite their disagreements. Friends like Adrian Boult, Kurt Hahn, Vincent Massey, J. L. Garvin, both respected and loved him. He is remembered at Printing House Square (a few critical colleagues excepted) as an outstandingly just man – a reputation not easily or often acquired in Fleet Street. He was always welcome in London to the select circles where men of influence met regularly to eat,

---

* Robert McGowan Barrington-Ward was known to all friends and colleagues as B-W, and this abbreviation will be used henceforth.

drink and talk together: Grillion's, the Literary Club, the Beefsteak, the Circus.

What did he look like, this quick-minded, charming, conscientious journalist who had no serious rival for the succession when Dawson came to the end of twenty-five years as Editor? Colleagues remember best the keen often worried look of searching and brilliant brown eyes, heritage of a Spanish ancestress; also the alert, bird-like carriage of the long bald head, and the brisk, precise walk of the Light Infantryman. He was short, slightly but strongly built, incessantly energetic. He was generally seen (as Low's cartoon shows him) in double-breasted black jacket and pin-stripe trousers. With Anthony Eden hat and rolled umbrella, walking the mile and a half from his St James's Square Club to his Blackfriars office, he might be taken for a Regular officer. If he sometimes dangled and fidgeted with his spectacles he was never seen with hands in trouser pockets, or propping up a wall or perching on the corner of a desk. B-W, like Dawson, was always on the go, a live wire.

One might suspect, watching the nodding head and the raised eyebrows, a certain wariness and lack of humour, only to be disconcerted by the merry smile that transformed the whole face after a flash of wit or repartee. Whatever he was talking about seemed at the time grave and urgent; he sometimes sounded sententious as he handed back an article or corrected a proof, saying that this or that simply could not be done in *The Times*. Yet among family and friends he was gay, relaxed, full of fun for his three children. Some thought him a typical Englishman; but he felt most at home in his mother's Cornwall and there was a strong Ulster strain in him. As well as kindness and sympathy, there showed puritanism and the tension that goes with it; the newly appointed women's editor noticed it when she proposed to write on her page about cosmetics and underwear. Such matters, he said, were better 'left behind the bedroom door'. At a desk he was more impressive than standing; but at Westminster he had been adjudged a strict prefect, something of a martinet, and he was an excellent infantry officer. For what it is worth as evidence of character, his handwriting was beautifully neat and well-formed, even in the hurried jottings of daily diaries.

Some friends of B-W think that Dawson made too great

demands on him, even exploited his passionate sense of duty to the office. The diary will throw light on this; but it may be observed that deputy editors aspiring to the chair are likely to seize any opportunity of showing their stamina and capacity. B-W, who was a most loyal assistant for fourteen years, may have deferred too much to his chief's judgement; but Dawson was a formidable personality and brilliant journalist, with twenty years of editing behind him, who had stood up to and broken with Northcliffe, and then returned to the chair on his own terms. At the farewell lunch given to him in 1941 by his staff the menu offered a tribute in verse by one of his colleagues:

> The glancing smile, the devastating glare,
> The Jovian nod, the rapt Olympian air,
> The eagle puissance, ample graciousness.

Awe in his presence was understandable.

Entries in B-W's diary for June 1938, when he was Deputy Editor and had an opportunity of leaving *The Times,* show what the man felt for his newspaper. They are presented as a foretaste of much more to be quoted from its pages:

Reith rang me up at the office in the morning to thank me for the leader and to tell me that I was being mentioned among possible candidates for his job as Director-General at the BBC. Was I prepared to stand? I had not been prepared to leave *T.T.* for the job of No. 2. Would I for the job of No. 1? I replied that I had no promise of the succession at *T.T.* in my pocket but that I felt I had a duty to the paper. Would I decline an offer of the post, he then asked. This seemed a large question to answer off-hand. I hesitated and he said he understood.[1]

B-W then went into a nursing home to have a cartilage removed. He was looking forward to a rest, he noted, for 'I have been rather over-driven at the office the last few days and my margin is smaller than it should be.' There, while he was still seeing no visitors, the offer was repeated by telephone, Reith having now spoken to J. J. Astor, Chairman of *The Times.*

Reith rang me up. I said we mustn't start from false premises. I was tied to *T.T.* by duty and interest and they had first claim upon me. I had a certain expectation of succeeding G.D.—when, I did not know. But I could not refuse an offer from the BBC on the grounds that *T.T.* wanted me. It was for *T.T.* to say that. He said that he had been staying at Hever for the week-end and had begun to talk to John Astor: had said 'We want a fellow like B-W.' John had replied 'Oh, don't go and take him.' Then the conversation had been interrupted. Reith asked me, should he talk to J. J. A. [Astor] or G.D.? I said that, in G.D.'s place, I should wish to be consulted first. There we left it.

I shall hear no more. D.G. of the BBC is a job I should in many ways like to do—one worth doing apart from the pay. But my goal and my training have been *The Times*. It is a far harder job and the financial reward is less, but I haven't the least doubt that I want, and ought, to take it on if the opportunity is to come.[2]

Three days later Dawson called on him at the nursing home. It was Sunday morning.

Then G.D. who opened up at once on the BBC. Ronnie Norman and Lady Bridgeman had been at him about my possible candidature for Reith's job. They had said (echoing my talk with Reith) 'If *The Times* claims him, of course we give him up.' 'Oh no,' G.D. had answered, 'he must be consulted himself.' He [Dawson] didn't intend to go on much longer and he knew of no one else to take on after him, though he added ' I don't nominate my successor.'

I said I thought duty and interest held me to P.H.S. My training and experience fitted me for work there particularly, and editing *T.T.* is the bigger job. He told me to think it over and he would talk to John Astor . . .

If I stood for the BBC job and were selected, I should come into £8,000 a year and should have given up 'the most exacting of all work'—executive night-work in journalism. But it would be *il gran rifinito,** after all, to abandon a life's ambition on reaching it and to leave *T.T.* before younger men are ready to take it on.[3]

Early the following week the episode was finished, with B-W still in bed.

Reith rang up: 'Well, that's definite, is it?' Myself: 'Yes. It's a great job for any candidate to think of, but feel that my business lies at P.H.S.' He then went on to say that he would have loved handing over to me. The thing was his child. He felt I understood it and I was always 'so decent' to himself.

I hope I *am* right. My motives are mixed. I feel I should have shirked something in giving up *T.T.* I feel too that *T.T.* gives me a better and more direct way of having some hand in the events of one's own day, and that is not, I hope, a contemptible ambition.[4]

*'The great refusal' of Dante's *Divine Comedy*, Inferno 1, 60.

The diary shows how exercised was B-W's conscience by this episode, which may, however, have hastened the offer of the editorship. But nearly a whole crisis-riddled year was to pass before Dawson, giving his deputy a lift home in the office car, said that he had offered his resignation to the Chairman to take effect before the end of 1939. Not entirely surprised, but sad at the thought of breaking the long partnership, B-W said he could hardly conceive of the office without G.D. Knowing Dawson's dislike of a 'scene' he said no more. A fortnight later, on 18 May, Astor offered him the editorship, which he at once accepted.* War was less than four months off.

Taking over in 1941, the new Editor was to have four years of that war and three only of peace before dying on holiday in East Africa of cerebral malaria. It was a short time to show what he could do on his own; during the whole of it limits were set to experiment and change by strict newsprint rationing and by the slow economic recovery of the nation. Yet his was a measurable and memorable achievement. It is the task of the biographer not only to explain – and if possible to defend – his work of the thirties in foreign affairs and in the general conduct of the paper, but also to compare with it his work of the forties. His thinking and behaviour during both periods were rooted in the same principles, in the same hopes, but the achievements have been very differently judged.

What his hopes were he set down in the diary on his fiftieth birthday, Sunday, 23 February 1941, a few months before he became Editor.

My life was really forfeit in 1914 and it is the merest, the least deserved of flukes that I have survived to enjoy so much of which war robbed the pick of my contemporaries. The more reason to remember the mission which August 1914 and survival have to-gether set men like me—namely, to strive for the creation and organization of peace, above all things, and for the liberating truths at home, at whatever cost to conventional opinion. Revolution cannot do it. It is to be questioned whether revolution as such has ever achieved anything *on balance*: but evolution, active and painful evolution must. On my own humble anniversary it is well to have this old resolution sharp and clear again.[5]

---

*A detailed account of events leading to B-W's accession is given in Chapter 17

'An old resolution', we notice, made in the trenches twenty-five years earlier; and the 'liberating truths' are those he discussed with his Greats tutor at Balliol. Both before and after the Second World War, which he had vowed to prevent, the man was guided and sustained by these convictions. His perplexities, the strain on mind and nerves, were to some extent created by the steadfast effort to apply to the brutal political facts and men of 1936 and 1946 the aspirations of 1916. It is in the light of this self-dedication that his career must be judged.

1

A Nursery of Nine

'A real son of the manse,' said one of *The Times* staff returning from his Editor's memorial service at St Paul's Cathedral in March 1948. The error was easily made, for it was in a Cornish rectory that B-W had spent his vacations from Oxford and it was the quiet and beauty of the garden and small farm at Duloe between Liskeard and West Looe that he longed for as he wrote home in 1915 from the trenches in Flanders. For fifteen years of bachelorhood Duloe was home, and friends from pre-war Oxford and post-war London who went to stay there may easily have come to think that it had always been so. For only rarely did Robin mention the house in Worcestershire where he was born in 1891, the fourth of five sons. It was not until he was eighteen and in his last year at Westminster (1909) that his father was presented by Balliol College to the living of Duloe, having just been ordained at the remarkably late age of sixty-four. Perhaps, however, there was not in those days all that difference between a parsonage home and the household of a deeply religious Inspector of Schools, save the frequent absence of the father on his journeys and the resulting dominant influence of the mother – to which all who knew them testify.

Childhood was spent in a large house just outside Worcester called Thorneloe Lodge, where Mark James Barrington-Ward and his wife Caroline kept three servants and a gardener, and brought up nine children in modest comfort on an earned income of less than £1,000 a year. They lived there because the father's work lay in Worcestershire and the industrial parts of Warwickshire, inspecting and examining in schools. It was the exciting period when the great Education Act of 1870, brought in by Gladstone's government, was for the first time bringing a school within the reach of every child. Payment to the new local school boards was by results, so the opinion and favour of Her Majesty's Inspector was sought even more eagerly than it is now.

Affectionate, self-sufficient, ambitious, energetic, high-principled are the words that fall together into a picture of the family after one has talked with Robin's surviving brother and the clan of cousins. They reared one another as large nurseries do, in a self-disciplining community, Robin being helped and curbed by brothers Fred, Lance and Michael, from eleven to four years older than himself. When they had gone to school and university he became in turn the mentor of the sisters and John. Life in two acres of garden and a coach-house was simple, noisy and gang-like; football on the tennis lawn, cricket balls hit into the greenhouses, no special holidays, music and theatre made at home, little entertainment and no great need for friends.

Caroline Barrington-Ward's simple rule was 'Always be kind to everyone'. There was a notably sweet nature in this very beautiful woman, fifteen years younger than her husband. She had lost her father young and had known hard times working in London before she married. The whole family was deeply devoted to 'Mater' and the eldest boy confessed to feeling relief when he saw 'Pater's' Gladstone bag standing packed in the hall for one of his visits of inspection, leaving them with her alone. Michael, looking back, feels sure that these journeys were important for the family finances because the Inspector could live – and probably save – for a few days 'on expenses'.

Mrs Barrington-Ward, partly brought up in an uncle's vicarage, had a passion for self-improvement. Correspondence courses that she took led to an invitation to study at Cambridge, which she refused. Family legend says that Edward Elgar, related to the tuner who came to look after the two pianos at Thorneloe, once praised her performance and understanding of music. There was plenty of singing and acting as well as playing in the house.

The Inspector used to sing sentimental Irish songs to his children, accompanied by himself on the concertina, while they danced around the inner hall. If his wife did not read indus-triously to her children she certainly made them work at their books. It was she who noticed in *The Times* the advertisement of Tancred Law Studentships at Lincoln's Inn, won first by Fred and then by Robin. She was ambitious for her boys, as was her

9

husband. If he applied the spur, hers was the coaxing voice and firm but gentle hand on the reins.* Gwen, the eldest of the daughters, understandably a little jealous of Mater's absorption in the boys, wrote as a student at St Andrew's some verses in caricature.

> Oh how I love my dear, dear boys,
> For Heaven has me endowed
> With five good sons
> All virtuous
> Of them I am so proud.
>
> My girls are all quite nice and good
> As far as girls do go,
> But after dreaming of my boys
> I find them very slow.

And of Robin, his elder sister wrote:

> And there's Bob the pretty
> The flower of the flock,
> He's always been a gentleman
> Since the time he wore a smock.

Apple of his mother's eye though he might be, Robin was sent away at the age of six to board with her brother, the Rev. Lewis Pearson, headmaster of Market Bosworth Grammar School, where Michael already was. He was to be prepared for Westminster where Fred and Lance had won the title and emolument of Queen's Scholars, worth £90 a year towards total expenses of about £120. But the uncle's disciplinary methods were too stern, the boys were unhappy, and there was a quarrel between the headmaster and the Inspector. Robin was taken away after two years and returned to Miss Robson's

---

*What his mother meant to B-W was poignantly revealed in his diary when she died in 1938.

'As I said my last good-bye, the nurse spoke of her hands. The youth and grace of them were touching. None of her children has those hands. And the same loveliness was in her mind and spirit. Strong, beyond belief, in her character yet wholly self-effacing, almost too much so, all her life, with the impeccable wisdom of the heart. I never knew her do an ill-judged thing, much less, of course, a mean one. Not a scrap pietistic, but a Christian in every line of the grain. Infinitely sensitive, without the least touch of sentimentality, sweetened with an endearing sense of the ironic, always able to laugh at herself. Always forward-looking. A very good brain which among all the cares of a family of nine was never allowed to rust . . . As near a saint as I am ever likely to know. If there is anything worthwhile in us, she made it.'[1]

dame school at home. After a year there he went to Winton House, near Winchester, to join Mr Johns, an admirable schoolmaster and distinguished naturalist.

How could the Inspector with nine children afford the fees of such a good preparatory school? He advertised in the *Guardian* for a school that would prepare 'a promising boy' for a scholarship at Westminster, hinting possibly at some reduction in fees. A reply came from Mr Johns, who said he would be happy to undertake the preparation of Robin 'upon favourable terms provided that the present state of his work is such as to hold out a reasonable prospect of his success'. He mentioned that an assistant master, who had won a First at the university, would take two or three boys into his house where they would receive special coaching. A second letter from Johns then explained that 'the material upon which I have to work is of the dullest sort; and of forty boys or more I seldom have half a dozen who are capable of doing anything like scholarship work . . . so that my staff of Honoursmen is somewhat wasted and a really bright boy would be most welcome.' Robin duly won his scholarship at Westminster at twelve and was happy with Mr Johns, whose enlightened methods gave him a good knowledge of flowers and birds.

What sort of man was Robin's father? 'Hot tempered but quick to recover,' says an elder sister Phyllis. 'Strict but with an Irishman's twinkle in his eye,' says the elder brother Michael. 'A typical usher priest, who drove his sons and wore them out,' says a director of *The Times,* who disliked him. 'More of an Army Chaplain than a clergyman, with a piercing eye and clipped moustache,' says a niece. 'A high-principled man,' said all the teachers he had to do with: and a much-loved Rector of Duloe, who more than did his duty to the sick and unhappy and the young, said his parishioners. When he died, the *Cornish Times* carried a long obituary notice which mentioned 'outspokenness abrupt at times and never varied to suit occasions; exactness in transactions of every sort; vitality, warm impulsiveness and optimistic temper; passionate love of flowers and all Nature.' The writer of the tribute, it must be revealed, was Robin, and it presents a formidable personality.

Pater's memory was excellent, and he would never let uncertainty or vagueness of statement pass unchecked at meals: he would jump up immediately and verify in his books of reference. Hospitality was second nature to him and he was the most entertaining company. Add to this catalogue of virtues the intellectual record: at Oxford scholar of Hertford and First in Natural Sciences; first head of the Modern Side at Clifton College; thesis for Doctor of Divinity submitted and accepted at Oxford when seventy-six – and we see an heroic Victorian, with exceptional vigour and application and an appetite for academic and wordly success. (A visitor noticed that the members of the family, though as individuals very modest, often sang one another's praises.) It was Pater who used to tease Robin as a small boy about his handwritten *Thorneloe Chronicle* and say he would be editor of *The Times* one day. A curious prophecy to be heard in a family which could not afford *The Times* at threepence and took instead the *Standard* and the *Illustrated London News*.

The boys were rather amused by their father's belated enthusiasm for the priesthood and visitors found no marked religious atmosphere in the household, although the blaze of coloured academic hoods when the Doctor of Divinity preached and his five graduate sons sang in the choir of Duloe Church was one of the sights of south Cornwall. The Christianity of the Barrington-Wards was practical and personal. If at the last moment anyone jibbed at joining the family party to Matins or Evensong, Mater would say 'England is a free country, but please do not hang about in the hall.' Robin was influenced by his father's simple faith, which in him grew into a well thought out modernistic position which he was always ready in middle age to discuss on long walks with his own sons Mark and Simon. But here again one suspects the stronger influence was his mother, who wrote to him in 1924, 'I am sure you are happy, because you are so kind to people.'

These were people of the professional class, with no private means or influence to help them,* living far from London, who knew that each must earn his or her own living, and win as best it could be won what Cicero called 'comfort with honour'. The adjective 'worldly' is used with hesitation of a priest, but friends remembered how Pater had named his eldest son Frederick Temple, after the Lord Dufferin who had given him his first job; and one of his nieces remembers

---

*For a few years at Duloe the Rector took two or three private pupils for coaching, sent to him by A. L. Smith of Balliol.

with amusement the crest painted by the Rector on the doors of the old Ford in which he drove around his parish.

The stock they came from was an interesting mixture: Ulster on the male side and Cornish on the female. The Ulster line goes back to one of the earliest Plantations, successful middle-class all the way. Robin's grandfather was partner in the printing firm of Marcus Ward and Sons in Belfast, famous in the sixties and seventies for its services to art and education, for its Christmas cards, calendars and colour printing. Walter Crane and Kate Greenaway, creators of the modern illustrated book for children, worked for Ward's in London. Robin's father Mark could presumably have made a career in the firm; but a quarrel had split the family and he came to England to finish his education and recorded his renunciation with the prefix Barrington.

Robin's mother traced her family back on the one side to John Brendon, a yeoman settled in the Cornish parish of St Dominic, who built himself in the mid-eighteenth century a house called Westcott. On the other side she claimed as ancestor Sir Henry Trecarrol, of Trecarrol near Launceston, who built the church of St Mary Magdalene in the town during the reign of James I.

With such a background the Barrington-Ward boys, although without social pretensions, could feel at ease in any Edwardian company.

John, the youngest of the five boys, who became a Tutor of Christ Church and was the finest Latin versifier of his time, once spoke to an interviewing journalist of a Spanish streak in the family. It was true enough and it may have shown itself in the eyes of Robin and others. For Eleanor McGowan, daughter of Robert McGowan (1753–1817) married a John Veacock, descended from a Spaniard called Vicoq who is said to have come in the early eighteenth century from Spain to Ireland in the train of the third Earl of Donegal. The matter is worth mentioning only to show the variety of strains which went to make a person whom some thought of as a typical Englishman of the upper class: Cornish, Ulster, English and Spanish. Perhaps they help to explain the mixture of brilliance and conventionality, of obstinacy and open-mindedness, of open-hearted charm and intense reserve which showed themselves as his character matured.

13

As we watch Robin moving industriously, and not always easily, towards eminence it is well to keep in mind the stimulus of those accomplished elder brothers.* Fred, eleven years older and regarded as the 'signpost' of the family, had been Queen's Scholar at Westminster; then, at Oxford, Scholar of Hertford, Vinerian Law Scholar and All Souls Fellow – all before Robin had left school. He was to become K.C. in 1919 and to challenge counsel like Patrick Hastings in success and wealth. There was a sad decline in his later years which gave Robin much anxiety.

Then there was Lance, seven years older, for whom Robin felt the greatest affection and respect. He had given up his scholarship at Westminster for health reasons and moved to Bromsgrove School. As medical student at Edinburgh University he worked his way quickly up, with an early FRCS, to be chief surgeon at the Children's Hospital in Great Ormond Street and at the Royal Northern Hospital. He was surgeon to King George VI and Queen Elizabeth. In 1909 he played in the England Rugby team. Socially Sir Lancelot was the most accomplished of the brothers.

Next came Michael, four years older. King's Scholar at Westminster and sent to Edinburgh University (on Fred's advice) to study engineering. When the 1914 war came he was Assistant to the General Superintendent of the Midland Railway. With a DSO and the rank of Lieutenant Colonel he was Director of Operations at the Ministry of Transport in 1919. When he retired with a KCVO in 1953 he had been divisional general manager of the London North-Eastern Railway and a member of the Railway Executive for six years.

Last came John, three years younger than Robin, who also had the help of Mr Johns in winning a King's Scholarship at Westminster and was the best pure scholar of them all. In 1914 he won both the Hertford Scholarship and the Chancellor's Prize for Latin Verse at Oxford. After the war he was a Student and Classical Tutor at Christ Church, and had Quintin Hogg as a pupil. The only disappointment in this brilliant academic

*He used to say after he became a journalist that 'introduction with us is nearly always a process of identification. On a golf course: "Are you the K.C.?" No. "Then you must be the surgeon?" No. "Or the railwayman!!" No. "Then you are on the *Observer*." Yes.'

career was his failure to be chosen as headmaster of his old school.

They made a distinguished company, these five sons who touched the world of affairs at many points, when they met together at the Windham Club in the twenties for the annual birthday dinner to their father, now a canon of Truro. One may doubt whether any of them would then have picked Robin, the youngest but one, to achieve the greatest eminence; but it was already clear that he was the brother who would do most for the lame ducks of the family – organize an income for Mater, help the unmarried sisters in their careers, reorganize the finances of Fred. He was a man to whom people found themselves naturally turning for support and understanding. Garvin was to cherish his characteristic of helpfulness; so was Geoffrey Dawson. It was inherited from and nurtured by his mother, perhaps the most important contribution made by family life to the shaping of the future editor.

2

King's Scholar and Captain

'He's small but he's very consequential.'
College butler at Westminster

Robin was small and remarkably young – only twelve and a
half – when he arrived as a boarder at Westminster School in
September 1903. He was the fourth – and not the last – of the
five Barrington-Ward brothers to win the cherished title and
emoluments of King's Scholar, which provided in College an
almost free education. His second brother Michael was still in
the school and as he walked for the first time – a little
frightened and awe-struck – up that gaunt stone back stair-
case, with its high rail, which led to College dormitories, he
would have seen on a board the name of his eldest brother Fred
as captain of the King's Scholars in 1898–9. Westminster,
despite its intellectual and social prestige, was a 'poor man's
school' in which eighteenth century traditions were still strong.
The sons of professional men, who made up most of the 270
boys in these famous buildings, were left outside the classroom
largely to govern themselves. Any boy who came to the top as
captain of the school or head of his house, as Robin was to do
in the next five years, needed courage, personality and
managing qualities above the average, especially if he was not
a star performer in games.

For the forty King's Scholars in College, and for those in the
boarding houses, it was a tough and often cruel society, competitive and hard-working. Life was easier for the day boys,
who went home of an evening in their top-hats and tails – one
of the capital's minor spectacles – to take part in the life of
their families; if, that is to say, they had any spare time. For it
was stated in the school rules that 'except for very young or
forward boys, the preparation of lessons at home ought not
to occupy less than two hours and a half hour each day, while
backward boys and those in high forms should be ready to give
more time to it'.

16

The forty in College formed a privileged, self-contained, somewhat aloof, society which looked down on the day boys. Westminster was run very much as a boarding school and the domination of College in the memorable past had been as much social as intellectual. King's Scholars and Boarders lived and fed in the primitive, uncomfortable style then accepted without question in the great public schools.

I am glad [Robin wrote home in his first term] that Westminster was made out to be such an awful place when I was at home.... I find it an Elysium compared to the vivid description of it given me.... The food is chiefly tea, beef, bread and butter, which is at all events wholesome.[1]

But Old Westminsters of Robin's generation – men like Lord Adrian, the physiologist, D. M. Low, the biographer of Gibbon, and Sir Adrian Boult, the conductor – say without hesitation and qualification that he, like them, was happy. They were, it is true, unlike Robin, home boarders and therefore did not experience the bullying during the idle weekends in College; but against the dull grind of the largely classical curriculum, the limited opportunities for games, the poor teaching – with one or two exceptions – in modern subjects and the philistinism of many of the boys they bear no grudge or grievance.

Like most of the older public schools which found it difficult to adapt their ancient buildings to changing conditions, the school had gone down in repute and performance during the nineteenth century. In the forties its numbers were down to sixty-seven; now they were rising. When Robin joined, Dr James Gow, the new headmaster, had been there only two years. Coming from Nottingham High School, he had been expected to show impatience of the ways of a privileged community which had spent three hundred years in the shadow of the neighbouring Abbey. Instead, in his first year, with the help of the school's most popular assistant master, John Sargeaunt, Gow reasserted for the Coronation of Edward VII an ancient privilege of the King's Scholars which, after sixty years of Queen Victoria's rule, had almost slipped from living memory. Pressed by Gow and Sargeaunt, the Court of Claims confirmed the ancient privilege of the KSS to be the first to acclaim the Sovereign, as he entered the Abbey, with their 'Vivats'. Gow arranged that some town boys should be admitted to the

17

Triforium, in addition to the forty King's Scholars, thus assembling a formidable battery of voices. So it came about that when King Edward reappeared from the Chapel of the Confessor, to pass down the Nave to the West Door, Dr Gow called on his Westminsters for three cheers. 'The effect,' said an eye-witness, 'was electrifying. A mighty burst of acclamation rolled around the Abbey.' This unrehearsed scene was entirely unauthorized but was, fortunately, highly pleasing to the King. Twenty years later, Robin, then assistant editor of the *Observer*, wrote in a memoir* of this robust and vigorous headmaster that 'Dr Gow braved the occasion with a masterful indiscretion'.

For most of the King's Scholars the education was overwhelmingly in the Latin and Greek classics, although there was a modern side for science and languages. The 'grand old fortifying curriculum' eventually presented to the boys of the Sixth and Seventh some glimpse of the beauties of philosophy and poetry, and it imparted incidentally some knowledge of ancient history; but the emphasis was on the meticulous use of Greek, Latin and English words, on the writing of versions and translations and – most difficult of all – on the composition of verses. This required of the pupil real application and of the teacher stern drilling: it was a process of learning to learn, and of fitting words together which was good training for a future journalist. What was the point of it otherwise few people ever asked. What had been in medieval times a vocational training for the new men coming into the service of Church and State had become the traditional preparation for scholarship and degree examinations, which in turn were the qualifying tests for such professions as teaching, the law, politics, civil service, literature and journalism.† A special History Sixth had only just been formed by Gow, mathematics ceased in the Sixth and formal English teaching in the Seventh was no more than the occasional essay set by the headmaster. There was simply a recognized ladder to be climbed and Robin set about climbing it, as his brothers did, with determination. He was to learn the

---

Selected Adresses of James Gow (Macmillan, 1924).

†Lord Adrian, O.M., former Master of Trinity, Cambridge, and one of the outstanding scientists of his generation, found Westminster "very weak on mathematical teaching, except for the teaching of one or two boys who specialized in it. I never got much idea of what it was all about and used to regret my ignorance later on.' (To the author, November 1969.)

handling of English, like most writers of his day, by turning it into Latin and Greek – and vice versa.

The Abbey itself was the school's chapel and each day began with a short service in the Poets' Corner. This, on important Saints' Days, was moved to the Choir where, however, they were not invited to sing. If the intellectual and social life was narrow, an important stimulus to some boys was the King's Scholar's right of access to the House of Commons. In white tie and gown he might walk straight up to the Strangers' Gallery at Question Time, or during the debates in the early evening, and listen to Joseph Chamberlain, Asquith, Lloyd George, Balfour and other giants of the Liberal-Tory duels of that exciting time.* His friend and contemporary, Lawrence Tanner, says that by the time he left school he had heard in the House every political speaker of any merit. Robin's ambition to practise politics – and journalism as a way of getting into politics – may have been inspired by these experiences, for he was very active in the school's debating society, which caught something of the flavour and style of the Chamber three hundred yards away.

There were also the compensations of easy access to the city – by leave of course – visiting museums and galleries, auctions at Christies, plays and – with his older friend, Adrian Boult, then lanky and delicate – as many concerts as he cared to visit. There would be invitations to lunch and dine with friends and relatives.

Educationally, the memory that Robin's contemporaries most cherish is of being up to J. S. Sargeaunt in the Sixth for English and classics. Sargeaunt ('You spell my name, please, by writing "large aunt" and changing the first letter to "s" ') believed in teaching by digression, in any direction that his richly stored mind inclined to: botany, eighteenth- and nineteenth-century literature, history, contemporary happenings. He would come from Abbey to the classroom and ask 'What do we mean when we say "I believe in the resurrection of the body?" ' and for two or three hours would pursue his thought, ending up perhaps with the latest news of the digs at Herculaneum. One long lesson is recalled which began with a dis-

---

*When he was fifteen (in 1906) he wrote to his father: 'I shall go into the House this week to hear Mr Chamberlain whose ardent follower I am . . . You see the most awful looking tramps about. Labour Members no doubt.'

cussion of vegetables in Latin poetry and ended with the Duke of Connaught. He had little or no control of his form in detail but mastered it by his knowledge, wit and humour. Sargeaunt's wise and humorous face still presides over his old classroom from a plaque under the window, reminding Westminsters of the only assistant master who has rated an entry in the *Dictionary of National Biography* as well as a leading article in *The Times* when he died – written of course by his old pupil, R.M. B-W.

This inspiring teacher, who had been President of the Oxford Union in Curzon's time, had an infectious enthusiasm for English history and literature of the Augustan and later ages. H. W. Massingham said that his general knowledge of English literature was only equalled by Asquith's. . . . 'Literature meant to him what it meant to Dr Johnson – the noblest expression of the views and emotions of educated men of the world on the life of this world and the next'. 'When he talked,' wrote Douglas Jerrold who sat under him in the Sixth, 'he was quite literally inspired. He lost himself in the majesty of noble sentiments nobly expressed and attained an eloquence quite foreign to his individual personality.'[2]

The historian, David Low, a friend and exact contemporary, says that when Robin went to Oxford he was as good a classic as many of his year and at school in 1907 had won the much-prized Mure Scholarship. Sir G. G. Williams, another contemporary, a distinguished civil servant, says that the teaching of anything but the classics was bad. When B-W and others failed their Higher Certificate exams in non-classical subjects, they were deprived of their gowns for a couple of weeks as a punishment. In the top form, where they were prepared for their university scholarship examinations, they went 'hour after hour, four and a half days a week', to I. F. Smedley, a brilliant Cambridge classical scholar with a fine liberal mind, but 'rather a fusty schoolmaster'. There they were crammed and drilled, translating at the rate of 30–40 lines an hour. The sheer monotony of it provoked from Robin (scribbling in form *sub rosa*) a series of satirical sketches of Smedley's classroom ways, which Low and Williams edited and had set up in booklet form by a local printer. Here, if anywhere, the future journalist reveals himself. Brilliantly observed, with that cruel attention that boys apply to any eccentricity in those who teach them, the frailties of Snogger – as the master of the Seventh was known – still raise a chuckle from the non-Westminster reader. 'Idylls of the Idle, by One of Them,' it was called, 'Edited by More of Them.' What follows is B-W's picture of a boy called Wade translating from Latin:

IDYLL XIII

Wade: 'Me miseram-Er-wretched me!'
Sn: 'Ah! no, no. Do-er-do try and put some spirit into your translation. Ah-um-mum-er-ah-mum-er "what a wretch I am"-(hastily)-um-ah-well that's not very good-er-ah-"what a"-well-ah-"what a poor"-can anybody offer any suggestion for this? Um-well-"what a wretch I am"-(sniffs defiantly)-that'll ha-have to do. What does our man say?-of course you must not take his translation as dogma but-hum-well-"alas, also"-ah-(scratches the sides of his head with both hands)-well-(quickly) it's a small point-it's a small point-go on-go on-' (and so forth for three hours).

To judge by this little book of thirty-three pages, with its bow of blue ribbon, Robin had his full share of impudent mischief and was not easily quelled. On one occasion, as a quite senior boy, he was rebuked by a master called Fox for talking during one of those long sermons in which Canons Resident indulged on a Sunday afternoon. He went immediately to Dr Gow and complained, so it is said, of the master's behaviour; so that when the formidable Fox went to make his report he had a cool reception from a headmaster already apprised of the incident.

From the memories of contemporaries there emerges a short, wiry, determined, ambitious boy, with good looks, charm and self-confidence. Douglas Jerrold says B-W dominated the school in his last year 'with more than Roman gravity'. Lawrence Tanner, who kept a diary during his and Robin's last year at school, noted how 'B-Ward told us of a delightful description of himself when he was a junior by Flynne, the College Butler: "He's small but he's very consequential." It is so true.' This was written in November 1908, when Robin, then seventeen, thought of Low, Tanner and himself (Captain of the School as well as Captain of College) as 'the three top people'. A few months later Tanner noted (13 March 1909): 'Of course he rules College with a rod of iron, he is horribly drastic. I was astonished at the way he leapt on small juniors for various small things this afternoon. I shouldn't like to be a junior under him at all.'

If he was a martinet in authority – and freely used the cane – he had not been a bully. J. R. Wade, who was in the election junior to his, writes:

Westminster at that time was a pretty hard school. If the second election kept their juniors in order, so in their turn were the second election kept in their place. It was one of the duties of the second election to initiate the juniors into the ways of school and particularly College. This duty was often carried out in a very bullying way and our lot of second election certainly were not very gentle. Robin, however, was not among the bullies.

Adrian Boult, two years older than Robin, remembers him before he held the highest office as a relaxed, amusing and charming person. When they shared a tent at O.T.C. camp at Bisley, Boult wrote a musical setting to verses by Robin, who acquired such facility through his classical training that he was in his last year at Oxford runner-up in the Newdigate Prize for a poem on a set subject. Low, on the other hand, as Head Town Boy (*Princeps Oppidanorum* he was called) shared authority with the Captain of the School and remembers him as 'the most mature and statesmanlike schoolboy I have known. He was astute in handling boys *and* masters, who often had less breadth of view than he had. That is not to say he was pompous or a prig. Far from it: he was full of fun and had a pleasant gift of schoolboy ribaldry.'

Yet beneath this self-confidence there were the doubts of a thoughtful and essentially humble person, which revealed themselves – as we shall see later in his diaries – on the threshold of achievement. In the last term before his final promotion he wrote home: 'I sometimes feel inclined to renounce all idea of becoming Captain and to go and do something that will effectually prevent it. . . . The labour entailed is dreadful, besides which I am only too conscious of being unfit for the post.' (July 1908.)

Sir G. G. Williams relates, as an example of Robin's authoritative ways, that he protested to the headmaster about the inadequate and sometimes disgusting breakfast of porridge, sodden toast and tea which was all that the boys were offered day after day. Gow had to admit that he would be unable to persuade the Governing Body to make improvements, but gave the Captain of College £20 out of his own pocket to bring in some extras. With this money Robin and a couple of monitors would go foraging in the local markets and in the Army and Navy Stores close by in Victoria Street for eggs, bacon and sausages with which to vary their menu.*

His independence and strength of character showed themselves when the time came to decide for what Oxford college he should enter. The normal and obvious course was to compete for a closed scholarship at Christ Church, where Westminster enjoyed three privileged awards a year. But he had other ideas. He did not want, he said, to spend his Oxford days hemmed in by Old Westminsters. He had ambitions for the Union and politics, and for these the outstanding college was Balliol, then at the height of its academic and social supremacy. Gow firmly told Robin he was not good enough for Balliol, which attracted the best scholarship candidates from all over the country, and warned him that, if he failed there, Christ Church would be little inclined to accept another college's reject. None the less, he was determined to break with Westminster tradition, as was his friend Low. Both were successful, and Low became a scholar of Oriel at the same time that Robin became, to his immense pride, a scholar of Balliol, one of the highest distinctions that an ambitious and gifted schoolboy could then attain.

What Robin took away from Westminster is not easily separated from what he brought with him, but this much is certain: that he felt and expressed great affection for the school; worked for it continuously, even when most heavily burdened on *The Times;* and wrote movingly and affectionately about Gow, Sargeaunt and others. He was on the Finance Committee of the governing body from 1936 to 1946 and was the heart and soul of the Appeal which put the school's finances on a sound basis.† If he suffered in his early days, being

*'At Westminster,' wrote Philip Guedalla in the 'Isis Idol' of 4 May, 1912, 'he became a Leader of men, strong and silent, whose speech was as strong as his silences.'

† After the severe air raid of 11 May 1941 B-W went down to the school. 'I found School and College burnt-out shells, Little Cloister a shambles, the house of the Master of the King's Scholars less seriously damaged. A truly tragic scene in that quiet, innocent and sequestered setting. . . . I am not very sentimental but I came away sad. So much destroyed. All that lovely panelling with the blazoned arms up-School, most of the names. Still, the walls are strong.'[3]

small and very young, he neither spoke nor wrote about it later unlike his contemporary at St Paul's, Compton Mackenzie, who has recorded in *Sinister Street* the life of a London public day school at that period. Perhaps after Market Bosworth Grammar School and the harshness of his uncle, Westminster seemed mild. Perhaps, like so many sensitive and intelligent public-school boys of that time – and even of today – the memory of the last year or two of exciting intellectual awakening, of gradually growing responsibility, of sudden emergence from servitude to mastery, of prize and game-winning triumphs, grew over the scars of what had been humiliating and hurtful. If Robin came out on top of that community, it was not through physique or athletic success, but through intelligence and personality.

Add to the benefits of that experience a memory well-trained in storing facts; wits sharpened in argument and repartee by verbal fencing over translation and composition; working vocabulary enriched with metaphor and example and quotation, which would be immediately recognized by all educated men and women of his age; sensitiveness to rhythm and balance in a sentence, which was to display itself at length in leading articles for the Press. Altogether it was admirable equipment for the serious journalism of his day, with its 1,200 word leading articles and long, narrow columns of print.

He would probably have included some appreciation of what he learnt in self-confidence and bearing from his five appearances in the annual Westminster play, faithfully reported both before and during his years on *The Times*. In 1908 it was Terence's *Andria*, with Robin in the leading role of Davus, the slave. It was a great occasion, because on the first night HRH Princess Henry of Battenberg was present. In accordance with ancient custom for the reception of Royalty, the Princess, escorted by the headmaster and the Captain (R. M. B-W), was lighted across Yard by King's Scholars with torches. His performance, and that of J. L. Benvenisti, the other chief actor, were much praised. 'Benvenisti,' Sargeaunt remarked, 'is a born actor. B-Ward of course is not, but he has brains and can apply them, and consequently has made himself very good.' That may serve, perhaps, as his favourite teacher's epitaph on Robin's school career.

3

Days at Balliol

Oxford in 1909 was a university where the average tutor thought of himself as *in loco parentis.* Jowett, whose ideas were kept alive in Balliol by A. L. Smith, the historian, used to say 'I should like to make all my old pupils properly ambitious, if I could, of living like men and doing silently a real work.' Yet the disciplinary rules were still those of schoolboys, and the substantial section in some colleges of semi-serious rich men and lowbrow games players made undergraduate society as worldly as it was academic. Indeed, it was perhaps the leisurely and unscholarly who gave to that life in term-time the magic that Edwardian writers have tried with passion to record. Even Lord Birkenhead, who knew the Oxford of the twenties, has lately written in his *Life of Walter Monckton,* one of B-W's most intimate friends:

Fresh from the restrictions of school or a narrow home they passed through a magic gate into a new world, a place of beauty and freedom, where every taste could be enjoyed, a world of leisured ease, of fires in panelled rooms, of grey college walls, and of bells 'pouring on roses and creepers'.

A student of our own day, social conscience awakened, would have noted the service received by undergraduates from poorly-paid scouts, with whom they enjoyed a pleasantly feudal relationship: breakfast brought to rooms; clothes tidied; the personal attention of mostly bachelor dons, with a tutor-pupil ratio which would bring rebuke from Whitehall; the high number of cubic feet per student's room in college or digs. Also the anti-social behaviour at Balliol of such rich men's clubs as the Annandale, which regularly smashed glass on an epic scale; and the curious preponderance of public-school men in a college which had a reputation for radicalism and socialism.

25

But there were other reasons why Oxford was the Mecca of ambitious young men. It had the intense life of a capital without the bustle and noise of a city. The links with those who ran the nation and the Empire were close and continuous, rivalled only by those of Cambridge. There were generous and radical aspirations in the air, generating the ideas which within half a century were to transform the university.* Dons like Caird and Lindsay were appealing for social justice in terms which would still not sound strange. Yet, even though so many, here on the threshold of public life, were serious-minded and purposeful, there was endless gaiety, games-playing, acting, rowing, riding, dining and drinking. Their time was full.

Indeed, for B-W it was too full – 'too many irons in the fire' he confessed – and the impression given by his letters is of what we call today a 'rat-race': the demands of examinations pressing against the duties of running several societies, editing magazines, speaking in debates and all the other activities which dons assured anxious parents were just as important as study. There was also what he called in after years 'the pinch of poverty'. His scholarship was worth £80 a year but his expenses were around £200; he was one of a parson's nine children, only two of whom, his elder brothers, were earning their living. Yet it occurred to no one that he should earn money in the vacation, for this was regarded as the proper time for catching up with one's books.

A classical scholar of the 1909 entry was bound to feel, when he arrived at Balliol in October, that he had little time to lose. Only eighteen months off was the first appointment with the examiners, the exhausting and comprehensive test of his mastery of Greek and Latin texts, and of composition and translation in prose and verse, called Honour Mods. True, much of it was no more than a continuation – for some a boring repetition – of work done in the sixth form; and good classics from good schools were expected to get Firsts, very much as good oarsmen from good schools were expected to get rowing Blues, not without concentrated effort but without great difficulty. Candidates had to get through the whole of Homer,

*Robin's friend Kurt Hahn, advising General Ludendorff on how to attack the morale of the British at war, could never forget the society of Christian and liberal gentlemen with which he had so recently lived at Christ Church and found the outlook of a Lloyd George or a Northcliffe abhorrent and inexplicable.

Virgil, Cicero and Demosthenes. If they had as well social tastes or athletic and political ambitions, that was more than enough. Moreover, the Balliol scholars of B-W's year were an exceptional lot, who were to collect eight Firsts and three Seconds between them.

Beyond Honour Mods, another seven terms away, was the test which contemporaries believed to be the most exacting and honourable of all academic tests: Greats, or the Honours School of Literae Humaniores. To get a First in this examination on the civilizations of Greece and Rome, in which one could specialize either in history or philosophy, was to be virtually certain of a good job in the running of the country or the Empire, in the professions or even in politics. It is impossible to exaggerate the reverence with which the good 'Greats man' was regarded in public and academic life. Although the kind of ingenious mind that performed best in the linguistic exercises of Mods could not always adapt itself to the more reflective study of Plato and Thucydides, the man with a chance of a First in the one was expected to hope that he might achieve the double. To say that a man was a 'First in Mods and Greats' was to credit him with both soundness and brilliance, a combination that the British Establishment found irresistible.

If B-W cherished at any time that ambition, it must have been more because Balliol expected the best of its scholars than because he really valued academic success above everything else. For it is evident from his letters to his parents that he went there rating success as a debater at the Union above prowess in Schools, and that they understood and accepted the reasons for his preference – even if he was the first of the family to show political ambitions. Here and there, when he sees his examination prospects darkening, there is a hint of excuse or apology; but always the plea is that speaking in debate and the effort of becoming President of the Union are 'not altogether a waste of time'.*

His plan was to succeed at the Union quickly enough to allow him the last twelve months or more of his four years free

---

*Sir John Masterman, the former Provost of Worcester and tutor in History at Christ Church, has told the author of two or three cases in which a pupil likely to get a first in History deliberately chose to put the Union first – and was not discouraged by the College. All became Ministers later.

of all distractions to make a good job of Greats. This might, however hard he worked, harm his performance in Mods, but the risk had to be run. A few days after term began he wrote to his father:

All kinds of people have called on me—even a fourth year man, a most exalted personage, President of the Union, with whom I brek tomorrow morning.[1]

This invitation to breakfast probably came from a Balliol man, for the college had had a run of presidents. Mr Ivor Brown (a contemporary of B-W's both in college and at the *Observer*) points out that, although there was no Union set at Balliol, 'there was Union loyalty in the form of a collective college vote. Most members of the college were also members of the Union, with probably a Liberal-Socialist majority; but a Balliol man was expected to vote for a Balliol candidate irrespective of his politics.'

Three weeks later, a letter to his sister Phyllis, to whom he could always show off a little, said that he felt 'as if I had been born in Balliol. I know now practically everyone I want to know in the College.'* His maiden speech at the Union, on the motion that democracy was a discredited ideal, was judged interesting but rather long-winded. Early in his second term he is assuring his mother that he had been working 'pretty hard' but 'had made a fairly (apparently) successful speech in the Union, as a result of which next Thursday I tell for the Ayes again, which means that I have caught the new President's eye.' Shortly afterwards he wrote to his father, who could be counted on to understand.

You will be glad to hear that I received an invitation today from the President to speak 'on the paper' next Thursday in support of the party system. Needless to say I accepted 'by return'.[2]

The university magazines, whose comments on Union debates were read by the politically ambitious as closely as a newspaper's racing tips are read by hopeful punters, had begun to take notice. The *Oxford Magazine* said that to hear B-W speaking on Britain's need of dreadnoughts had been a pleasant

---

*This is perhaps a tribute to his own special qualities, for Balliol, with under two hundred undergraduates, was then a congeries of social cliques or circles, distinct though intersecting.

experience and that it was time he appeared 'on the paper'. Sure enough he did. Then his speech on the party system, mentioned above, was described by *Isis* as his best yet, 'very humorous and racy'. Advancement had begun according to plan. Calling himself a Tory Democrat (on which one heckler commented 'There ain't such a beast') B-W had the best of both worlds in a college which was markedly liberal and socialist in sympathy. He knew how not to antagonize people although supporting the view that 'Liberalism is in theory a pestilential heresy and in practice a pitiful illusion' or demanding that English society should have 'a larger element of Puritanism which would keep the spirit of the nation healthy'. The famous charm was working; for his age he was judicious, though there was plenty of gaiety in him – and music – when the occasion offered.

He had a voice better tuned and managed (thanks to his mother) than had most of his friends. He is therefore remembered as the natural leader of the impromptu singing that would break out in someone's room, or sometimes on a noisy Saturday night in the back quad joining the college to Trinity. There Balliol men would taunt their neighbours with the song called 'Gordooley', the origins of which were until lately quite unknown. Its refrain was:

> Gordoo . . . ley
> He's got a face like a ham
> Bobbie Johnson says so
> And he ought to know.

This crude doggerel had originated at a party in the late nineties when an undergraduate of New College, called Bobbie Johnson, was wining with Balliol friends. Someone mentioned the name Gordooley* and Johnson remarked, 'I know him; he's the fellow with a face like a ham.' As Johnson himself was thought to look rather like a ham, this was too much for the company, which rushed into the quad and sang for the first time what became a festive anthem of Balliol on noisy nights. Trinity used to retaliate – though the habit may well now have ceased – with

---

*Who, then, was Gordooley? According to B-W's contemporary, Mr Norman Knight, this was the nickname of a Trinity undergraduate called Arturo Mario Galletti di Cadhilac and was taken from a then popular cigarette. Galletti. taunted from across the wall by Balliol for years, sent his own son there in 1926.

> Bloody, bloody Balliol
> Bring out your black men
> And teach them to row.

sung to the same lilting tune.

At one moment success seemed to be coming too fast for B-W: already in his third term friends were urging him to stand for the Secretaryship (one of the offices through which one progressed to the chair). But he decided 'not to rush things too much'. The first part of the letter included an urgent request for money ('I'm afraid you will find me rather an expensive luxury') and he thought it wise to add that he had been 'working tremendously hard, harder than ever yet at Oxford'. The Dons were 'beginning to put the screw on a bit'. This was in June 1910, during his first Oxford summer, the most delightful and distracting period in any freshman's life. Depressed and penitent, he writes to his father:

Sometimes I almost feel inclined to entertain the unworthy wish that my luck had never brought me here. The standard here is far above that of any other college and anywhere else one might be a shining light. The fact is I haven't *read* nearly as much as these other people, though that can be rectified. Anyhow, I think I ought, with luck, to get a First in Mods, if I go on working as at present. My first two terms I was at my old game of a multiplicity of irons heating indifferently in the same fire; but that I am getting out of.[3]

As a sign of resolution to reform he is moving his room next term from the front quad, so vulnerable to casual visitors, to the back quad where he will have the hospitable bachelor, Cyril Bailey (his Latin instructor) below and the much less sociable Pickard-Cambridge (his Greek tutor) next door. 'What an atmosphere,' he writes: 'I'm afraid I rather reacted at first after a strenuous year at school and now the tightening up process has really begun.'

Perhaps writers on Oxford as it was just before the First World War have underrated the seriousness of many of its intelligent young men, who were warned by the newspapers of their day – more serious and ample than ours – of the dangerous world they were living in. Their endless discussions in a score of college clubs like the Arnold and the Brackenbury at Balliol were not all froth and epigram. It was, after all, a dramatic period of change in politics.* Lloyd George was challenging in the most caustic and ribald terms the power and wealth of the landowning class. The Lords were at logger-heads with the Commons on vital constitutional issues; the Labour Party was emerging; Europe was taking up positions for Armageddon; there was much industrial unrest; and radicalism and pacifism were stirring many consciences. True, undergraduates did not demonstrate against the Czar's treat-ment of Russian intellectuals, or against German behaviour in south-west Africa, or against Belgian atrocities in the Congo; but they were aware of the problems and dangers. The Bracken-bury Society, which several times met in B-W's room, defeated by twelve votes to four in November 1911 the motion that 'A European war is much to be desired at the present time.'

In spite of his efforts in the final months of reading B-W got no more than a Second in Honour Mods to the great dis-appointment of his college and school. It was a shock to open the telegram from the college porter which arrived at Duloe on an April morning saying:

Firsts Asquith, Bell, Brown, Fyson, Grenfell, Ridley, Williams yourself second Hancock.

We can imagine the Rector's blunt disappointment, the mother's gentle sympathy with dearest Robin. A letter from his tutor Cyril Bailey contained not one word of reproach:

You mustn't reproach yourself with anything in these last months —you worked like a horse and fully deserved to be rewarded; you must not let it damp you for the future; you must just make up your mind to show people that you aren't a second-class man. . . . Poor old thing! It's simply beastly and I wish I could be with you to cheer you up a bit. I shall write soon to your people. Yours ever.[4]

He returned to Balliol for his second summer term to find the Union prospects good, and there was comfort in winning a Tancred Studentship at Lincoln's Inn, where Fred was now a well-known figure. This added £100 a year to his income and was the cause of his being admitted at once as a student of the

---

*Lindsay, later to become Master of Balliol and a thorn in the flesh of his old pupil at the time of Munich at *The Times*, seems to have been the only Socialist don at that time. But the Fabian Group was strong among undergraduates. The leading Socialist personality was G.D.H. Cole, a Balliol contemporary of B-W's, who never sought a political career.

Society. He records eating his first dinner 'among a large throng of my blacker and yellower brethren' and 'walking this pleasant, green place' wondering about his future. Was it to be the law or politics? There is no mention yet of journalism.

The third year begins and the rat-race was keener. The 'brekking', the lunching, the dining, the conspiring, the speech writing were at their height; for the plan was to make such a mark this autumn and after Christmas that the presidency would be his in the summer term. So in November 1911 he writes that 'with luck and a decent speech' he hopes to get the office of Junior Librarian. He explains to his parents:

> Then there will be a rare old tussle for the final office. I should very much like to hold it for the summer, so that I may have all next year cleared for action. But that is problematical in the extreme.[5]

For his twenty-first birthday in February 1912 Pater sent a guinea, with his best wishes for the Presidency and a 'double first':

Dearest Robin,
I send you my warmest congratulations on your coming of age. You are not an heir, as regards this world's possessions, but I hope you inherit a sound constitution and sound principles, and I trust that you may yet fill a distinguished place among your generation.

To which Robin replied:

> Thank you for your wish for the Presidency and Greats. The one now depends on the other. If I can get the former this term, all may be well with the latter. But I have a *very* hard man to beat against me, who has already stood. Balliol I know will vote solidly for me, but success is doubtful in the extreme. We have just had two Balliol Presidents running.... But I should be foolish to throw up the Union now that I have got so far. In some ways it is more important than the other. Meanwhile I hope—possibly in vain—for both.[6]

As things turned out, he was correct in his judgement. It was his connection with the Union which brought him the chance of joining *The Times*. Presidents, and even junior officials of that body, could by standing tiptoe see into the public life they wanted to enter. They corresponded with politicians, barristers, writers, hostesses. For debates they met visitors, dined them, breakfasted with them and saw them off at the station. Meetings in connection with the Union led to other meetings. One peer enjoyed his visit so much that he offered B-W a job as his private secretary. And at All Souls, visiting Fellows like Geoffrey Robinson (Editor of *The Times*) would hear the gossip about the coming young men, perhaps glance at the university papers. The Union was as much a paddock for inspecting likely Tory and Liberal politicians as the Workers' Educational Association was later on a recruiting ground for Labour candidates to Parliament.

A visit by Hilaire Belloc – a great master of the Union – gave B-W his chance.* He felt more confident now and wrote to his mother, 'Look out for a wire on Tuesday morning. If I can do it, then I shall have a year free from all distractions and also the knowledge that I shall not altogether have wasted my time.' His speech was brilliant, his success assured. On 5 March 1912 the telegram duly arrived. 'Elected President maj. 105 Robin.' A handsome victory for the man and his solidly voting college. In May, the journal *The Varsity* carried the usual anonymous Open Letter of welcome to the new President, written – as B-W well knew – by his great friend Walter Monckton, soon to be President himself. That friends should build one another up was part of the game. It gives a vivid and affectionate picture of Robin at twenty-one:

In politics you revel. Did you not work day and night for the Tariff Reform League, whose principles you have since renounced? Do you not keep your weight down by giving vent in the Union to those paroxysms of rage which are the birthright of an Ulster man? And now, as Treasurer of the New Tory Club, you smoke the fattest cigar in Oxford; as secretary of the Chatham you inculcate the most heterodox principles, and finally you have become President of the Union by one of the most shameless jobs which have ever disgraced ... but we are getting on and this is the new style. So, to revert to the old, by the charm of your manner and your personal attractions, combined with a thoughtful though humorous outlook, you won the suffrage of your friends, coerced your enemies, and so, like the Chancellor, you have 'got home'.

*Thirty years later, dining with the Douglas Woodruffs, B-W met Hilaire Belloc again. 'Looks more John Bullish that ever. He seems to spare himself the effort of dialectical talk – all his half-affectations have become realities to him, dogmas indeed. He is walled in. However, he was amusing at times. He professed not to "write" now. "I dictate at top speed for money," he said, "and defy the reviewers."'

For the '*Isis* Idol',* Philip Guedalla depicted him as 'at home with cows, rural audiences, and the Union, and at ease at the table, or in the Chair. ... Like Clifton Chapel he stands four-square to all the winds that blow. ... He never goes to bed and very rarely gets up.'

Having written so much to his parents about his ambition, he seems to have fallen silent about its fulfilment, but he is proud of getting Carson for a debate and F. E. Smith has offered to speak on Welsh Disestablishment.

By the end of May he is thanking heaven that there are only four more weeks 'of this life of multifarious interests and occupations'. We know that he was a dignified and successful President, presenting good fare for Union members, and that his interventions were often witty and devastating. Guedalla said that he succeeded because 'he meant what he said and said it clearly, sometimes with heat'.

With the summer term over and the main purpose of his Oxford career achieved, B-W moved into digs in 20 Holywell, with four others, and settled down to carry out his good resolutions. He decided to get some coaching for Greats from a friend at Balliol, G. N. Clark† (who had won a First in Greats and in History) so as not to 'fall out of the second class'. And one afternoon he joins A. L. Smith, the future Master, on a walk and discusses his future.

He approves of my idea—get called to the Bar, perhaps try for an All Souls Law Fellowship (??) and start in life as a journalist. I am to see Sir E. T. Cook.'‡ A.L.S. was very nice about it. I shall get Fred to talk to him.[7]

Even in that ambitious family, B-W seems to have realized, the thought of an All Souls Fellowship for him would cause surprise, for the interrogation marks are his. It looks as if he was then looking to journalism, as so many had done, for a way of

---

*A long-standing feature of the *Isis* magazine was a feature article of the kind now called 'Profile' in which an undergraduate personality was described, criticized, flattered and made fun of by an anonymous friend or rival.

†Later Sir George Clark, Fellow of All Souls, Provost of Oriel, Chichele Professor of Economic History (1931–43), Regius Professor of Modern History at Cambridge (1943–7).

‡Editor of the *Westminster Gazette* (1893–6) and then of the *Daily News* (1896–1901), Edward Tyes Cook, of Winchester and New College, was one of the distinguished gentlemen editors of the turn of the century. His advice would be much valued by an Oxford aspirant to Fleet Street.

earning a living while acquiring a reputation at the Bar – as a convenience and not as a profession. His brother Fred liked the idea, and suggested he should get his scholarship at Balliol extended for a fifth year so that he could read Law. The question was whether Pater could afford it.

Social life went on, however, in spite of Greats, and B-W was notorious among his friends for the number of irons he kept in the fire. Although not a 'Blue', he was elected to Vincent's Club, an unusual tribute to social rather than athletic qualities. Rhodes Scholar from New York, Whitney Shephardson, who lived in the Holywell digs, has described how 'my dear Robin was on a spree at just the wrong time'. For it occurred to him that he might 'have a whack at the Newdigate'. The subject set for the poem was 'Oxford'. He took it in his stride. M. R. Ridley won the prize, but Robin was *proxime* and some thought that his submission showed more imagination and understanding than Ridley's.

Among the visitors who dined at No. 20 was Edward, Prince of Wales, then an undergraduate at Magdalen.* The Rector must have been delighted with this account from his son in a letter of 1912:

Last month Hansell came to dinner. He is a charming man and the ideal Royal tutor—devoted, I think, to his charge. Last night he came again bringing the Prince. It was not an official dinner at all—just a private visit from one undergraduate to others. There were just the five of us and these two.

We all liked the Prince immensely. He is small and young-looking even for his years (18) but in other ways quite 'grown up'. He is quite intelligent and anxious to do the right thing—but all most naturally and unaffectedly. We had very much our ordinary dinner and after dinner the 20 Holywell Band—we are all fairly musical, one or two brilliantly so—got under way. We have a number of cardboard trumpets. The Prince promptly took one and made as much noise as anyone. He said he liked 'a good row'. So we had a ragtime, comic songs and choruses, and he joined in merrily like a man. He was quite reluctant to go, enjoyed himself tremendously, and is coming again.

*The inhabitants of No. 20 had a wide range of interests and rarely dined together. 'When we did,' writes D. Norman Smith, the Organ Scholar, 'it was difficult to avoid talking somebody's "shop". We therefore formed ourselves into a vocal-cum-bigaphone band. We had outsize wind instruments made of cardboard and we worked up quite a decent repertoire, our star number being "The Rosary".'

It was impossible not to like him. He is clean-looking and jolly with no 'side' at all. If I get a chance, I will get Pater his autograph. I think the nation will and does owe a debt of gratitude to Hansell for bringing up the future king so sensibly and normally.* We treated him just as an ordinary undergraduate.[8]

With only six months to go before Schools, one senses in his letters a note of resignation, if not of despair. He cannot afford to go on with Clark's coaching, which has helped him very much. 'I have,' he tells his mother, 'all my Roman and Greek history to do and a number of texts, while the philosophy is, of course, limitless.' By all accounts A. D. Lindsay was not a good tutor for anyone who needed cramming; stimulating for first-class people whose chief interest was in metaphysics, but too diffuse for the kind of examinee that B-W had let himself become. This is reflected in the next two months. 'I am becoming a better philosopher,' he tells Phyllis in February 1913, 'but I shall have to work overtime until the exam. Still there is no doubt, viewed apart from classes, that it is a fine school to take. If I take Law after, and do well at it, Greats gives me a big pull in an All Souls Fellowship.' Over-ambitious, one feels, and more than a little conceited. If there were illusions, he was too honest to persist in them, and can watch them crumbling away. With three months to go, he confides to Phyllis:

I shall have to stick sternly to Greats now though I have absolutely no enthusiasm for it. It is a most depressing school. . . .

With two months to go he writes of the 'crowning floater – but at all events a degree and no more Greats!' A week or two later he writes to father, preparing him for the worst. 'A First,' he said, 'is out of the question for the main reasons I have already given and for the one true reason that I haven't sufficient intelligence to get a First – not in this school at all events. Law, I rather feel, may be a different proposition.' (14 April 1913.)

None the less the announcement of a Third Class came as a real shock to pride. Again Cyril Bailey wrote to reassure him:

*Mr. Henry Hansell of Cromer, an old Magdalen man who was tutor in the Royal Family.

I am so terribly sorry about this because I know how much it will distress you and make you think horridly self-reproaching things about yourself. I cannot understand it myself. I had very much hoped that Greats might compensate you for your disappointment in Mods and it had never occurred to me that this might happen.

All I can say now is, don't be too wretched about it. I'm certain that for all Oxford has said officially about you, you will show in life that you are a really first-class man and will do good—I believe great—things. I don't think you have anything really to regret. . . . Just look to the future now and get back your confidence.[10]

If the college was disappointed that a scholar should fall so low, worldly wise men would say that a Third was a sign of underworking brilliance, while a Second was a sign of over-working mediocrity. His father's comment, telegraphed, was characteristic:

Only temporary check. Lucky not fatal.
Other battles to win. Pater.

The disappointment affected his career only in so far as it made it less likely that he would stay at Oxford to read Law in one year, and more likely that he would seize an opportunity to make a start in journalism. Ned Grigg,* impressed by the young President of the Union, whom he had met on a visit to Oxford, had promised an introduction to the Editor of *The Times*, should he want to work with a newspaper while reading for the Bar in London. This offer he now took up, knowing that it need not commit him to a life in journalism: had not men like Asquith, Haldane, Morley, Amery and Winston Churchill, each in his different way, earned a living with their pens while preparing for the House or the Bar? Grigg kept his word and within six weeks of going down, after an idyllic holiday at Duloe, enjoying the family, the farm, the sea, the neighbours, he was writing his first leading article for *The Times*.

One of his contemporaries, looking back fifty years, said in the jargon of the sixties: 'Robin had been well groomed for the Establishment.' Is this a fair and accurate judgement of

*Edward William Grigg, then in his early thirties, wrote most of the articles on imperial affairs in *The Times* between 1909 and 1913. He had begun there as secretary to the Editor, Buckle. Dermot Morrah, who knew him as one of the most active figures in the Round Table group, says that Grigg could think on his feet with the most astonishing fluency. In debate 'he could master even Bob Brand, who had the best brain of the lot.' Entering politics he later became Lord Altrincham. B-W could hardly have found a more effective sponsor.

what life in Balliol and Oxford did for him? That it gave him immediate access to the friendship and advice of influential men is true. That he developed a personal style of sociability and authority in the intellectual hurly-burly of the Union and other societies is also true. That he was mature and self-confident for his age – despite the disappointment in Schools – is apparent. But this was a time of liberal ascendancy in Britain and the qualities required for admission to the Establishment were not those of today, when the Tory radical is a type much less rare than it was in B-W's youth. Despite his intense loyalties to family, school, regiment, college and newspaper – loyalties to which he devoted much of his spare time – he was never entirely an Establishment man.

It was this apartness, perhaps, that put him most in debt to Balliol. He had a taste for general ideas not common in Englishmen of his type, certainly stimulated by the Greats curriculum. His friendships – notably with the Canadian Vincent Massey and the American Whitney Shephardson – liberated him from any class-consciousness he may have brought from Westminster. The wish to achieve something in public life – and not for himself alone – was part of the ethos of his college. His conception of journalism was from the first to the last public-spirited. In all these respects he felt that his college had made him; and nothing gave him deeper satisfaction than the Honorary Fellowship with which Balliol saluted him not long before his death.*

Surely the most unusual testimonial of all, preserved in his papers, is a letter from the Manager of the National Provincial Bank in the Cornmarket congratulating him on working for *The Times*. He informs B-W, in passing, that he is overdrawn £281 against his father's guarantee of £175, and asks as a 'pure matter of form' for a covering note from Fred until salary cheques start coming in. Interest will be at five per cent. But, knowing how expensive London can be, this philosophical manager writes that 'You can take your time reducing your overdraft.' *Credite posteri!*[12]

---

*'Really staggered to find a letter from Sandie Lindsay on behalf of the College offering me an honorary fellowship, a distinction I never dreamt of. The dissipation of energy in 1909–13 which bought me academic disaster was rewarded at the time by the offer to extend my scholarship for a fifth year, and now by this. One coal of fire after another. And I owe to Balliol pretty well whatever else has come to me.'[11]

As an example of B-W's skill in versification I have been allowed by the Librarian of Balliol to extract portions of his 'House of Belial', written in the spring of 1913, in which he satirizes the college and its dons.

Where Oxford lifts to Heav'n a crown of tow'rs
And idling wastrels snuff the passing hours
There stands a college, built on wondrous wise –
(Who dreamt that stone could thus as brick disguise?),
A sham-Bavarian, pseudo-Gothic inn;
Where one style stops and th'other styles begin
That none can tell. And wondrous 'tis within.
Within 'tis wondrous. Here the meek Hindu
Is seen with German, Japanese and Jew,
With Slav, with Berber or with swart Afghan,
Aztec and Moro, men from Yucatan.
Here Melanesians, natives of the Cape
Jostle with Pigmies, cousins to the ape;
Or here the Ethiop wears his native smile,
Beams on a savage from a Leeward Isle.

And some there are, that come of Albion's land,
Mixed with the alien horde, a motley band.
Aristos some, that awe us with a nod,
Others are out-at-elbows, scantly shod,
The first adored by graduate and don,
That lick the very earth they walk upon,
The second, beings none could ever know,
Spend three laborious years in work and go.

See Smug, our great historian, gatewards walk!
A tutor, slow to wash and swift to talk.
Has he not told you often how a score
Of Earls, Dukes, Viceroys, Marquises and more,
Princes and leaders of our native land,
Received their infant schooling at his hand?
Committees, Councils – Smug will welcome each,
Only provided he may make a speech.
Swiftly he rises, slowly sits he down,
And wags his hair-girt tonsure dirty-brown.[13]

4

The First Bantling

To a generation which is told that two years' experience 'in the provinces' or training at a technical college is an indispensable qualification for appointment to editorial posts, the story of B-W's entry to Printing House Square will read like fiction. In 1913 the trade union spirit had made so little progress that brilliant young men from the University might be installed as aspiring editors and future newspaper executives over the heads of older and technically competent men. Intellectuals like William Beveridge and R. H. Tawney could write articles for newspapers like the *Morning Post* without the slightest intention of becoming professional journalists. Brains were recruited where they offered themselves and first-class minds were going cheap. Even Geoffrey Robinson (he later changed his name to Dawson), who took the chair at *The Times* for the first time on 23 September 1912, had been only five years earlier a young civil servant working in South Africa for Alfred Milner when he was appointed, without any newspaper experience, Editor of the *Johannesburg Star*. Northcliffe, a professional if ever there was one, had no hesitation in choosing this young Fellow of All Souls to edit the great newspaper of which he had secured control four years earlier.

When Robinson (known to his friends as Robin) met young Barrington-Ward at lunch with Ned Grigg, he was a bachelor of thirty-nine living in Smith Square, Westminster, finding his way confidently and skilfully around the political and social elite of London. He had been Editor a year. He was deeply interested in imperial affairs and of necessity involved at that time in the burning question of Ireland's future. So the ancestry and views of the young Oxford Ulsterman he had been invited to meet may partly account for the rapid decision he made in his favour.

B-W had expected no more than to be looked over and given a few words of august advice. He was therefore surprised at the Editor's first suggestion, that he should send in one or two leading articles to show his paces. Then, as lunch drew to a close, Robinson said suddenly: 'Why not come down to the office with me now and try your hand at a leader? I don't promise to put it in but you can try.' What else could B-W do but accept, 'palpitating with a great fear'? So to P.H.S. he went with Robinson, was put into a room by himself, and was given some articles to read in proof entitled 'Tunnel or Ferry?' He was to comment for *The Times* on the facts and arguments about the projected Channel Tunnel there presented. It was a severe test for a novice of twenty-two, even if this was not to be the first leader.

Three hours later, when the Editor came up to see how he was getting on, about seven hundred words had been written. 'Excellent, just what I want,' said Robinson and told the writer to get himself something to eat, as there was plenty of time to finish. B-W used the dinner interval to send a hurried note home:

I have now to go back and finish and hope to get done by 10.30 p.m. I don't know what luck I shall have. He told me at lunch there was no vacancy. That may have been to protect himself. But at all events he said 'It'll do if you finish by 11 p.m.' and that looks as if he *might* print it. At all events if you see a leader tomorrow entitled 'The Channel Tunnel' you'll know that your most obedient wrote it. . . . But I don't suppose it'll see the day. You can bet I am writing with every oz. of me applied.[1]

But it did see the day, all 1,100 words, and the very next morning. This was a triumph, coming a bare week after the deep disappointment of the Third in Greats; and one can imagine the delight with which the Rector and Caroline Barrington-Ward heard of Robin's success and read and re-read the article. Although it had the reader sitting for much of the way on the fence, he was let firmly down on one side at the end, with the help of sentiments about connections with the Continent which have lost none of their appeal today.

The real truth is, we believe, that there exists a half-articulate feeling, deep-seated in the heart of the nation, instinctively urging it to repel without question an attack on its individuality. It is

41

difficult for Continental peoples to realize the peculiar quality which the possession of an island kingdom breeds in a race. The moral effect of the 'continuous road into Europe' would be immediate and striking; but might also be disastrous.[2]

How fluently the young man already used the editorial 'we', how confidently he wrote of what was deep-seated in the nation's heart, how skilfully he planted right at the end that last word 'disastrous'. The next morning Robin described to his mother what it was like to compose with people standing at one's elbow fidgeting for copy. The Editor had come up to congratulate him on his style and Grigg had said it was a 'triumph' to have his 'first bantling' accepted straight off.

Soon afterwards B-W was given sub-editing work and went on writing minor leaders, but without any promise of a place on the staff. Financially the free-lance status suited him well: in December, for example, he earned over £25. He could run the small flat he had taken in Harley Street and get on with his reading for the Bar. Following Robinson's advice, who said that experience on an evening paper would be useful, he made inquiries and at the office of the *Pall Mall Gazette* he saw J. L. Garvin, a well-known and successful editor, who took a liking to him, gave him a lot of good advice and said, 'People I don't like I don't want to see. I like you. Come and see me whenever you like. I mean that.'

Then in February 1914 B-W was formally appointed to *The Times* at £240 a year as secretary to the Editor. A letter home described the job thus:

> ... something of a diplomatic position. I have to deal with all the things that come in, with the veiled personages who converse darkly with the Editor of *The Times* etc. etc. and write some of his letters for him. Hours 7 p.m.-2 a.m.... It's quite an important position.[3]

It was indeed – like being head of a Minister's private office – and from it he must have been an enthralled spectator of the mounting crises of that winter and spring: confrontation and near-civil war in Ireland, the struggle between Lords and Commons over the powers of the peers, the growing tension between Russia and Austria-Hungary in the Balkans, the naval rivalry with the Germans. He watched at close quarters the Editor's relations with Northcliffe and had dealings with Wickham Steed, Valentine Chirol and other famous personalities on the staff.

B-W's own writings, as might be expected from someone so junior kept busy with secretarial duties, were of a minor order ranging from leaders on 'Tottenham Court Road' to 'Classics and Modern Life' or a light piece on the conventions of letter-writing, or rather letter-ending, called 'Yours Very Truly'. One of these caught the eye of Northcliffe, who liked a 'light leader' and the author was asked down in July 1914 for a weekend at Sutton Place, near Guildford, where he was much impressed by the luxurious appointments and pleased by the attention shown him. Doubtless he heard the great man prescribing for *The Times,* dominated still by those obstinate 'black friars' of the old regime, the topicality and vigour of the *Daily Mail* and felt, perhaps, that he was one of the up-and-coming young men that the new one would turn to. It was not to be, however, for within a few weeks he was training not twenty miles away from Sutton Place to be an officer in the New Army.

5

Into War

Like most young men of his generation, B-W at twenty-three had no doubt about the justice of the cause for which he was volunteering to fight in August 1914. He had thought carefully about where his duty lay and what would be the effect on his career at the Bar. In the slightly pompous style a young man of twenty-two would adopt towards a sister he writes that 'both from the material and the moral point of view it is the right thing to do. . . . The present is a time rather for the protection than the study of international law.' He had no doubt, too, that Germany would be quickly defeated. In a letter of 11 August he wrote that many well-informed people believed that it would be a short war.

If, as seems likely, we retain command of the sea, Germany will be at starvation's door in about three months. And that takes no account of the financial situation. But much depends on what happens in the eastern theatre of the land War. . . . I hope the French may be able to roll the Germans up on their own account.[1]

It was all to be appallingly different for the next four years.

By September he was doing his elementary officers' training at a camp on top of the Berkshire downs near Didcot, sharing a tent with two Balliol friends. It was a 'great life', rising at six, training for four hours before lunch and for two hours after it; then after supper a lecture and lights out at 10.15 p.m. Only a fortnight later – such was the training of those days – he was at Aldershot in Marlborough Lines, with his chosen regiment, the 6th Duke of Cornwall's Light Infantry, then part of the 24th Infantry Brigade. This, he said, was second on the list of the New Army, the first being the 23rd, with the Rifle Brigade and K.R.R.s. He had his own tent and an efficient soldier-servant and lived on 'about 2s a day, with pay and allowances of 7s 9d'. His fellow officers were mainly Regulars and ex-Regulars and if the mess was not intellectually high-powered, it was at all events a very cheery place.

As a subaltern he commanded a section of 60-70 men:

It is a real interest for me to have a body of men for whose efficiency one is responsible. My platoon is taking shape like anything. The men are keen to learn because keen to get to the front.

Before the end of the year they were training, in an ankle-deep quagmire on Witley Common, a draft of eighty raw recruits just arrived from Bodmin: 'proper old backwood Cornishmen, at present awkward and amusing young ducklings'.

Next spring, B-W was in France writing from behind the front in the Bailleul area, and he described for the first time to his mother what he was facing: 'Guns, rifle and machine-gun fire are more or less incessant. But the extraordinary thing is that the nearer you get to the trenches the safer they seem. . . . Most casualties occur of course in attacks.'*

Then it was June 1915 and the bombardment of Ypres infuriated him.

A melancholy sight to-day, on this clear, baking hot day. Two hours ago stood the cathedral tower of Ypres a white landmark among the trees. Now it exists no longer. The Huns had it down— God knows why—in an hour. It makes me savage to see such useless and irreparable destruction.[2]

Not until July does he hint at the ordeal of life in the trenches. The D.C.L.I. had returned after seven days in the line 'very weary but fortunately intact'.

We went through two bombardments and a certain amount of gas —from gas bombs, fairly ineffectual. . . . I do not regret having joined the infantry. I don't pretend to be anything of a hero—far from it! —but I do think that fellows who write home, as some do, and deliberately advise their friends to join the A.S.C. or R.A.M.C. are skunks.[3]

*B-W was the moving spirit in a regimental magazine for the 6th D.C.L.I. called 'The Red Feather'. It was a lively, newsy production of which the last issue, written in a rest area after the recapture of Delville Wood in the Battle of the Somme, exists in proof. Third Army later forbade such magazines. When it was represented that 'The Red Feather' had discreet and honourable seniority and should be exempt from the ban, the request was in B-W's words 'brutally and wantonly refused'.

Experience built up in a cruel crescendo. From his letter of 3 August his mother learnt for the first time in detail what her son had faced at Bullecourt:

We have been through a hot time since we [were?] called suddenly about 3.30 one morning from our rest camp, which we had occupied for only two days. 'Stand to. The Germans are attacking the -Bde.' Off we marched. We halted about three miles up the road and got our orders. Trenches had been lost and we were to support the counter-attack which had been hastily organized. We marched up pretty well across the open, swept with shrapnel; and some good fellows dropped there. Eventually we reached the firing line, supported the counter-attack and moved on to hold the line when it failed.

However, we roughly organized our line—and then we got it. For 36 hours the bombardment continued not of course at full strength all the time. At 2 a.m. the Germans attacked again, using liquid fire. Our guns were splendid, our ammunition seemingly endless— Thank God for it! With rifle and machine-gun fire helping the artillery we beat them off. The men and the N.C.O.s rose to the occasion. By this time we had practically no officers, it was night, we were sodden with fatigue, and the enemy were using their bestial device. Yet the men hung on as best they could and it was a good best.

Our casualties have left us sick and sorry, but there is only one thing one can do and that is to remember what one is out here for and to get everything going on a new basis as soon as possible and as efficiently. All were fine fellows and good officers and everyone of them died doing his job and doing it bravely.[4]

Later that month, while B-W was back in hospital with trench fever, disaster overcame his battalion in the cellars of the Cloth Hall at Ypres.

A superior intellect [he writes bitterly in a letter home] put them into cellars by the Cathedral ... packed like sardines. They got 15 crumps among them and I hear the losses are heavy, many killed. Rumour said many things which I refused to believe because I did not want to believe them. Major Barnett [who had recommended B-W for his gallantry in action] and Blagrove killed. Two of the straightest, finest, bravest fellows you could know. I was devoted to both and after all we have suffered this almost breaks my heart.

This is strong language from a son who made a point of sparing his parents anxiety in his letters.

From now on the freshness of style in the letters faded under the pressure of what had become bloody routine. Sensitivity was being blunted. In February 1916 he writes about the 'first real rest we had since we came out', billeted in a 1686 chateau which he admires; later he wrote about 'a lovely spring day and sun and blue agree in condemning war as something too futile and wasteful for words'. He had heard of the heroic death of his Oxford friend Gilbert Talbot and of the tributes written about this legendary figure. That spring B-W was put up for a staff job as G.S.O. III in place of a major from his own regiment. He was 'almost installed on this pinnacle of glory' when it was learned that Corps had put up another candidate from another division.

I am not entitled to any grumbles. And a man does not leave his battalion without many, very many regrets and misgivings, and returns to it with corresponding pleasure.... I don't want you to gather from all this rigmarole that I covet a cush job far from the madding trenches. As you know, I have never asked for or lifted a finger to get one. But G.S.O. III ... would have been a good job.[5]

He was to fight another eighteen months, either with his battalion or his brigade, before becoming one of the General Staff. After reading in August the memoir to Gilbert Talbot which the family had sent him, he was reflective about himself and the past but optimistic about the future.

The reading of an analysis of someone else's character, particularly someone well-known and a friend, turns one to self-analysis also and to painful recognition of how much one lacks that one ought to have. The reading of it has done me good. It brings back to me the period of my life which at the moment I most cherish, 1908–9.... I have always enjoyed and do enjoy soldiering so long as I have something to do. It is when you have nothing to do that you begin to notice that precious time is flying and that you are not growing any younger.[6]

It was now the Battle of the Somme.

Stirring days these last. Two battles fought and two battles won. The Division has done splendidly. Everyone has come brilliantly up to scratch and the troops—as one knew they would—have done most gallantly fighting their way irresistibly through heavy machine-gun and artillery barrages and through a notorious crumped wood, full of fallen trees, wire, shell-holes and horrors.

On 3 January 1917 B-W was awarded the MC and this led him to speculate for the first time in these letters 'That war "must always be" is a disgraceful proposition which I hope this war will utterly discredit.' Promotion to Brigade Major came at last, a job which still took him into the front line but offered scope for ideas and initiative. Major Anthony Eden testified that he was an energetic, indeed brilliant, officer. B-W clearly enjoyed relating the unceasing demands of the job, which was not without risks.

Dearest Mater,
    The Bde. Major salutes you. I was sent to this Brigade (same division) a week ago or more to act for a fellow going home and was appointed to the job almost at once. All very sudden and surprising. . . . We started Brigade training (we are still out of the line) just as I arrived; that meant all kinds of tactical schemes and things, endless work—and interest.
    Of course I love the job. Apart from being a rather rapid and flattering step ('flattering' is used advisedly) it is a job which gives great scope though its demands on one's energy are unceasing. But my idle nature never did produce anything unless someone or circumstances kept my nose to the grindstone. . . . I am a happier and prouder man than I have been for some time. A baser voice adds that my income is now about £550 a year—till I am dégommé.[7]

In September just after a big battle he writes proudly about his men:

It was a triumph. The men were beyond admiration; they meant to fight; they did fight; and they carried all before them. All objectives taken, and counter-attacks most bloodily repulsed. Now *we* shall be quiet for a bit. . . . I am in my usual state of mixed feelings after a fight, glorying in the success which one has taken a minor part in helping to prepare and downcast for the death of many whom I got to know in the Brigade and liked.[8]

He survived unscathed the great German offensive and British retreat of March 1918 and on 3 April wrote home from his HQ thankful to have survived what had nearly been a great disaster.

I have not exactly been *in* the great battle, but concerned in it. I have had a front seat in the stalls and our proximity has been a sufficiently anxious matter to keep me in my clothes for a fortnight.

He takes the opportunity of speaking up for Lloyd George.

'Five good sons all virtuous'. Robin, second from the right with Pater, Mater and his four brothers at Duloe, Christmas 1913.

Robin, aged twenty, scholar of Balliol and President of the Union.

BW-, *centre*, as a subaltern in the 6th Bn Duke of Cornwall's Light Infantry, Aldershot 1915.

'Garve', Editor of the *Observer*, as B-W would have seen him at their first meeting in 1913.

I am deeply interested in politics at the moment. I believe Lloyd
George will weather it yet. People who suggest a change of government forget what Lloyd George means, more than any British
politician (mustn't call him statesman until he's dead) since Salis-
bury, to our Allies, especially France and U.S.A. They regard him
as a force and I think that to a great extent he is and that outweighs
many disadvantages, and even actual and historical mistakes.[9]

In July 1918 for the first time B-W was removed completely
from the perils and hardships of the front line. He was
appointed with the rank of Major to the staff of the Inspector
General at GHQ, General Sir Ivor Maxse. 'I feel very frightened
but will do my best,' is his first comment. 'It's no use disguising
the fact that these comforts, this security, this semi-permanence
and this absence of noise do *not* constitute soldiering.'

In fact, it is clear from what his friend Archie James (then
the airman on Maxse's staff) and others said that B-W did
there a most valuable job, helping to draft and write the
manuals of infantry tactics with which, at long last, the General
Staff were trying to cure British infantry leaders of their preference for attacking in long, close waves of men, offering
maximum targets for the German machine-guns. He and his
three or four colleagues visited corps and divisions in the line
to look for new tactics and fresh ideas, which were then brought
back to Maxse's staff for study and development. B-W was
regarded by the Regulars with whom he worked as an outstanding officer, who should have made a career in the Army.
Witness the letter he received from his intelligent and enterprising chief:

...I cannot let you depart without writing to tell you how
greatly I have appreciated all that you have done for TRAINING in
France. Nor do I think it right that you should exchange Khaki
uniform for civilian clothes without a word of recognition of your
conspicuous success as a *soldier* in the Great War from start to
finish. Without the advantages of preliminary training you have in
every rank shown great quality.[10]

But he had other ideas for his future and was determined in
October 1918 to try again at the Bar.

Whatever I decide to do I shall start on it the first day I land in
England. Great pressure for the first few years may make up for
what one would have done in a more leisurely way perhaps during

49

five years wasted. — Not really wasted even from the most selfish point of view. Other parts of one have probably been developed that five years of peace would have left fallow. At all events experience will show.[11]

On 29 November comes the entry which finally draws the curtain between Major Barrington-Ward and the young man who was to join the *Observer* as assistant editor to J. L. Garvin.

The Masters of the Bench of Lincoln's Inn have granted my petition and will call me to the Bar without more ado. Under F.'s good guidance [his brother Fred] that is a valuable step taken. I propose, on going to the Temple, to lie low for at least six months and study my trade — and then one can start making a little money again.[12]

The war had left him in politics a Radical. Only the Labour Party seemed to have 'principles and imagination'. He would vote for Lloyd George and Labour. People must not think that they can 'flop back into the old ways'. After a visit to the old battlefield around Ypres, where he had first stood in the trenches, he wrote to his mother, 'People who decry honest peace efforts should be made to spend a night in a shell-hole. The League idea is practical politics: peace has to be organized on new lines.'

What was the effect of the war on this sensitive and thoughtful man, now twenty-six? Garvin noticed when he returned that he had lost some of his gaiety and lightness of touch. Kurt Hahn noticed the same. Archie James, who met him first in 1917, insists that his spirit survived the war intact. Adrian Boult, his school friend, thinks that his health was affected by his wounds and by his experiences in the trenches, and says Robin's doctor brother warned him, soon after demobilization, not to try his strength too hard.* The most lasting effect was not on his nerves or physique, but on his mind. The conviction in later years that the fighting had not been worth while because the peace had been bungled was burnt deep into him. It was at the root of his determination that war between the same contestants — the return match that some Germans dreamed of — must be avoided.

---

*It is curious that Phyllis, his sister, insists that 'Robin was always delicate.' For although he was seldom free from minor ailments in middle age he stood the ordeal of the trenches very well.

Later entries in the diaries will illuminate the effect on him of the war. It is sufficient here to record what he felt ten years later, after reading Siegfried Sassoon's *Memoirs of an Infantry Officer*.

A v. good war book. I have shared, less intensely perhaps, some of his feeling and experiences—except that, rightly or wrongly, I never doubted we were fighting for the better cause and believed the German creed denied us any hope of compromise. We were right to make victory definite, I believe, but the failure to make peace definite and to sacrifice self for peace as it had been sacrificed for victory was a crowning inconsistency for which we are paying now and for which our children may have to pay. The war, with all the crudities it threw up, was essentially fine in spirit. The peace was essentially vindictive and vulgar, bred by French blindness and ruthlessness out of British party politics. The peace has put many honest people wrong about the war.[13]

For years later, as Deputy Editor of *The Times,* he found himself trying to improve a colleague's review of the fourth volume of Lloyd George's *Memoirs.* It was October 1934 and he recalled that day seventeen years earlier:

On Oct. 30th 1917 the 174th Infantry Brigade lay beyond Poelcappelle and under *Passchendaele.* That day we were ordered to do an attack. We protested its impossibility to the Division, the Division to the Corps, the Corps to the Army, the Army to G.H.Q. G.H.Q. said it must go on. So the front line rose and were promptly shot down or slithered back into the shapeless shell holes, water-filled, in which they had to exist. This was all that happened or could happen in that enveloping waste of deep mud. I always thought it would be sufficient to remember Oct. 30th as a date on which G.H.Q. thought an attack practicable in Flanders. The date alone says enough. And here I am reviewing Lloyd George's strictures—not that LLG is a good authority—on Haig for his conduct of the whole battle.[14]

6

Garvin's Right-Hand Man

To-day is the day when shrinking begins. I feel a
normally sized being on Monday morning but by
Saturday midday a very small man tackling a very
big job.

B-W to his mother, April 1920

The prospect facing B-W at the end of 1918, as one of thousands
of demobilized officers, showed little choice. At twenty-seven he
was still without professional qualifications that would ensure
a fairly senior post, even though his outstanding war record
would count for something, and the number of contemporaries
from Oxford and Cambridge with whom he had to compete
had been murderously reduced. Less than a year as secretary
to the Editor of *The Times* had given him only a slender
stock of newspaper experience, and the obvious thing to do was
to return to P.H.S. But there were rumours of trouble between
Dawson and Northcliffe, and the portents were unhappy. The
Bar promised better. Perhaps, by working very hard, he
could revive his old plan of taking the Law School at Oxford
in one year and following in Fred's footsteps as a Fellow of
All Souls.

Before the war, at Oxford and in London, B-W had a footing
inside one or two influential circles where he was known as a
young man of unusual charm and promise. Grigg, who had
arranged his trial with *The Times,* had kept him in mind for
*The Round Table,** which was eager to exploit the demon-

*The quarterly journal *The Round Table* was founded in November 1910 by
a group of men associated with Milner, to give – in the words of its first issue – 'a
regular account of what is going on throughout the King's dominions, written
with first-hand knowledge and entirely free from the bias of local political issues
and to provide a means by which the common problems which confront the
Empire as a whole, can be discussed also with knowledge and without bias'.
Its connection with *The Times* was always close and Dawson, when he resigned
in 1941, helped with its editing for a while. Thanks to men like Brand, Lionel
Curtis, Grigg and Dawson himself it had an influence between 1914 and 1930 out
of all proportion to its modest circulation.

stration of power and unity that the Empire had given on the battlefield. B-W had made friends with J. L. Garvin. As he could not sell himself as a newspaper technician, or as literary critic or as a language specialist, he must start as a pundit or opinion-maker. He might even aim at becoming an editor, for if he modestly thought of himself as lucky to have survived the war, he felt none the less the need to catch up. Fred and Lance and Michael, each in his own way, had been forging ahead to eminence and high income.

At first the thought of making money quickly at the Bar prevailed, and in January 1919 he received in France the following letter from Dawson.

I will not pretend that I was not looking forward to getting you back on the staff of *The Times,* but from a detached point of view I think that your decision is absolutely wise. You are quite young enough to make a start on your own account, and I feel certain that you will make a success of the Bar. There is no reason whatever so far as I can see why you should not go on in the early years with a good deal of your journalistic work. I think I can put you in the way of it, either in connection with *The Times* or elsewhere, and you may be sure that I shall do everything I can. One further small point. Did it ever occur to you to go back to Oxford to read the Law School and then to take a belated shot at All Souls?[1]

Coming from a Fellow of All Souls as influential as Dawson, the idea of joining that choice society must have been attractive to someone who felt he had not done himself justice in Schools, even if it meant further delay in earning a living. Journalism in one form or another could, after all, be combined with the Bar.

Perhaps it was fortunate that he had given up the idea of a post at Printing House Square, for only six weeks later it was announced in *The Times* that the Editor had resigned and was to be succeeded by Henry Wickham Steed. If B-W had returned he would have found himself in an unhappy office, bristling with personal rivalries and emanations from an increasingly eccentric proprietor. Again Grigg came to the rescue, and a month later B-W was hesitating because he had been 'sounded about becoming the assistant to J. L. Garvin that, in the opinion of Waldorf Astor's friends, was needed on the *Observer.'* He wrote to his father on 4 February that he had 'an offer of an assistant editorship straightaway with the *Observer,* with the idea of succeeding Garvin'. A brilliant and exciting prospect this, for Garvin was the outstanding pundit of the serious Press, and his newspaper, which had been in B-W's schooldays 'derelict in the Fleet ditch' (Northcliffe's phrase), was now flourishing and influential. Sunday journalism, requiring – as he then believed – only three days' presence in the office each week, had particular attractions for someone who looked forward to having more than one iron in the fire. Negotiations began but it seems that the first meeting with Garvin went off none too well. B-W wrote to his father in March:

> I must have a clear understanding as to what the *Observer* offers me in the way of scope and responsibility. I haven't the slightest intention of becoming a leader-writer. In justice to myself that would be unthinkable, even though I get exceptional chances of saying what I want to say.[2]

He knew enough about Fleet Street to realize that a journalist who is not given specific administrative, as well as writing, responsibilities does not have his foot on the editorial ladder. In any case Grigg had hinted in writing at the possibility of eventually succeeding Garvin, then fifty-one. Who was to know that this opportunity would not in fact present itself for over twenty years? In the end B-W was given a trial run, which included a visit as special correspondent to the Peace Conference in Paris. He seems to have quickly won his chief's confidence, for in September the Editor was promising him a definite contract as Assistant Editor, 'with the reversion of his position after some years', but warning him that the *Observer* must have clear priority over his articles for *The Round Table.* 'An exceptional prospect at my age,' B-W writes home. To this any ordinary parent would have replied, 'I should think it is,' but this was an exceptional family with no mean ambitions. We know from the diaries of his sister-in-law, Fred's wife and the daughter of A. L. Smith of Balliol, that the family debated earnestly whether the opening was good enough for Robin. Journalism, she noted, seemed 'to lead nowhere': a strange illusion in a generation which must have known that John Morley, Alfred Milner, Asquith, and others eminent in public life had worked in their youth on newspapers. So it is not surprising to find B-W, when he has his contract, writing to his mother somewhat defensively:

You will be interested to hear that I had yesterday a long, friendly and intimate talk with J.L.G. . . . The upshot is this. He has offered me a contract of three years, or of five years, whichever I please. The first three years at £1,000 a year, with not less than £1,200 a year for the next two. This for four days' work a week, Wednesday to Saturday. I am to be Garvin's complete deputy and take his place and responsibilities when he is away. I am normally responsible for three columns a week—I have often done four, as you know—and have a regular share in administration. I hope you will agree with me that this is highly satisfactory.

I shall almost certainly take the five-year contract. The K.C. advises it. I shall only be 33 when it comes to an end. I am not likely to be offered the Premiership or the Presidency of the League of Nations in the meanwhile! Seriously, if something very advantageous offered itself before the contract expired I don't think either the editor or the proprietor would stand in my way.[3]

The KC who advised acceptance was, of course, his brother, Fred, then reputed to be earning £30,000 a year. One cannot help smiling at the eagerness with which Robin assures his mother that if something better turned up before the five-year contract had expired neither Garvin nor Astor would stand in his way. For this was a magnificent opening for a bachelor with only one year's experience of newspaper work. The *Observer* of the twenties was a distinguished journal, read by a thoughtful, liberal-minded stratum of the upper and middle classes, and not directed particularly at the young and progressive.* Its readership, as distinct from its circulation (100,000+) was around 300,000. It was noted for its ample and high quality critical pages in which St John Ervine wrote about the theatre, Ernest Newman (and later Percy Scholes) on music, with J. C. Squire doing the book of the week and many celebrated literary names contributing reviews. The literary editor was Viola Garvin.

Just what opportunity was given to B-W to form and express opinions and to learn how to run a newspaper office can be seen from his letters. What he does not record is the influence of Garvin's unique style of talking and writing, designed to persuade the listener or reader in a determined, lengthy, sinuous

*Mr David Astor, the present Editor, describes the paper's political attitude in Garvin's day as 'maverick Tory'.

way, like a serpent coiling itself round a victim but with no intention to crush. To ears attuned to the styles favoured by Mr Luce and Lord Beaverbrook, the manner is often long-winded, pompous, emotional; but its effectiveness survives and there is no doubt that its impact, like that of a fine sermon, made many a Sunday memorable. His big signed article on the leader page represented passionate belief in the effectiveness of regular argument directed at a select circle of influential decision-makers and opinion-formers, in which everyone assumed that everyone else had either read or heard about the weekend pronouncement of the sage of Beaconsfield – where Garvin lived from 1921.

The Garvin offering was introduced each Sunday with towering, sometimes sensational headlines in six or seven decks. To write them was not the least of his assistant's worries. A specimen from August 1920 reads as follows:

THE COAL CRISIS AND THE WIDER MORAL
WAR AND PEACE — AND SOCIAL JUSTICE

THE DESPOTISM OF DIRECT ACTION
RUSSIAN METHODS AND BRITISH FREEDOM

CROWBAR OR BALLOT BOX?
THE SUICIDE OF VIOLENCE

Today a writing editor directing his Sunday newspaper from his home in Bucks thirty miles from London would have tele-printer, closed circuit television, and the use of the M4. Garvin was content with the telephone, with visits by colleagues who caught a train at Marylebone and reached Gregories by taxi, and his own one or two visits weekly to the office. Hardly a Saturday afternoon passed without last-moment anxiety about the arrival in Tudor Street of 'the article'. Would it be late? Would it need cutting? Would the author alter it near edition time? How would it affect the rest of the leader-page contents?

Two staunch men called Robert Bell and Howard Gray got the *Observer* out: collected the material, prepared it for the printer and saw it through the presses on Saturday nights. Bell was in charge of the shaping and day-to-day organizing of the paper. 'He knew exactly what he wanted done and got it done promptly and without fuss, which is a rare thing in a news-paper office,' said one of his contemporaries. Formally they were subordinate to the new deputy, but he had to learn from them, and in this potentially embarrassing relationship – familiar to all graduates who have come into journalism at the editorial level – B-W's niceness was decisive. They were soon good friends and Bell was his constant companion in a feast of visits to the Old Vic's Shakespeare productions.*

B-W occupied himself mainly with matters of policy, with finding the best writers and the most topical and suitable ideas for feature articles, reviews, letters, notes, criticism. This meant having a wide circle of acquaintance in political and literary London, leaving him less of that leisure for reading that he had looked forward to. His own writing was for the leader page and he had to be ready on Fridays to produce two or three columns on any aspects of home and foreign affairs, political or non-political. A letter to his mother after half a year of this responsibility describes the editorial function as seen from the deputy's chair:

I haven't been doing much of interest except my work, which involves little physical effort but a wearing sense of responsibility — the racking of brains to think of the right person, the right topic, the right thought and the right words at the right time. In fact the exercise of judgment, assisted only to the smallest extent by routine. The editorial position is — anyway, in my case — peculiarly solitary. There is no one to advise beforehand but, what is more unusual, no critic and no immediate and related result to test your work by when it's done. However, I find each time it falls to me to do this job that I gain in confidence, or perhaps callousness and possibly cunning! It must be a healthy process on the whole. . . .[4]

It is pleasing that the young man who was so frank about his confidence in one day succeeding Garvin was able also to be candid about being a 'very small man tackling a very big job'. Quite frequently the Editor was away and B-W faced the problems of deputizing for a dominating personality of immense experience and 'unpredictable impulses'.†[5]

*Adrian Bell, the novelist of rural Suffolk, recalls seeing his father and B-W together in 1919–20. 'B-W's tact and considerate approach quite disarmed my father, who could have been a little chary of the new presence in the editorial sanctum where he had sat so long at the head of the day to day running of the paper. Garvin only turned up about twice a week – if that. There was no mistaking if He was there – he never stopped talking for one minute.'

†On this judgement Garvin's daughter, the late Mrs Katherine Gordon, commented, 'I do not think Garve was impulsive at all; he used to turn and

It is possible that his experience made him more of a loyal chief of staff than an assistant editor should be.

The doors of post-war London society, still mourning after its fashion a legion of distinguished dead, were opening to this well-placed, good-looking, intelligent, charming bachelor, with an address in Harley Street, where he shared a flat with Lance the surgeon. Down at Duloe, the family read with some scepticism his weary complaint about the capital's social round in the season:

I find 'the Season' (or whatever you like to call this period of gregarious manifestations of activity) cuts into the time of even a person so far removed from its centre current as I am. It brings to London so many people who want to see you and whom you want to see again. It brings dinners in its train at which you meet more of them and so on. I shall be glad of empty August.[6]

I went to the Balfour reception at the Astors last week. The only interest (I find) in that form of entertainment is the visible presence of all the nobs, from the P.M. downwards—it was like a political film, a sort of quintessence *Who's Who*—but for me, not aspiring to be a Creevey, that interest is limited. You can't talk with anyone on those occasions or do anything but walk around and shake hands —two fairly mechanical operations.[7]

He had quickly formed a warm friendship with Lady Astor, his admiration for whom is expressed in diaries and letters. At her houses in St James's Square and at Cliveden he would meet, among a great variety of people, older friends from *The Round Table* like Milner, Grigg and R. H. Brand (later to be one of his directors at *The Times*), Philip Kerr (later Lord Lothian) and his old chief Geoffrey Dawson. These were powerful backers for a young man. Lloyd George used to say about the *Round Table* group led by Milner:

It is a very powerful combination ... in its way perhaps the most powerful in the country. Each member of the group brings to its deliberations certain definite and important qualities and behind the scenes they exercise much power and influence.[8]

They, too, believed in the power of ideas in politics and the possibility of persuasion by the right kind of journalism, even

turn things over in his mind for very long periods, and when he finally came out with his resolution or answer, it was a kind of shyness that made it burst out, so that people thought what was the product of long thought was said on impulse.'

if the prose of their quarterly was as different from Garvin's as a Fabian Society pamphlet is from a main article in *Tribune*. B-W was learning early the business of ideological conspiracy, an experience valuable to him twenty years later at *The Times,* when he encouraged E. H. Carr to recruit for the paper a brains trust of like-minded young 'Radicals'.

At this time he improved his understanding of foreign affairs by travelling in the holidays. He notes in August 1920 that he is going with Adrian Boult to stay with his Oxford friend Kurt Hahn, then working at Salem, near Lake Constance, for Prince Max of Baden. 'You probably know,' he writes to his parents, 'that no journalist is worth a – or has any prospect of – high advancement who doesn't know his foreign politics really well.' He had been greatly stimulated – and confirmed in some of his basic ideas – by his visit the previous summer (June 1919) to the Peace Conference in Paris where he had been talked to by a number of important people. Breakfasting with that ubiquitous enthusiast Lionel Curtis (who had offered him the secretaryship of *The Round Table* the previous day) he had met some of the Yugoslav delegation, and in the afternoon he attended 'Colonel' House's daily meeting with the American newspaper men, who were all 'much concerned with the liberalization of the English treaty-making spirit and anxious for news about modifications'. That appealed to him as strongly as a talk with a M. Champenois dismayed him.

He gave me the French point of view pretty straight and I loved it no better than before. Suspicion of Germans for ever, only to be satisfied by military and economic repression; disappointment with the British for not being whole-hoggers; positive dislike and distrust, perhaps even envy of the Americans.[9]

This is a portent of later pro-German views.

B-W noted with pleasure that the younger men in the British and American delegations, which included old Oxford friends – some of them Rhodes Scholars – knew each other intimately and were 'really one in thought, feeling and friendship'. To keep this relationship alive plans were being made which led eventually to the creation of the Royal Institute of International Affairs at Chatham House, St James's Square, the brain-child of Lionel Curtis, and the Council of Foreign Relations in New York.

To return to the summer of 1920, when he is off to the Continent for a long trip ('Must get grip of foreign affairs'). He notes at the end of August that he thought of tearing his diary up: 'Too priggish by half'. Then decides it is better to keep it for that reason.

Not much in the facts to alter. Save as to my relations with J.L.G. They are now rather those of father and son. I like and admire him enormously. He seems to trust me—perhaps rather more than I deserve. He is a genius: he is also a gentleman. As for Bell I never met a man I liked and respected more or with more cause. The O. is a happy and therefore all the more efficient family. It is a pity the Astors don't realize how much work is done there and in what spirit.[10]

The *Observer*, unasked, had given him a ten per cent salary increase back-dated to 1 March with a further ten per cent to come next March. Garvin was clearly pleased with his recruit, and the following year he told B-W he would leave him in charge for three months in the summer: 'I know it's a nuisance but I've never had even two months' rest since 1903. I should have six, but shall prefer to take half next year again.' No wonder the Astors had thought it was time to have an assistant editor!

B-W wrote fully and entertainingly to his mother about his London work and his weekends with people like the Astors. Nancy and he were getting along very well.

I had a jolly weekend at Sandwich [in August 1921]. Just saw Astor who left for Jura soon after I arrived. Grigg and Philip Kerr were staying there. I bathed and played golf. . . . I am invited to go down regularly for weekends. It would be pleasant but I don't think I can quite manage that. Other considerations apart, either I should have to be richer or fares and tips must come down. Butlers, chauffeurs, footmen make for the comfort of the stay and the discomfort of the Exchequer. I really grow more and more fond of the lady member. She has the pluck and vitality of twelve men, great charm and wit, a very good heart and a very quick feminine intelligence—not the blue-stocking kind, man-made at Somerville and Girton.[11]

Lady Astor begged me to stay over Tuesday [in October 1921]. The Crown Prince of Sweden was there and she needed my help to entertain him. So I could not leave her in the lurch. The result has been a somewhat compressed and intensive week. I hope you ap-

prove of its fruits. I wrote the main article and nearly all the notes
—I thought it a rather interesting paper.[12]

A rare comment on politics and on the problems of helping
Nancy Astor in 1922 hold her seat at Plymouth . . .

I am sick of stale talk about people's war records. A good war
record is an honourable fact. It is not an argument to support a
political candidature when we need brains and character and
experience to solve some of the greatest problems and the most
critical in our history. They require politicians, i.e. men who have
given some serious study to the arts of government . . .
If a General Election comes I fear I shall be dragged into the
Plymouth fight. I could conscientiously vote for the lady M.P. and,
were I a free man, I could equally work for her. But I confess to
being proud. I don't like going down as a salaried member of the
Observer staff because I have no wish to figure as anyone's political
lackey. However, I can't refuse on that ground and there is no
serious political difference giving a ground on which I could refuse
—which makes it all the more difficult.[13]

So electioneering he went. After visiting Duloe for the
weekend, he writes from Plymouth to ask his mother to send on
'an old brown check cap, suitable head-gear for democratic
occasions!' Such is electioneering, he says; 'I am getting a bit
notorious here. Now I am introduced as "your old friend Mr
B-W" and people address their questions to me by name!' He
was required 'to wrestle with the Communists on North Quay on
Sunday morning'. Again at the election of 1924:

They all know me now and bay for me. . . . They were very good-
tempered. I spoke for 30-40 minutes. The rest of the two hours was
heckling, questions and answer. This is what they enjoy. It is as
much a game to them as it would have been to the Athenians. At
the end I'm hanged if an unknown member of the crowd, now about
1,000, did not come forward and propose a vote of thanks which was
carried! I think, if I get on with the crowd, it is because I try to
answer fairly and don't aim first at squashing the heckler with
personal retorts.[14]

The political life does not seem to have tempted him, but
he was to complain bitterly of the social labyrinth in which he
had been caught and from which he never escaped.

Dined by myself, at last, thank Heaven. . . . I must get more time
for reading; yet, if I cut dining out, I miss things that I ought to be

in touch with. Haven't read a book for days and always late to bed. Cannot write without reading.[15]

S.O.S. from Lady Astor, begging me to go down to Cliveden to-night. I had asked to be excused till to-morrow morning. It was represented to me that they would be a man short. So I felt obliged to go. Great rush. Had to throw a good deal of work on Grey. Found a large party. The Queen [Marie] of Rumania, her sister Princess Beatrice, wife of the Infante Alfonso of Spain (himself also there), the Neville Chamberlains, the Samuel Hoares, the Ormsby-Gores, Brands, Geoffrey Dawson ... Philip Kerr.[16]

Certainly this was company not to be missed, especially when the proprietor's wife commanded.

The year 1926 brought a unique test of B-W's nerve and authority. Garvin was away in Aix-les-Bains when the National Strike began, immediately posing the question of how a paper was to be produced and got onto the streets. Urging his chief not to return, B-W gives in his letters a vivid report of what had gone on in Fleet Street and Tudor Street, where there had been crowds of four or five hundred men, all mostly quiet. *The Times*, in spite of an attempt to burn their printing department, had produced from their presses a double sheet paper of four pages, but it was unlikely that they would be able to repeat the feat (in fact they did so throughout the strike). The Berrys, in spite of having produced a *Financial Times* of four pages, were doubtful about getting out the *Sunday Times*. At the *Observer* they had tried in vain several outlying printers, because they felt the risks of trying to print on the spot were too great. So they were planning a single sheet through Roneo reproduction, with 'tabloids from Paris, Berlin and so on'. With volunteer cars they hoped to get a miniature *Observer* distributed to a sixty mile radius.*

However, owing to the dangers of disorder, B-W thought it possible that the Government might prohibit the appearance of any metropolitan paper except their own *British Gazette,* for which they had commandeered the office of the *Morning Post.* Its first number, wrote B-W, was a 'disastrous, partisan and provocative sheet'. He found the whole business 'loathsome – a

---

*On 9 May was produced a single sheet, printed both sides, $16\frac{1}{2} \times 12$ ins., and on 16 May two sheets (four pages) each $16\frac{1}{2} \times 12$ ins.

kind of mocking and distorting mirror of the war'. 'The sight of our own special picket,' he added, 'the most reluctant and unhappy picket ever seen in an industrial trouble, would move your heart. Our strikers have addressed to the office a most appealing and disarming epistle.'[17]

7

Back on the Ladder

How B-W came to leave the *Observer* for *The Times* after eight years there with Garvin is not entirely clear. Grigg may well have been again the intermediary, but B-W was meeting regularly, in *Round Table* and Astor circles, his old editor, who would read as a matter of course each Sunday what his former secretary was writing in the *Observer*.* He would know of B-W's growing reputation. The diaries show that Dawson was with him in July 1926 at a dinner-party to see Lady Astor off to the United States and there asked why he ever left Printing House Square. He seemed to be 'implying a shortage of lieu-tenants there, and said B-W 'should have been high in the hierarchy by now', B-W reminded Dawson that he himself had been parting with Northcliffe in 1919 and had advised acceptance of the *Observer*'s offer.[1]

The wish to get back had never faded. B-W records a talk over lunch in 1924 at which Garvin told him 'he did not want him to go and edit *The Times* just yet.' On which the diary comments: 'It seems only the remotest of possibilities. But that, or politics, I hope. These things best left to the future to take care of.'[2] There is no doubt that he came home from Tudor Street sometimes weary, stale and depressed, and that he had to work excessively at those times when Garvin was busy with his *Life of Joe Chamberlain* or editing the *Encyclopaedia Britannica*. There was work enough then at the *Observer* for two assistant editors. The paper was being produced on a shoe-string. Holidays were arranged without proper plan and crises like that of a Saturday in 1926 were not unusual.

*Adele Barrington-Ward remembers meeting Grigg at lunch and being asked by him why her husband had not gone back to *The Times*. She replied that it was because he had not been asked.

Worked all day and late. Wrote the whole editorial page—5 columns. Only once before have I done this. Usual supervision at night at the office as well.[3]

Garvin was now close on sixty but showed no desire to retire. He remained the dominating character who once said to Victor Gollancz over brandy, 'Do you know, looking back over the years, I think I have never been wrong.'[*] There was no sign of decline in a man who could ring up on Saturday morning and say he was sending up by car for that issue an article on the war, the main article on Ireland, and a memoir of an old friend. 'No one else in journalism could do it,' his deputy remarked. The succession was fading into the distance, a happening which is not unusual when an editor finds an efficient deputy whom he likes. 'Garvin might go on for a decade or more.'

So at thirty-six B-W felt he was in danger of falling out of the field of future editors. When his contract had expired at the end of 1924 he was offered a new one of five years with a rise in salary; but Garvin himself asked whether it would be wise for his deputy to tie his hands for so long. 'This is just like his generous heart, the finest of chiefs,' B-W noted. His affectionate relations with 'Garve' were the intimidating obstacle. A remarkable letter of 1924 from the older man in his Carlyle-like style sounds like father writing to son.[†] (B-W had been unwell and the suggestion is that the proprietor had been unreasonable. In fact, Waldorf Astor was a most considerate man, except in his sometimes tiresome demand for attacks on the drink trade.)

[*]An article in the *Belfast Telegraph* by a former member of the staff of the *Observer* in March 1948 described B-W at this period: 'As he sat, silent and still, in the room in Tudor Street, while the Garve introduced me to him in about a million clattering words . . . the chief impression he made on me, on everybody, was of quietness of mind and spirit. I soon learned to think of the Garve and B-W as the two halves of our Ulster people: Garve as the highly articulate Roman Catholic Ulsterman, B-W as the silent Ulster Protestant . . . . Not mark you that B-W had nothing to say or that he seldom spoke. He could talk well and effectively. The Garve, too, could listen intently, though few will believe this, and he very frequently did. But garrulity seemed to be the characteristic of the one, as silence seemd to be the characteristic of the other . . .'

[†]Garvin had been stricken and stunted by the death of his son in 1916, leaving him as 'the last male of my race'. B-W was the first to become the confidant and steadying sympathizer that he needed, as well as the understudy in the office. Later the role was filled by his stepson, Oliver Woods, who followed B-W to *The Times* in 1936 and had a distinguished career in the office and abroad as its specialist on Commonwealth affairs.

Great Cumberland Place

My Dear Boy,

I know: it's a hair shirt; but life is difficult at phases and demands tremendous patience biding the hour. You have done the right thing and I think the need won't recur. You see I talk to you like Ulysses, which in our sphere I am—much-travelled in a profession needing far more dangerous navigation than any other. You are a safeguard there you see. It's important.

Heaven knows it's hard on me too. When I finished my six intense columns on Saturday night and then looked at the news pages, and you were not there, I felt irrepressibly tired and lonely. The camel's back didn't break but felt the last haystack on top of the load. I got home at one in the morning and sat up till between three and four, too firmly quietly done to go to bed ...

It's not only your prized work I miss: its grip and sense and truth. It's you, as well. Even if I do as much, it's easier when you are there. I dare say you know I have come to love you like a son, which perhaps is natural in the circumstances. There's no other young man I care for half as much—no not half, nor nearly half—satisfied, proud of our fights together for that 'which is most worthy to be blest'. I'm the last male of my race, and when the stock has been strong that is humanly a hard thought though philosophically a very foolish one. All I can say is, your coming has made it easy to bear. It's much to say. You understand. I feel I have got a soul's son, out of Westminster too, if I have none of my body. But when you are not beside me in a crisis everything is heavier again. But you'll soon be back—thank God.

Your affectionate,
J.L.G.[4]

The conversation with Dawson bore fruit in April 1927 when B-W visited him at his house and was offered an assistant editor's post at *The Times*. The Waldorf Astors had been consulted, he was told, but not Garvin. Two days later B-W himself told his chief, who was angry and very much upset at the idea of losing 'the only right-hand he had ever had'. Then came from P.H.S. the formal offer of £1,500 a year and £500 expenses, a useful if not substantial rise, which B-W after consulting Walter Monckton and having a 'good sensible talk with J.L.G.' accepted.

During the last two years, important events had been changing his social life. In January 1925 he set up a bachelor household on Haverstock Hill in a cottage costing him only

£65 a year. The privacy after Harley Street, more particularly the garden, gave him the keenest pleasure. There was main road traffic past the front, but at the back french windows opened into a garden with an old vine, which he dug up, and two pear trees which were in full blossom for his first spring there. The teaching of Mr Johns came in useful. He ordered sweet williams, larkspur, Canterbury bells and 'other delights'. 'If I had more time or less conscience I should be all the time in the garden. . . . I think of Pater every time I go into the garden and wish he were here to advise.' He went to concerts and plays, played cricket for the *Observer* on Mondays, kept up with old friends now married, like Alister Wedderburn, or making their way, like Adrian Boult, conducting his first orchestra in Birmingham. He was able with small dinner-parties to return some of the hospitality he was offered.

Life was very full and mostly pleasant, but he longed for the leisure to get down again to his books. Lance gave him a small Conington's *Horace* which he read riding up and down in the tube. His weekends were nearly always taken up with 'useful' country visits. The conscience which drove him at his work, drove him in his leisure. One wonders whether the presence of Pater was not felt at his shoulder long after he died in 1924 and the Rectory ceased to be home. He was deeply affected by the break with Duloe, 'the one spot in the world which has everything palpable and impalpable to content me and to which I belong'. So were the brothers, and a scheme was suggested – but quickly dropped – to buy the Rectory and keep it as a home for Mater. Instead, she had to be brought north and was settled at Pinner, close enough to London to enjoy some of the social life with her sons.

Most active in this respect was Lance, the surgeon, whose accomplished and musical wife, Dot, gave dinner-parties and dances at 85 Harley Street, which went with a rare swing. It was at one of these in July 1926 that Robin met Adele Radice, daughter of a distinguished Indian civil servant, a friend of Garvin's daughter Viola with whom she had been teaching at Putney High School. The eligible bachelor of thirty-five, who had shown little interest in women, was, in his own phrase, 'pole-axed'. She, on the other hand, was at first no more than interested in a partner whose dancing with a woman slightly taller than himself was much less attractive than his conversation. With a season in India behind her and a gay time at Oxford studying History, Adele at twenty-eight was a mature young woman who had friends and interests in common with Robin. She was described by his eldest brother as 'beautiful in an Italian and statuesque way' with dark hair and remarkable blue eyes.

After the first note in his diary that he had met Adele and 'had no difficulty about a partner' there are significant blanks for over a fortnight, at the end of which he wrote, 'These have been the best and worst weeks of my life.' To fall deeply in love for the first time while working at full stretch for Garvin must indeed have been an ordeal. Greatly daring he took one Friday evening off and dined at the Café de Paris to meet her again: 'I got all I had a right to expect of the dancing that I wanted.' He danced, too, with Geoffrey Dawson's wife, Cecilia, thinking to himself that she must wonder how the assistant editor of a Sunday paper came to be out dancing on a Friday night. By the end of the year – with his debts only just paid off and his future uncertain in his own mind – he had married Adele at All Souls, Langham Place. They went off for a sight-seeing honeymoon on a continental tour prescribed by 'Garve'. His letter of congratulation on their engagement is worth quoting:

My dear B-W,

This wonderful news of yours causes me so much personal happiness that I smile almost enough for you to see it in Cornwall. And my wife rejoices and so will Viola when she knows. I remember Miss Radice distinctly but also my girl has always talked immensely about her and always in her praise, and I am satisfied that you are a lucky man, and tell her from me that I know she will be a happy woman . . .

I've always said about love that it doubles the delight of the reason as well the joy of the heart.

The holiday must be a long one—one to remember for scene as well. . . . So my dearest B-W, the *best to work with me for all the true causes* that ever I have found, I can only say God Bless you from a full heart and remain steady.

Your affectionate,
J. L. Garvin[5]

So is the letter from Nancy Astor, now losing one of her best-liked and most reliable bachelor guests.

From: *Mirador, Greenwood, Virginia*

What better place to write a lover than from Mirador! I am truly glad for you, glad for her, and sad for us! I know just what these happy marriages mean. In fact it's notorious that *I* prefer my friends unhappily married. However you seem to have taken all precautions and she sounds charming—*tho'*, you *can't really* be trusted to judge of her just now. I know *no one's* plans interest you now *but* the point of telling you mine *is* that I hope you will soon bring *her* to see us at Cliveden—I hope you know that my love and best wishes for a *long* and dreary married life go with this hasty line. Why the young woman should be so lucky I know not. I hope she's not an R.C. Anyhow you could never be.

With love to you both,
yours,
Nancy Astor[6]

When B-W, in May 1927, duly took Adele with him down to Cliveden for her first visit, she recalls the awe-inspiring and forthright manner in which her hostess greeted her, leaving her almost speechless with nervousness. But Nancy Astor's charm quickly worked and they spent an enjoyable weekend in that splendid mansion. When B-W talked with her about his change of job, she said that her husband 'was rather upset about it, but she was rather pleased – partly for my sake, partly because I should be better able to edit the *Observer* one day (?), partly because I should be a channel for her good causes on *The Times*, and partly because I was too much enveloped in J.L.G. All amusing reasons. She was in excellent form'. B-W was doubtless aware of a further cause of friction between Waldorf and John Astor: that the latter refused to allow the former's newspaper to be printed on the presses of *The Times*.

After a very rushed spring and summer in 1927, house-hunting and widely entertained as newly-weds, leaving Haverstock Hill and a tearful housekeeper, there came the moment to leave Garve. Lord Astor gave a farewell dinner-party at 4 St James's Square on 12 October at which most of the *Observer* staff were present. Whatever slight irritation between the two branches of the newspaper-owning Astor family had been caused by the transfer of a favourite from one to the other had subsided and all seemed nicely set for B-W's new start.* But he was not starting as fresh as he should have done. Up to the last minute he worked hard for Garvin. He was feeling the strain of moving to a new job and Adele was expecting her first child. He felt as if doomed never to rest.

Working seven days a week, sleeping upstairs, rather tired and at times a little too sorry for myself. Feeling the need of normal life and a holiday.

And there, so far as the diary and the papers go, the story of his time in Tudor Street ends.

What mark did B-W leave on the *Observer* and what mark did it leave on him? The second question is more easily answered than the first. It gave him the supreme qualifications for his next job: confidence that he could write at short notice on any subject under the sun, especially politics. Week after week his political notes on the leader page – 'terse, tight, right' Garvin called them – had been the tastefully, efficiently arranged dish of vegetables beside the great, savoury Sunday roast cooked and carved by Garve. When the chef was away, B-W or some outside person would perform instead. So the new assistant editor of *The Times* had tasted the joys of broad columns and ample space. He had been trained in intensive night work on Fridays and Saturdays and he was used to supervising the whole range of a serious newspaper's features – literary and social, men's and women's features, political and economic, home and foreign. He was, in fact, a pioneer of 'weekend' features.

As for leader-writing, Garvin had claimed in a letter to Northcliffe to have revolutionized the art: 'a touch of the poet, a touch of the prophet, and a touch of the wirepuller too (for I know what politics are and must be)'. B-W was an apt pupil and caught something of the oracular style. He had seen in operation Garvin's flair for the interesting topic – that curious ability, formed of intuition and experience, which enables a man to choose unexpected themes to write about which other

*Mr David Astor thinks that B-W was wrong in believing that the move caused irritation between the two branches of the family. He explains that Lord and Lady Astor were on much closer terms, both political and personal, with Dawson than with Garvin, and seldom met John Astor, owing to a family disagreement unconnected with the newspaper, but arising from their father's acceptance of a peerage.

journalists at once recognize, on seeing them, as the only right ones. Garvin did not underrate the importance of topicality, but he was a master of the art of timing, which is quite a different thing. He would create news by advancing a view or a theory at the right moment; and he would never hesitate to make his argumentative article into a narrative one if it suited his purpose. Stanley Morison declared that it was Garvin who taught B-W how to address a special audience instead of preaching to the public at large, and we shall see later how the pupil sometimes wrote with echoes of the master. 'Consistency,' Garvin had insisted, 'compels conviction', and B-W was to prove consistent to a fault.

There was one serious weakness that the new Assistant Editor brought with him: a habit of over-centralizing authority and overworking, of trying to reconcile the conflicting roles of office administrator and policy-making writer. If B-W had a natural tendency to fall into this error, the shoe-string methods of the *Observer* turned it into a habit which was to damage his health and, in the end, his performance in the office. But in retrospect B-W felt nothing but gratitude to Garvin, far apart though their views moved after the thirties. When on 23 January 1947 Oliver Woods rang him up to say that his stepfather Garve was dead B-W was deeply shocked. He wrote that night:

Can't take it in. What has he not meant to me and my family? He is one of the people to whom I owe anything I have done. A great human figure. It is hard to think of my world without him. 28 years almost exactly since we met at the Café Royal and dined together on the evening of my joining the *Observer*.[7]

8

Interlude

To look, at this stage of the narrative, a few years back and a few years forward from the date (1927) when B-W left the *Observer* for *The Times* should make it easier to understand by what experience of events and in what controversies his attitude to Germany – and to world affairs generally – was formed. Although simplification invites immediate and violent disagreement, only the simplest and most general survey is attempted. The purpose is not to impose a dogmatic view, but to recall the time-scale of events, the speed with which in only twenty years – within the middle age of B-W – a peace settlement turned into world war. Anyone recalling and reflecting on the pace of events between 1945 and 1965 will realize how little time there was in Britain between 1919 and 1939 for the changing of convictions and the transformation of national policy by democratic process.

To an extent that we can now hardly imagine the great power situation for a few years after 1920 looked relatively simple. Russia was out; Japan was not to show aggressive symptoms for another ten years; Germany was prostrate and in disorder; what had been Austro-Hungary was balkanized. Apart from local difficulties in the Middle East and India, the central security problem was to decide whether the peace of Europe was to be indefinitely maintained by France, with British approval, holding down Germany. The League of Nations, it is true, was being built up as the guardian of security everywhere; but by 1924 it was clear that very few nations would take their obligations seriously, even in their own local part of the world, by actually enforcing peace. The optimism of Britain – its determination to economize and relax – was reflected in the notorious 'Ten Year Rule', by which the British Cabinet directed the Service Departments year after year to base their estimates 'on the assumption that the British Empire will not be engaged in any great war during the next ten years'.*

This was, too, a time not only of withdrawal by the United States from the Europe and from the League that it had helped to create, but also of acute rivalry with Britain in naval armaments, in the course of which the Americans unwisely forced the British to jettison the friendship of Japan.

It was against this background that B-W in the *Observer* was commenting on foreign policy in the post-war years. The great debate was about whether to support victorious France or to succour defeated Germany, between the idealism and the *Realpolitik* of the Versailles Treaty, between conciliation and repression; just as we in the sixties discussed whether the Russians or the Americans started the Cold War, so scholars in Europe and the USA were discussing whether the Germans really alone caused the 1914 war. Always in the foreground, too, was the hope of restoring prosperity abroad by creating confidence, and so bringing economic recovery at home. To this discussion B-W brought three qualities. First his recent experience as a front-line soldier who had survived with the determination that the sacrifice of his generation should not have been made in vain. (Corporal Hitler, it should be remembered, with a very different mentality and background, had the same idea.) Second, he had a certain liberalism of outlook and believed that everyone might be persuaded in the end by patient reasonableness. Some part was played in this by the Ulsterman's obstinacy (revealed in that long upper lip of his), and he did not change his mind either quickly or easily in a period when events moved fast. Then, too, there was a taste for broad general ideas of policy, which had tempted him into journalism and was encouraged by seven years' close association with Garvin, the great generalizer of his day. A minor factor, revealed in his letters and diaries, was the memory of

---

*This rule was not abrogated until the end of 1932. Thus, when the estimates for 1933 (Hitler's first year in power) were being prepared it was assumed that no great war was likely before 1943. As Stephen Roskill points out in his *Naval Policy Between the Wars* (Collins, 1968), this rule was 'wholly empirical and not based on any scientific analysis', yet it gave the Treasury the whiphand whenever increased arms expenditure was proposed. The rule may have been known to a few editors and journalists concerned with defence; it was known to Colin Coote when writing for *The Times*. But it seems never, or seldom, to have been referred to in public or parliamentary debate.

dishonesty and muddle among statesmen that he took away from the Paris Peace Conference when he visited friends there.

To this store of ideas, impressions and prejudices B-W added an informed interest in the Empire, which outside *The Round Table* group was rare in that generation of journalists. Questions of definition and demarcation of the powers and responsibilities of dominions overseas were appearing which seemed more important and more tractable than the problems of Europe. The idea of the Commonwealth was gestating. Dawson – and to a lesser extent B-W – has been criticized for this imperial attachment; but to them it seemed obvious that, for example, the future of India and South Africa was no less important than the future of Eastern Europe and that relations with Canada and Australia might be the key to cooperation with the United States in the Far East. In this respect they were stronger on geopolitics and more far-seeing than some of their critics. Besides, Europe seemed to be settling down. By 1927, when B-W had gone to *The Times,* the Locarno Treaties (under which Britain joined with France, Germany and Belgium in mutual guarantees of frontiers) had begun the process of conciliating Germany and breaking up the encircling French security system, which he believed to be untenable in the long run. The switch of policy had taken just about as long as it took to decide and carry out after the Second World War the rearmament of Federal Germany. Now another five years were to make it clear that German rearmament under National Socialism was the new problem.

The resurgence of national feeling among Germans even before 1933 was, and could reasonably be treated as, a sign of the urgent need to reach with them an arms agreement and territorial settlement. On this possibility the Berlin and London offices of *The Times* saw eye to eye. But for anyone committed like B-W to the diagnosis that German behaviour was largely due to injustice still to be righted, it was not easy to decide when to change the attitude. (So long as you hope a mental patient will recover under treatment you hesitate to certify him and put him away.) The question between 1933 and 1936 was whether Hitler might not after a while settle down. History suggested that revolutions often run out of steam. If there was to be a change in the conciliatory attitude to

Germany, how soon should it come and how quickly would British public opinion accept the implications? That was the British Government's problem – and it was also B-W's. Not being a Jew or a left-wing radical, he was not prepared to change his attitude just because the new rulers of Germany were Fascists and – as the 1934 purge reminded him – gangsters. He objected just as strongly to the methods of Stalin.

By this time the pattern of international affairs had been made more dangerous and complicated by Japan's defiance of the League in Manchuria and by the antics of Mussolini in the Mediterranean. Whitehall – and B-W certainly knew this – assessed the strategic dangers at that time, largely in naval terms, as coming first from Japan, second from Italy and only third from Germany. The Anglo-German Naval Agreement of 1935 was approved in the light of these priorities and the speed at which Germany might rearm was underestimated, largely because it was judged by the inadequate pace of our own production in the aircraft, tank and ship-building industries.

Once the need for rearmament had begun to press itself on ministers – and on Printing House Square – the question was asked 'How much will the public take?' What rearmament could a National Government get away with short of splitting its ranks? And what could a country showing the first signs of recovery from the economic disasters of 1931 afford for modern weapons? Allowance has to be made here for the difficulty of quickly jettisoning the policy followed for over a decade. For *The Times* to change its course was like turning a battleship – it needed time and room. Moreover, that influential part of opinion which was against war and armaments, which had backed the Government and *The Times* in their League policy, and agitated for the first dismantling of the peace treaties, needed a lot of convincing that collective security might mean actually fighting.

Britain having failed to lead the League into effective action against Japan – it would have been an impossible exercise of naval power without some American cooperation – it was not surprising to find France hesitant about, and under Laval actively hostile to, sanctions against Italy, her neighbour in the Mediterranean on whose goodwill depended all possibility

75

of communication with her alliance system in eastern Europe.* Between 1935 and 1937, therefore, *The Times* found itself in the difficulty that it still wished to try out on Nazi Germany the effect of an active conciliatory policy (ways of accepting some German rearmament and removing 'discriminatory' clauses of the Peace Treaties were being actually discussed between London and Paris, with German knowledge) while also advocating cautiously rearmament by Britain. Against this policy those who had never trusted Germany, or who were naturally pro-French, and those who wanted a holy war against Fascism – especially in Spain – began to join hands. The temperature was raised even higher by the intense anti-Fascist propaganda of Communist parties everywhere, which expressed among other things the fear of war in the Soviet Union, then going through the crisis of the great purges.

By the end of 1936 it was clear from Abyssinia's fate that collective security against an aggressor was not going to work as had been hoped. Hitler, by moving troops into the demilitarized Rhineland in March, had shown that he was not going to wait for concessions in Europe to be made at the leisurely pace of the Foreign Offices. But he was expressing, sincerely or not, a detailed interest in the organization of Europe's security through a 'new Locarno' which tempted those who still believed in 'appeasement' to test his sincerity by attempts at negotiation. The French decision in 1935 to sign a pact with the Soviet Union, thus strengthening the 'encirclement' by democratic and Bolshevik forces against which Hitler so shrilly protested, gave him a plausible excuse to stall on such negotiations. Encouraged by the refusal to use effective sanctions against Italy, he set about revision of the treaties in his own gangster fashion, using the techniques of cold war and guerrilla to prepare the way for the Reichswehr and the Luftwaffe. It was by these methods that were accomplished the *Anschluss* with Austria, which so many friends of Bruening's Germany had said should be allowed to happen

*As a young reporter believing ardently in collective security, the author was deeply shocked when a sardonic Laval assured him, in an interview at Geneva (not for publication) not long after the Walwal incident, that the French Government believed that Britain would take no action against Italy and did not want to. 'Are we to push Italy into the arms of Germany?' he asked. The answer was not at that time obvious. A report on the conversation was sent to London.

peacefully, and the taking over of the Sudeten areas of Czechoslovakia.

Meanwhile, during these last five years of the thirties, Britain faced outside Europe other demands on her limited forces, as the chiefs of staff pointed out persistently to ministers. Japan's attitude was causing serious anxiety; Palestine was a running sore; there was an incipient Italian threat to Egypt and there were doubts about the safety of Mediterranean sea routes in war – unless Mussolini could be wooed away from Hitler. Above all, there was intense but carefully concealed anxiety in Whitehall over the difficulties of defending against air attack London and the ports and the other great cities. It was not only a question of fighter aircraft and the radar organization to guide them, or of anti-aircraft guns and the men to fight them; how was the public to be persuaded to organize street by street for its own civil defence?

It is difficult to recapture now and present in words the indifference, cynicism, laziness and scoffing incredulity with which the first local organizers of air raid precautions had to contend. They were symptoms of the reluctance with which most of the population recognized that 'standing up to Hitler' meant gas masks for the children, air raid shelters in the garden, and war – war which the Navy had for centuries kept at a distance – to be fought on the very doorstep of home and place of work. B-W, so cautious about rearmament of the forces, never had the slightest doubt about advocating a prepared and self-confident civil defence.*

*During three of these years the author spent several holidays working with the paper. In December 1937 he made a detailed survey of the state of air raid precautions in various key areas of the country, which was published in three critical turnover articles in January 1938.

9

Return to P.H.S. (1927-34)

B-W needed almost as long to advance from Assistant to Deputy Editor of *The Times* as he had taken to prepare himself at the *Observer* for his return to Printing House Square. That was not his fault but the predictable result of the post-Northcliffe regime. Assisting the Editor, and often sitting in for him at night, was George Murray Brumwell, thirty years older than B-W. As Associate Editor under Northcliffe he had once had hopes of the highest position. Now his chief function was the detailed scrutiny of proofs and pages that had to be made between tea-time and edition-time.

Unconcerned for most of the week with policy-making, Brumwell exerted great authority by simply taking the time to detect inaccuracies, breaches of the office style book, offences against taste and abuses of the English language which others had let pass. He would never have allowed 'Oxbridge' into the paper; 'ground to a halt' would have been changed to 'stopped'; the 'lovers' lane' in which reporters place murders and assaults would have been called 'a secluded spot'. To be sent for by this bulky, bald, deep-voiced man and to be told, as he stared ferociously over his roll-top desk, that one must understand once and for all that *The Times* never used this or that expression, was alarming and salutary.* Most people stood in awe of 'old Brumwell'.

*Five written rules shaped the character of the paper at this time. No sensationalism; no colloquialisms; anonymity; rigid separation of news from features; clear lines between reporting and comment. Each of these rules was from time to time broken, but some of the reputation of *The Times* for accuracy and objectivity rested on what was later to be known as 'stuffiness'. A distinguished author would be allowed to sign an article, but never a member of the staff; the timing of a leader or the coverage of something like the Everest Expedition could be sensational but not through exaggeration of style; a new coinage like 'body-line bowling' would be admitted on probation, but would be used for a long time between quotes. It was the exceptions that made the rules so fascinating to those who had to apply them.

Every newspaper needs a Brumwell and everyone in the
P.H.S. knew that the high standards of accuracy, the consistency
of style and tone in *The Times,* owed much to this man. For
Dawson – like Delane a news-gatherer – was not one to spend
much time on textual criticism and close reading of proofs,
although he was a most skilful mender of other people's headlines and comment. For practical purposes Brumwell was playing the Deputy Editor's part when B-W returned, so the arrival
of the promising young recruit from the *Observer* must have
been a warning to this survivor of pre-war days that his
seniority would be coming to an end.* This alone would
account for a certain suspicion and irritability towards the new
day-editor; but Brumwell also had at home a constant anxiety
about which he never complained: an invalid wife whose
condition had long made a trial of most of his leisure. No
wonder that he would sometimes reappear at work without
explanation on a day he had agreed to take off, making the
new man feel distrusted or disliked.

The office where B-W arrived in the autumn of 1927 was
a place of long, dark corridors, high-ceilinged and linoleum-
covered, in which one heard the machines pulsing in the distance. Messengers of all ages disappeared into great square
rooms, with heavy latching doors, full of light and cold, big
enough for a writer to walk up and down as he pondered a
paragraph. Each had its lavish coal fire and tall, double sash
windows overlooking Queen Victoria Street and Blackfriars
Station with glimpses of the river and Westminster. Each had a
number and an identity: home subs, foreign subs, conference
room, special writers' rooms (two or three together). Some contained long rows of wire-protected shelves containing the
paper's excellent library, into which John Maywood, head of
the Intelligence Department, vainly tried to guide back copies
of books sent for review to members of the staff.

A small room on the first floor at the back was the Editor's,
overlooking Printing House Square and the Walters' old private
house. It was uncomfortable and unhealthy, B-W used to complain, for you were frozen on one side by the window and

---

*Before 1914 Brumwell had made up the paper and Dawson had for No. 2
G. S. Freeman, an Assistant Editor. The great improvement in the appearance of
The Times between 1908 and 1914 was largely due to Brumwell's efforts as its first
night-editor. He was known as the 'beautifier'.

baked on the other by a coal fire, but it had the compactness of a captain's day cabin. Within its modest dimensions Dawson had perfected an adroit manoeuvre to get rid of anyone who stayed too long. He would rise suddenly from his chair, walk quickly round his desk, causing the person opposite him to rise and turn, and then place a friendly hand on shoulder or elbow with which he coaxed or propelled the visitor to the door. This piece of ring-craft could be performed only in a room where the stranger quickly got the feeling, as it were, of the ropes at his back. B-W, in the day-editor's room upstairs, never achieved such prompt dismissals. Being a kind and polite man, he would seldom do more than glance at the clock over the fireplace and hope that the caller would take the hint.

On 11 January 1929, eighteen months after his arrival, B-W was asked by Dawson for the first time to edit. We can imagine the pride and pleasure with which he came downstairs to take over at last in the coveted seat. Word would go round the office: 'B-W's in the chair tonight.' Eyebrows were probably raised among the old stagers and B-W may have felt slight embarrassment as he passed colleagues in the corridors – for his moments of triumph were generally followed by moments of self-questioning. The various stages of editing would be familiar from *Observer* days – even the thrill of seeing not long before midnight 'my first paper'. But this was *The Times* and in all this satisfaction there was one flaw:

> Brumwell took a day off – not even a proper day since he was in the office in the afternoon. I don't think B. trusts me very far. Anyhow all went off well.[1]

The absence of Dawson in India for three months during 1929 might have been expected to give B-W a real chance as deputy to Brumwell, but instead the diary notes the night-editor saying to him one evening:

> Jenkins said to me at the office that Dawson was likely to be annoyed to find that Brumwell had not given me any chance of training on as deputy. The fault is not (so far as I can judge) mine. I volunteered to take a night every week for about six weeks and then desisted. It is no good making myself cheap.[2]

This lack of understanding with his colleague became, not surprisingly, something of an obsession. He had never before

The Deputy Editor outside his Regent's Park house in the late thirties.

A Working Dinner in the Ladies' First Aid Post at Printing House Square during the Blitz, 8 November 1940. The host is the Chairman John Astor; on his right is Geoffrey Dawson, the Editor. Opposite B-W is John Walter V.

The Day Editor's room on the second floor at Printing House Square, after the bombing in 1940. B-W worked here for thirteen years.

found it difficult to get on with anybody. To his slight disgust, he found himself resenting the changes that this man made in his leaders: 'he had hung a turgid peroration' on a leader about the death of Marshal Foch. When current gossip in March 1929 said that Dawson was to go to All Souls as Warden, leaving Brumwell or B-W to succeed as Editor, the diary noted:

Brumwell could not at his age expect many years of it, but how many months could I stand under Brumwell? Working with Brumwell, who is the most conventionally minded, not to say narrow, man I have ever struck, has been a growing burden since Christmas.[3]

Later he was to qualify this uncharitable judgement. However, he learned with relief in February 1934 that Brumwell had asked to be pensioned. When he retired at the end of the year the way would be clear to bring on younger men, one of whom would release B-W from some of his daytime chores for more editing and leader-writing.

B. and I have never got on and I have long abandoned the efforts I made several years ago to get on terms with him.... But his timid, vigilant and exhaustive caution has a good side and has often been very serviceable. He is about the only man in the whole of my experience that I have failed to get on with. But I have tried latterly not to forget the trials, most loyally borne, and the homelessness of his home.[4]

When B-W asked how this retirement would affect the Editor's plans to visit South Africa in the New Year he was told he would have to carry on in the chair. A month later, however, Dawson had cancelled his Empire Press tour, partly because the Prime Minister did not like the idea of his being away during the debates on the Bill for reforms in India. B-W was naturally alarmed and puzzled, even though the value of Dawson's powerful advocacy of Baldwin's Indian policy against Churchill was apparent.

He told me he thought the burden of the whole office, unassisted, would be too much for me. I said I faced it with equanimity and was clearing my decks for it now. On the other hand I realized that we should have the India Bill (which is his particular affair) and controversy in full blast. But he insisted that he could trust me to look after all these things and that what really troubled him was the feeling that he was going off at a busy time on what was merely a

81

jaunt. It appears that Stanley Baldwin, when he saw him this week, expressed alarm over the plan.

I suppose I may as well accept the explanation offered me without looking for another less favourable to myself. At the same time I suspect he thinks that I have been too deeply absorbed in the History and in special numbers lately. But only because someone must look after them and they must do us credit as far as I can contrive, not from any preference of mine. I would rather be wholly absorbed in policy but, while G.D. is here, I neither need nor can be.[5]

This passage reveals the strength and weakness of B-W as a future deputy. His readiness to take on for several weeks the duties of editing by day and by night was ill-judged, as Dawson must have realized. Already, by trying to write important leaders in the evening after a full day's work he had forced on himself that conflict between administrative and creative duties of which he had complained on the *Observer*.* He would doubtless have argued that writing articles as well as deciding to introduce the crossword puzzle into the paper for the first time (on 23 January 1930) and organizing with Stanley Morison the changeover to the new type, or arranging features like the serialization of Garvin's *Life of Joseph Chamberlain* and James Barrie's special Christmas story was just what he had been used to on the *Observer*.

Five years after his arrival B-W was feeling the strain of these day duties. After hours spent with two of the staff planning a special number on the English Home (a task for a features editor on any other paper) he grumbled to himself: 'I could wish I had something nearer to my heart to busy me. It all seems a little remote from the steps of the editorial throne, and in the meantime I get less and less of the editorial practice which I had so fully at the *Observer*.' Yet the way to establish his position was to make himself indispensable by taking off the Editor's shoulders duties that did not interest him. So well did he succeed after the first four or five years that people said Dawson was exploiting him. Be that as it may, never was a deputy more ready to be exploited. Frequent mentions in the diary of meals missed, of late arrivals at parties (sometimes

---

*One administrative achievement of these months was the capture from the *Daily Telegraph* as defence correspondent of Basil Liddell Hart, who was invited on 26 November to join the staff. See Chapter 15.

his own dinner-parties with Adele left to entertain six guests until after nine o'clock) and of first leaders written four in a row are written more in pride than in self-pity.

By the end of 1934 B-W was confirmed as second-in-command, and this is perhaps the moment to note the part played by chance in shaping this part of his career. Originally he had been engaged as a principal political leader-writer, but before his six months' notice to Garvin ended Gordon Robbins, *The Times*'s day-editor, had been tempted away into publishing. B-W, who had been thought of as an extra writer, therefore became an administrative replacement. Then came in November 1929 the death of Flanagan, the principal leader-writer.* He had written the series of leading articles which had (according to the Liberal press) 'stampeded' Britain into war in August 1914. His loss, following hard on the death of Harold Williams, the Foreign Editor, left a gap in foreign affairs comment into which circumstances, as well as love of writing, were to tempt B-W.

As day-editor, a post which combined the duties on another paper of features editor and managing editor, B-W became the channel through which management approached editorial with query after query. Now it was about circulation, which was flagging; now about the appearance and arrangement of the paper, which were out-of-date; now about planning a special issue, intended to encourage advertisers; now about the *History of the Times*, the first volume of which was to appear in 1935, the 150th anniversary of the first issue of the *Daily Universal Register,* and on which B-W did much editorial work.†

*Wolfe Flanagan was a much-loved office character. He arrived each night at 7 and would, when required, produce by 11 a distinguished first leader, written in longhand on half sheets of paper which were passed uncorrected to the printer. Before writing, this 'bowed frail little man with spiritual face and keen eyes and fine silver hair' would change his socks and put on black felt slippers, a black cardigan, and a white silk neckerchief. He would place a bottle of soda water on the table with his packet of sandwiches and then tie up the handle of his desk with his handkerchief to prevent its rattling. 'An example of journalism and contented anonymity at its highest,' B-W remarked. The soda water was presented to each leader-writer gratis by the management, which had long ceased to provide port wine.

†The extent of the work done by B-W on the *History* is revealed in a memorandum sent to him by Stanley Morison in November 1934: 'I don't know anybody else who would have consecrated himself so freely and fully to the dreariest form of all drudgery – the heeling and soleing of my thousands of hack paragraphs. You have made a flowing narrative out of a set of smudgy blue-prints.'

Each of these projects called for the qualities which had made B-W a successful Brigade Major. But the average denizen of Printing House Square did not respond to military methods. Tact and patience were needed, for example, to get the old and long-retired Editor George Earle Buckle working at the *History* with the ambitious, outspoken newcomer forty-year-old Stanley Morison; or to persuade John Walter V and members of the Board that the world would not come to an end if the title of the paper were improved.

It is not surprising, then, to find him grumbling about reduced writing opportunities. One day he took up an old *Round Table* and re-read one of his articles of ten years ago. 'I wrote better then,' he remarked; lack of practice, he feared, might make him lose his touch. But these tasks were most important for the paper's future. The anniversary and the *History* were to provide prestigious and wide publicity through reviews and tributes from all over the world. The circulation drive was to help rescue the office from the worst effects of the slump. The change of type and title – the putting of news on the front page was not even discussed – made *The Times* for some years the best-looking daily newspaper in the English language. Indeed, when Stanley Morison in August 1929 first agreed to act as typographical adviser, he hoped if all went well to make it 'the finest piece of printing, without exception, in the world'.*

The withering criticism of the paper's appearance made at that date by Morison, then working with the Monotype Corporation on the design of new types, had shocked the management. At an office meeting on 24 October 1930 he proposed that 'the type face used in the editorial and advertising columns of *The Times* be redesigned and brought up to the standard obtaining in the average book as brought out by London publishers'. To consider the many questions of practice and taste which were raised, the Manager appointed a small committee of which B-W was chairman. He quickly became Morison's main supporter and the most persuasive influence in discussions between proprietors, directors, management, and composing room which occupied the next two years. With shrewd judgement of the traditionalist resistance of his opponents, Morison presented them with a magnificently pro-

*I owe this account of the Morison changes to his biographer Nicholas Barker.

84

duced essay on the history and principles of typography, holding back until the last moment his proposals for changing the
elaborate gothic title of the paper.

Endless trouble was taken over what must be for many years
an irrevocable transformation; even the medical aspects of
readability were considered with the help of the eye surgeon,
Sir William Lister. Morison urged the design of a type 'English
in its basic tradition, new, though free from conscious archaism
or conscious art, losing no scintilla of that "legibility" which
rests upon fundamental ocular laws, or of that "readability"
which rests upon age-long customs of the eye'. With the skilful
help of Victor Lardent, of the publicity department, the new
letters were drawn in pencil and changed again and again until
the essentials of Times New Roman were settled.

Feeling ran highest over the title and the heraldic device at
the top of the front page. John Walter V said the Gothic letter-
ing was the paper's trademark; to lose it might be disastrous.
But Morison was scathing on the subject and described the
titling as 'the most significant memorial of the lapse in English
taste' which came about in the middle of the eighteenth century.

The white line drawn or tooled on every letter, which connoted
gaiety to the post-Strawberry Hill generation of aesthetes, is to us a
repulsive toying with three-dimensional effects.[6]

We may doubt whether his opponents understood this historical reference, but it was with another item of historical
research that Morison clinched the argument. He was able to
prove that in the first issue of *The Times* in June 1788 the title
was in roman, clear and uncluttered with decoration.* Not
until three months later had it been changed to the sham
medieval. That helped to silence the traditionalists, who were
also defeated over the heraldic device which Morison showed
to have gone from poor to worse over the decades. Anyhow,
he said, the paper was not entitled to use it.

By August 1932 B-W seems to have succeeded in convincing
all doubters and on 3 October 1932 the paper appeared in its
new dress. The achievement was largely Morison's and it was
widely and enthusiastically acclaimed; but outside the profession of journalism and the industry of printing it was an

*The newspaper was first published in January 1785 under the title *The Daily
Universal Register*.

anonymous triumph. Nor were B-W's patient, diplomatic labours commemorated save in one or two paragraphs of his diary, which are sighs of relief at a job well done to maintain the 'aristocratic precedence' of the paper.

Having played a leading part in restyling the daily, B-W was bound next to examine the *Literary Supplement,* which now looked, compared with its mother publication, old-fashioned, grey and hard to read. It was still edited by Bruce Richmond,* who had helped to create it in 1902 when he was already an assistant editor to Buckle. He had been Editor of the *Times Literary Supplement* since 1902, presiding graciously and with distinction in his own exclusive corner of the world of literature and scholarship. Richmond was a man with whom it was impossible to quarrel; to persuade him to change his journal was therefore a delicate operation, the more so when he made it known in June 1934 that he would like to retire at the end of 1935.

B-W could hardly take the initiative until the title of Deputy Editor was given to him, so lifting him clearly above those senior men who had survived from the Northcliffe era.

Gave Bruce Richmond lunch at the Windham. He wanted to discuss the Lit. Supp. which has lost in revenue and circulation a

*As the origins and growth of the Literary Supplement are ignored in the *History of The Times,* it may be of interest to have the main facts about it recorded here.

Bruce Richmond had joined the paper in 1899 and retired in 1936, having received a knighthood two years earlier for 'services to literature'. Although it was he who won for the *T.L.S.* its prestige in the world of letters and scholarship, the creation of such a journal was the idea of Buckle's brilliant Manager, Moberley Bell who had run a separate publication called 'Literature' edited by H. D. Traill from 1897 to January 1902.

Books were reviewed each week in *The Times* but the space available varied with the volume of parliamentary reports. The October election of 1901 made possible ample regular space for reviews, which built up a goodwill with readers and publishers which Bell decided must not be lost, once Parliament made its normal demands again. So from Friday 17 January 1902 there appeared the first weekly supplement of eight half pages given away with the paper. It was immediately successful in circulation and advertising. From February 1914, it was sold separately, Northcliffe having insisted that *The Times* should have a book page like other papers.

In 1922 it narrowly escaped extinction when he ordered that issue 1054 should warn readers that issue 1056 would be the last. This sentence of death on the *T.L.S.* was removed from its front page by order of the Managing Director, Campbell Stuart, twenty minutes before it went to press.

(Sources: 50th Anniversary Number of *T.L.S.* 18.1.52; tribute to Richmond in the *T.L.S.* of 13.1.61; the present editor Mr Arthur Crook.)

good deal lately. He recognizes that the paper itself has been wise
to do more in the reviewing of books but thinks this has injured
the Suppt. He would deprecate — and so should I — sweeping changes
in the contents. It is, as I reassured him, still unique in the world
among literary reviews, the only one almost with a true standing in
literature.[7]

The first ideas of improvement were called for from Denis
Mackail, B-W's old friend of Balliol days, who had some
reputation as a novelist and reviewer. Typographical changes
apart, the details of which would be left to Morison, Mackail's
advice seems to have been that the now venerable journal
should become more popular in style with reviews of fiction,
use of pictures, fewer articles of purely scholarly interest,
removal of the long lead review from the front page, whence
it used to turn on to four columns or more of admirable prose
by Virginia Woolf, T. S. Eliot, and other outstanding though
anonymous critics.

Already, in a letter to the Editor, Richmond had offered a
different diagnosis. He pointed to the 'fundamental fallacy' in
the existence of the *T.L.S.*: that it had been 'called into existence
to relieve *The Times* itself of difficulties with which *The Times*
was no longer confronted'. Its *raison d'être* was disappearing.
More and more the daily newspaper's book page was doubling
with the weekly. Lighter books had been taken over, then
novels, then notes on forthcoming books. The feminine public,
those making lists for the lending library, the buyers of the
book of the moment, those who liked coffee-table books – all
were being attracted away by *The Times*. 'Were there really
enough people, interested in books but not readers of the daily
paper, to keep the Supplement going?' With characteristic
modesty, however, Richmond recognized the possibility of a
more enterprising and versatile editorial policy.[8]

The changes were agreed and the chair was eventually taken
in 1936 by a reluctant D. L. Murray, the assistant editor. As a
writer of successful historical novels, Murray naturally hesitated before accepting duties which would take him away from
his Brighton home and his well-organized and well-paid life.
He arranged with B-W that he should attend the office only three
days a week.

For reasons that are not clear, the restyled *T.L.S.* did not
give pleasure. Old readers were perhaps offended by the con-

cessions made to the young, who in their turn were not impressed. Perhaps Murray did not impart sufficient personality to the paper.* Its prestige among scholars waned. Circulation went on falling and only the outbreak of war in September 1939 stopped the decline. The newsprint restrictions kept its weekly size down to twelve pages, with considerable savings in costs; other newspapers left out or cut down their book pages; the number of books published declined; while the demand of the public for reading matter built up into the explosion of 1945 onwards.

Not surprisingly, as the war drew to an end, and as Murray became more and more eager to leave, B-W and Morison were forced to ask what was the lesson of 1939-45. Should the journal, while keeping and extending its changes in type and lay-out, swing back to seriousness (notably by restoring the long lead article) or should it make a further experiment in semi-popular treatment under a new editor? All trace of what must have been a famous office debate is now lost, but the decision was for seriousness and Stanley Morison achieved his ambition of becoming an editor in 1945. He promptly reversed the popular trend of which he had been an enthusiastic supporter ten years earlier. Circulation quickly rose to fifty thousand or more, riding a post-war boom not only in publishing but also in advertising. It would be wrong to claim for B-W great credit for this successful judgement. He always looked over the proofs of the *T.L.S.* but his role was only supervisory. But if prosperity had not been recovered and prestige maintained, B-W as Editor of *The Times* would have been blamed. The episode is fairly seen as an example of how his daily administration kept the office and its staff up-to-date and ready for experiment.

*Murray was Editor for eight years, from 1936-44. His chief assistants were Philip Tomlinson, Eric St John Brooks and Simon Nowell-Smith. Morison, who succeeded him, remained Editor only five years and was succeeded by Alan Pryce-Jones.

10

The Working Day

To write a leading article may take only two hours
to two hours and a half, but then all the rest of
your time you are a crouching tiger, waiting,
waiting, to make your spring.
                    Rev. T. Mozley on his own work at The Times
                                            in the eighties

The special strain of an editor's life has less to do with long
hours at the desk than with the daily effort to divide his time
between ephemeral and more long-term tasks. He is continually
chopping and changing the objects of his attention. If he watches
lovingly over his paper, keeping up its standards, measuring its
performance against that of rivals, he cannot afford to interest
himself merely in its comment, leading articles which are only
a small part of its content. He may by temperament and training
prefer policy-making to producing a paper – as B-W did – and
some editors have been politicians *manqués*; he may prefer
concepts to facts and argument to reporting. But interest in
news, in what has just happened and what may happen next,
is fundamental: a daily newspaper whose news is late,
inaccurate, biased, badly presented, incomplete, will lose both
circulation and influence.

So, to watch whether rival newspapers are covering the news
better – as well as interpreting with more flair the trends in
public interest and opinion – is something that every editor
must undertake. Each day for him begins at home, with a
scrutiny of his own last edition – if he has not seen it already
the night before – and of the six or seven national rivals. For
B-W as Deputy Editor this meant careful scrutiny of the *Daily
Telegraph* news pages, then beginning to challenge seriously
the performance of *The Times* in news, especially home news;
of the opinion and correspondence columns and some foreign
news of the leftish *Manchester Guardian* and *News Chronicle;*
of the news treatment and political line in Beaverbrook's

Express and Rothermere's *Mail*; perhaps of one or two provincial dailies, notably the *Yorkshire Post* and the *Glasgow Herald* (each a favourite stable for training *Times* staff). He probably also read with care the *Spectator, New Statesman* and *Economist* laid out each week on his desk.

To read the Press with a criticizing and comparing mind is a strenuous activity, quite unlike the ordinary person's reading of one or two newspapers over the breakfast table: as different as an inspection of troops by royalty is different from the inspection by officers before royalty arrives. It is a critical search for detail, to be at once appraised and to be used later for praise and blame. The same exercise is being simultaneously performed by a dozen of his heads of departments and assistant news editors: comparing treatment of general news, of sport, City, crime, Parliament, 'culture', calculating successes and noting clues to be followed in tomorrow's paper. Later in the morning there will be available for him, if he wishes to read it, a detailed analysis of what has been found. Yet only he, and perhaps one or two of his assistant editors, feels responsible for examining this day's paper as a whole, and for initiating basic thinking about the next day's. 'A good paper' is a phrase which occurs from time to time in the diaries; 'I left X in charge and he produced an excellent paper' – meaning that under X the staff did well those things the Editor likes to see done and the total impression made by the issue was of *The Times* as it should be.

From eight o'clock onwards, there imposed itself this intense tasting of newspapers, until 9.30 perhaps. Normally this stretch of work led to telephone calls or briefly dictated memoranda: office work began long before the office was reached. Then followed some tidying up of problems more easily done at home, free from interruption by heads peering round doors, swelling in-baskets, telephone calls, and odd meetings in passages. Came 10.30 and on four days out of five there were calls to be made on the way to the office at Blackfriars, some for news-gathering, some just social: half an hour with Walter Monckton or some senior civil servant; an hour with Anthony Eden or Herbert Morrison; a visit to a sick member of the staff; a quick look at a picture gallery.

Arriving at Printing House Square between 11.30 and 12, B-W would have a first look at his personal letters and memoranda. People with something to say to the public, who claimed personal acquaintance with the Editor of *The Times,* would mark envelopes 'personal', so ensuring that they would not go into the post-bag of the correspondence editor. They would include ideas for articles, requests for publicity for this or that event, suggestions of meetings inside and outside the office to draw the paper's attention to a point of view or a special piece of information – all would find their way into his personal budget to be weighed and answered. Meticulous in his dealings with correspondents, B-W would never think of adopting the celebrity's method of giving the secretary the gist of a reply and leaving her to compose the sentences. He would dictate with care, often with hesitation; or write in his own elegant and neat hand, without abbreviation or any other relief from the rules of acceptable prose. For the care he took he might have been doing a Greek prose at Westminster. Some letters would be marked to colleagues for comment and action; a beginning would be made on the more urgent replies; then it was time, most days, to be off to a luncheon engagement.

It would be almost always with someone whose information or views would be valuable; sometimes a formal occasion in the City or a party of political or diplomatic or merely social interest; most frequently tête-à-tête in a club or restaurant. B-W made a point of lunching regularly at the Beefsteak where he could keep in touch with typical and influential readers of *The Times.** Then, as now, editors took their time over lunch, as much for the sake of the talk as for the pleasure of the table. B-W watched carefully over his health and was by Fleet Street standards abstemious; but no one expected him back in the office much before three.

Then, if editing that day, he would take charge. He found waiting for him forty or fifty letters of the day – or of the previous day – from which selection had to be made for publication on the leader page and inside letter page. The top letter or the top topic would choose itself more often than not without difficulty. Sometimes B-W, impressed by some tip he had been

*'Curiously enough I have been beset with invitations, all of which I should like to have accepted, to lunch to-day. I have been asked by Gladstone Murray of the B.B.C. (to meet Stephen Tallents now director of public relations for the B.B.C.); by Admiral Dickens (to meet the D.N.I. Admiralty); by Paget (to meet the D.M.I. War Office); by Lord Astor; by General Higgins (his old Brigade Commander); and finally by Anthony Eden, just back from Geneva, whom I had asked to see.'[1]

given or some view he heard, would ask if there was no letter on so-and-so. 'Yes there is, but I was holding it up for a day,' the correspondence editor might reply. 'Let me see it and if it's all right we'll put it in at once,' B-W would say. 'Are you sure this is a balanced selection?' he would ask. 'Have we been fair so far to both sides?'* Or 'Is there nothing amusing, nothing to get the cranks writing in?' Not that cranks needed encouragement. 'Is there nothing light, no good little "funny" for the bottom page? Don't forget this is our gossip department.' Sometimes he would decide that a certain correspondence must now be closed, because it was getting repetitive, boring and keeping out better subjects.

B-W liked himself to devise the triple headlines for the top of the main correspondence column, counting the numbers of letters in each word for an exact fit, wasting precious time on a kind of crossword-puzzle thinking which has fatal attractions for every man who prides himself on his command of words.† (Dawson, too, was a keen and rapid headline-writer.) Then there would be letters of praise and complaint to look at, threats from solicitors and so on.

The letters done, after half an hour's intensive work, the

---

*Impartiality in the handling of letters meant different things to different people. A letter received from John Walter, Joint Chief Proprietor, in September shows the kind of attitude that the Editor might have to cope with.

'My dear B-W: Here is a small criticism which I submit for your consideration. In Saturday's paper there appeared a letter from Mrs Thirkell complaining of the theft of parcels in transit through the Post Office. Unfortunately for her, the letter was immediately preceded by one from Lady Lindsay protesting that her own parcels had never been stolen. To-day Vera Brittain writes to voice a similar complaint, but her effect is similarly spoiled by a letter from Mrs Cooke, which appears next to it, announcing that she herself has nothing to complain of in this respect.

Now impartiality is an excellent thing, but surely these two announcements do not merit equal publicity? The frequent theft of parcels in transit through the Post Office is a matter of increasing public concern. The fact that many parcels are safely delivered is far from interesting, might indeed almost be taken for granted.   Yours ever
                                                    John Walter'.[2]

It was on occasions like these that the paper sounded like the parish magazine of the gentry.

†The author once watched B-W puzzle for most of an hour over a title and headlines for three articles written on the state of air raid precautions. The leader-page article – known as the turnover, because it ran over to the next page – was only a column wide, and the problem was to find headlines with 10–12 letters and a top line with fewer letters than the second. With a smile of triumph B-W plumped for the initials only, A.R.P. – and so civil defence was known for some time after.

Editor would leave his desk and make a brief tour of the leader-writers. Men like Dermot Morrah and Philip Graves, Colin Coote and A. L. Kennedy, Harold Child and Charles Brodribb were mostly happy to share rooms for their work – mostly writing in longhand. There might be three desks to a room, each piled high with the books and litter of a specialist writer, and the conversation which the Editor held at one desk would certainly be heard by the others in the room. For major articles B-W would write some notes or have the writer down to his room and advise him with great care on the 'line' to be taken. (One brief for a Liddell Hart leader was longer than the article itself.) That is to say, the writer would give an expert view of what the facts and arguments were, and B-W would then select and simplify, building up emphasis on the point he wanted to see made. Leaders on topics that promised particular difficulty, needing discussion and revision, would be prepared a day, or even longer, beforehand. B-W was proud of what were often masterly displays of policy-preaching, the aspect of journalism he rated most highly and most enjoyed doing himself. 'On that subject,' he would sometimes say with a twinkle, '*The Times* has *pronounced* already.'

His tour concluded and friendly and informal contact having been made for the day with his chief advisers, it was now time to look at the news schedules from the Home and Foreign departments – detailed forecasts of the night's main stories and their relative importance, together with the estimate of space needed for Parliament – before going into the editorial conference. This the layman might imagine to be the occasion for debate and decision on the great issues of the day, the forum in which 'the paper's view' was formed. Far from it. Leader-writers did not attend the conference and policy discussions were generally impromptu, informal and inconclusive. This gathering of a dozen or more was first and foremost a clearing house, bringing together assistant editors, departmental heads and a few specialists to make sure that everyone knew what everybody else was expecting to do. For the first time the next day's paper was looked at as a whole. It was the moment when the day staff began to hand over to the night staff. Then the night-editor got his first vague outline of what his main pages might contain; the chief sub-editors of the various sections learned the size of the paper and realized within what space they had to condense, headline and perhaps lose matter to the 'Bill page' – that is to say, the main news page. The 'art editor' considered picture possibilities. The rough contents list in front of them made it clear what the feature articles were about, which books were to be reviewed, whose obituaries would be needed – and the Editor would himself announce the leader subjects. This would ensure that the chief subs sent to leader-writers copies of relevant messages and despatches, both from the paper's own correspondents and from the agency tapes – of which in those days there were six. The Foreign News Editor would sometimes telephone a foreign capital and ask his man there for notes to assist the writer, or he would drop in himself to tell what he knew.

After this 4.15 conference – generally an uneventful affair – the Editor had a couple of hours for seeing callers, talking with members of the staff and candidates for jobs, discussing problems with the Manager, while the printers got to work on early copy and the leader-writers drank tea. Ideally a leader should be in before 7.30, having been ordered three hours earlier; but it was often 9.0 or later before the main contributions had appeared. This could be annoying, for the tradition of the office accepted that the Editor should dine out. It was a vital part of his news-gathering and representative function. He could, however, always have a second 'go' at the leaders when he returned from dinner, or he could leave the shorter and less important of the four or five articles to be seen and passed by the assistant editor on duty.

So around 7.45 the Editor would depart in the office car to dinner with a fairly clear, if not detailed, picture of the night's news and likely developments. Dining out, for all practical purposes, meant work: agreeable fare and company no doubt but most of the conversation would be 'shop', requiring a constant effort to select and store away, to make judgements and make one's own contribution. The Editor of *The Times* was expected to take himself very seriously. With close friends he might relax, but with hosts who thought of him exclusively as the newspaper editor he had to watch for the motives, the 'plants', the lobbying, the arguments used. In London's hierarchical society, a hint was worth a memorandum and a wink was as good as a nod.

Back from dinner by 9.30, the Editor found on his desk

letters ready for signature, his second post (as it were) from the staff, queries arising from the night's papers, page proofs still damp for him to cast an eye over. An assistant editor would be combing through advertisements and editorial matter looking for errors of taste, instances of things that were 'not done' in *The Times*, overlaps and doubles, inaccuracies and misprints and other faults. There would also be points to discuss with the night-editor when the 'Bill page'* for the first edition was brought up: the relative space given to items, the look of the headlines, the policy implications of this position or that emphasis; and the night-editor would already have his views of how a better-looking job should be done for the next edition and, perhaps, for the final one, by remaking the pages.

More often than not, important news would start breaking late after dinner or important additions to a well-covered story would arrive. The Editor might order cuts to be made in a particularly long and diffuse despatch, which had just been scrambled into the first edition without time for it to be assessed and presented as a whole. It might be necessary, too, to change part of a leader in the light of the news, or to take one leader out and put another in. This required from him rapid re-writing and cutting, with corrections calculated to fill the right space so that changes in the page could be made with the least possible delay. Even the Editor had to take notice of the night-editor's scolding and grumbling about late copy, which might delay production and hold up his vans for the main line stations. If the paper were late, there would be trouble the next day from the Manager.

With every leader-writer getting things right first time, with the shape of the news changing very little between seven o'clock and midnight, and no personal or administrative problems of an unexpected kind arising, the Editor could get away from the office with a good conscience before midnight. But such a night, however welcome it should be to a tired man wanting to get home to wife and family, gave no real satisfaction to a conscientious newspaper man like B-W.† A 'quiet night'

*The main news page then was inside on the left opposite the leaders, and was called the Bill page because it used to contain the theatre advertisements for the night.

†It would be unfair to describe B-W as emergency-prone, but the kind of situation that arose is vividly illustrated from the diary of Good Friday, 1939. On Thursday the paper had the news of Mussolini's expedition launched against

meant more often than not a 'dull paper', uneventful news
shared with other papers, no topic to which the paper could
make an especially distinguished or expert contribution. A
worth-while or 'difficult' night was one of changes and uncer-
tainties, of long-planned articles being changed at the last
minute, of crisis and totally unexpected news (or news breaking
a day or two earlier than expected) changing the whole aspect
of the main pages. It might be the sudden, though long-awaited,
death of a famous man, as when Lloyd George died in 1945. *The
Times* having been warned through Tom Jones, and having prepared three splendidly detailed columns on the national leader
of the First World War, could achieve in its tribute a remarkable
superiority over other papers.

Some of the strain of this exacting day was, it is obvious,
self-imposed. It was not essential that an editor – even of *The
Times* – should dine out every night; or that he should return
night after night to the office after dinner. Proofs could be sent
to him by despatch-rider and there was a telephone for giving
instructions; he had good assistant editors, and B-W should
have known from his own days with Dawson just how much a
deputy can spare his chief. But this anxious wish to be personally involved in the daily creation of a newspaper is something that has to be experienced to be understood: it is a feeling
like that of the doctor for his patient, of the gardener for his
roses, or of the chef for the serving of the meal that he has
cooked – a conviction that there are always finishing touches
to be given and that only he can give them.

Dawson, with two decades of editorship behind him, had by
the thirties worked his way out of this obsession. He was happy
to delegate and get off to Yorkshire and, if he felt like it,
stay away a bit longer than he had said he would. He could
concentrate on essentials and leave himself free of anything
that did not interest him. Indeed, his more relaxed approach to
work could give the appearance of carelessness. B-W, on the
contrary, found it difficult to shake off the hounding conscience,

---

Albania, as had been predicted all the week. The next day B-W, having spent an
hour at the three-hour service at St Paul's, went to the office to find Albania being
literally overrun and virtually all the leader-writers away together. So Dermot
Morrah, a specialist on home and constitutional topics, was put on to writing a
difficult first leader over which B-W himself then toiled while editing. 'An
unsatisfactory night,' he wrote, 'at the office till after 1 a.m.'[3]

although there were signs towards the end of his life that he was beginning to do so as he realized he was overtaxing his strength. There was not in his case the lure and distraction of a permanent country home like Dawson's; he had country roots in Cornwall, but they were too far away to be developed. He never had a deputy as experienced, trusted and conscientious as he had been himself for Dawson.*

B-W was not normally a fast or easy writer, although no one could do more rapidly a late-night job of surgery or improvization. He needed the special emergency to spur him into disregard of the caution with which he approached most matters for comment. He had no use for the columnist who sees no virtue in consistency, to whom a good idea is one that startles and stirs talk, who maintains that readability is all and that one idea is as good as another. To B-W his pen was the pen of *The Times*; it must do its work with the deliberation and sense of responsibility that are attributed to the Lord Chief Justice or the Permanent Head of the Foreign Office, every sentence to be weighed. He was deeply conscious of being in the succession to Barnes and Delane, without having that sheer beefy recklessness which inspired the Victorians or the jaunty brilliance of Dawson.

These inhibitions made him not only a slow writer of his own articles but a zealous corrector of other people's work. They might fancy themselves as coiners of a phrase or masters of epithet: if B-W thought their style inappropriate to the paper he would not hesitate to change it – as he had a right to do. All this took time. To judge from his diaries he found special satisfaction in such work: there are frequent references to having to do a lot of work on this or that man's leader.

On this evidence alone of the working day at Printing House Square, it is fair to say that here was a man doomed to take too much out of himself. Brought on to *The Times* as a writer, he accepted from Dawson more and more administrative work in the day without giving up the writing at night. It is hard to blame him: this was the way to the editorship, to become indispensable. Far from giving up writing to become an editor,

---

*Already in 1926 at the *Observer* he noted: 'The worst of it is that decisions fall to be taken towards midnight when one is most tired. Things that a fresh mind might judge rightly, a tired mind often does not. Then worry follows in the train of errors and fatigue.'

he regarded writing as a prime function of editing. That is to say, he believed that the leading articles and comment of the paper must bear the stamp of the office even when the personality of the writer was as strong as that of E. H. Carr or Basil Liddell Hart. Here, perhaps, is to be found the explanation for that sense of strain day by day as B-W records the rapid shift of his mind from papers to people, from people to ideas, from concept to detail, from detail to sub-editing, from tactics to strategy and back again. One wonders how he found time to think. The answer is that thinking was done in those leisure hours of the weekend when he should have been resting and relaxing.*

*Six months before B-W's death his friend Stanley Morison wrote to the Chairman: 'The burden is very great. The constant interruptions, the switch of the mind from one topic to another; the innumerable decisions that have to be taken; the multitude of people to be seen and listened to; the many telephone calls – exact a fearful price from the Editor. I conclude that either B-W will stop the old routine or the old routine will stop him.'[4]

11

Peace by Concession
A Personal Creed

Isn't it enraging, what the French are doing in the
Ruhr? Can one ever get people to know what WAR
is and, by consequence, to rise up for peace? Have
our sons (if we ever have any) got to be killed in
the way I (for one) have seen hundreds killed, and
in even fouler ways than that, to suit the shortcomings of the French? I don't know what to
wish – whether that a few more people had *seen*
a man blown in half, or a man gassed, or had lain
several hours in a shell-hole with the half-buried
and long-dead dead.
Letter from B-W to his mother, 24 January 1923

Had he lived long enough to feel he could speak or write freely
about the thirties, B-W would not have left his Editor alone in
the pillory while he was pelted with accusations drawn from
such different sources as Claud Cockburn's *The Week*, the
memories of political and newspaper critics, the memoirs of
public men and women and the files of the paper itself. For it
was he who wrote most of the leading articles which argued
obstinately, through crisis and calm, for understanding with
Nazi Germany; and it was he who decided for the most part
what articles of a descriptive or argumentative kind should
appear on the right-hand side of the leader page. True,
Dawson bore the responsibility for the paper's policy, but no
editor exerts continuous authority over the whole range of
comment. At some points his personal inspiration or direction
will be looser than at others; and for Dawson in his sixties these
were Europe, the Far East, economics and social policy. That
is not to say that he was indifferent to Europe or quite ignorant
about its affairs. Had he not, after all, edited *The Times* with
distinction throughout the Great War in Europe, directing
eminent specialists like Wickham Steed? If his chief interest
abroad was in the Empire, and in what is now called the third

world of India, Africa and the Middle East, it was as much because the sheer scale of its future problems impressed him more than the quarrels of Europe as because his early career had been in South Africa under Milner. There was no careless indifference in the free hand that he gave to B-W, who remarked more than once in his diary that they saw eye to eye. Except, perhaps, for a brief period during Abyssinia's crisis with Italy, Dawson and his Deputy presented a solid front to their leader-writers and correspondents, many of whom were in varying degrees opposed to what was later called 'appeasement'.*

The tone in which the 'appeasement' articles were written was personal, at times passionate, and the arguments with which B-W pleaded his case were rooted in his own experience of the First World War, in his apprenticeship with Garvin at a time when the French were holding Germany down, and in his conviction that Britain could not afford, socially, morally or financially, another such ordeal. There is no evidence that his thinking was influenced, directly or indirectly, by meetings at Cliveden, which he visited only rarely after his marriage in 1926, and his contacts with Germany were at least as much anti-Nazi as pro-Nazi. To the warning advice that came from Norman Ebbutt in Berlin, in the form of memoranda and inter-views, he paid respectful attention; he always insisted, how-ever, that it was one thing to be reporting a foreign situation to London and quite another to be deciding in London what the British attitude towards it should be.† The first was the corespondent's job, and the second was the Editor's. If *The Times* decided that the policy towards Germany – or any other

*The only passage in the diaries where this fact is referred to is in an entry in 1938 after Munich. B-W took Casey and McDonald home to dinner with him and there resulted a 'lively discussion on foreign affairs. Most of the office is against Dawson and me.'[1]

†One of the higher skills of the foreign correspondent is to find ways of getting into his messages points of difference with his office. It can be done by use of parenthesis, by attributing the critical view to a third party or by warning the office in advance that what is coming is of unusual and exclusive importance. Ebbutt in Berlin was a master of such techniques. Indeed, the lateness of some of his despatches, which did not endear him to the sub-editors in London, was often due to the pains he took, with much puffing of his pipe and striking of matches, to construct unbreakable paragraphs. To be fair, the motive was more often than not the wish to be cautious and balanced in his judgements of a situation in which it was hard to trust sources and even harder to guess what was happening behind the scenes.

country – should be conciliatory, then it was expected that the correspondent should bear this fact in mind.*

Sitting at his desk B-W was exposed to pressures of which there is scarcely mention in the *History*: letters from influential British Jews making appeals for German Jews; visitors offering first-hand accounts of concentration camp experiences; organizations proposing demonstrations and protests of one kind or another; messages from or speeches by people who advocated what seemed to him reckless resistance to an enemy better armed and prepared than Britain yet was; strategic arguments against fighting a land war by the side of France from Liddell Hart; confidential memoranda on delays in British aircraft production from the aeronautical correspondent. He was not, like Kennedy,† a leader-writer ruminating in his quiet room, undistracted by the flow of office business, able to concentrate his attention at one or two places on the map. He was seeing and hearing things which must affect any broad judgement of policy; and, instead of passing them on for leisurely digestion by a colleague, was absorbing them into a mind which several times a week was switching late in the day from administration to editing – the very combination of tasks of which he had complained when on the *Observer*.

If the verdict of history goes against B-W for his advocacy of a European settlement in which Hitler's Germany might take part, then his habits of work might be treated by charitable men as extenuating circumstances. But let us suppose that it does not. Suppose that the evidence now appearing about the state of British armaments, the ineffective resistance to Hitler in Germany, the feebleness of France, the true Russian attitude to Czechoslovakia, the intelligence reaching Chamberlain and

*Ten years later B-W occasionally remarked to colleagues that he regretted not having paid more regard to the views of correspondents. In 1944 he backed the man on the spot in Greece with what many thought disastrous results. See Ch. 22.

†A. L. Kennedy came to *The Times* from Harrow and Magdalen, Oxford, in Buckle's time. He had experience as a sub-editor and abroad before the war, in which he gained the M.C. He rejoined the paper in 1919 and after further work as a foreign correspondent was made leader-writer on European affairs in 1923. He was allowed to travel to the League of Nations and foreign capitals and was well known in the diplomatic circles of the inter-war years. Kennedy had been a keen advocate of revision of the peace treaties, but had sharp differences over policy towards the Nazis with B-W, and even with Dawson himself, whose friend he was.

the state of British public opinion in those years – suppose that it persuades historians that 'appeasement' was in the circumstances the only realistic policy for a British – above all, for an imperial – Government, then it may be thought that *The Times,* as B-W believed, had done Britain a great service by supporting negotiations with Hitler up to the very last moment so that public opinion was convinced beyond any doubt of the necessity of declaring war in September 1939. If the pendulum should swing that far, then B-W will be praised for the devotion and conviction with which he laboured at a brief which, he felt, only he in the office really understood. The clarity and dignity, the balance and feeling of his articles will be praised. What some still regard as an almost criminal piece of advocacy will be recognized as masterly journalism. The most that the biographer of B-W can do meanwhile is to show wherever possible what charges against him are factually inaccurate; what his motives were and how he judged himself; what people and facts influenced him and how, clearly and without hesitation, he refused – as Dawson did – to take sides in the left-right ideological struggle of that decade.*

THE MEANING OF THE WORD

First of all it is necessary to ascertain what B-W himself understood by appeasement, a word which was not often heard in the thirties. It was most fully explained in a letter written on 27 April 1939, six weeks after the German occupation of Czechoslovakia had shattered his hopes and left in ruins the Munich agreement of Chamberlain and Hitler.[4] It was to George Ferguson, of the *Winnipeg Free Press,* a much respected newspaper which might be described as the *Manchester Guardian* of Canada. Dafoe, its famous editor, had persistently criticized British policy towards Germany, and this letter was partly directed at him. That B-W would have taken particular pains with this reply is certain. His frequent meetings with his old Balliol friend, Vincent Massey, Canada's High Commissioner

*It seems probable that parts of the chapters in Volume IV of the *History of The Times* dealing with the appeasement policy were either drafted or inspired by Wickham Steed, the former Editor and foreign correspondent. Steed took Dawson's chair in 1919 only to lose it to him again in 1922. His participation would account for some of the curious omissions and instances of bias which mark that volume. It is known that Stanley Morison consulted him a great deal.

in London from 1936 to 1946 had kept him keenly aware of the Dominion's wary attitude to commitments in Europe;* and, like Dawson, he never lost sight of the immense political and economic importance to Britain of North America's friendship. Besides, deep down in B-W was a dislike of being misunderstood by Liberals.

'Appeasement [he wrote] is a misleading term, even though it has had official sanction. *The Times* has declined to use it, implying as it does a policy of "buns to the bear" instead of an endeavour to secure by negotiation the removal of the causes of war.'† When collective security failed to protect Abyssinia, 'chiefly, though not wholly, thanks to the defection of France', it was seen that the League had also failed in securing reasonable revision of the peace treaties. So an attempt was made to find out whether some of Europe's major problems could not be solved by consent. That, B-W insists, was the origin of 'appeasement'.

It was an endeavour to discover, even at the eleventh hour, whether the Nazis were, according to their professions, out for reasonable change or whether they were out for mere domination. Chamberlain was ready to wait for the proofs and Churchill was not.

Churchill was ignoring, B-W goes on, the admitted blunders of 1919. The policy he was urging 'could have been represented as one of mere frightened encirclement' and 'would have ranked every German behind the Führer and left this country with an uneasy conscience and deeply divided.' Now (April 1939) the occupation of Bohemia and Moravia had shown that the Nazis were not bound by their own professions and that they were out for domination unless resisted. 'Very well, they must be resisted.'

---

*During the Munich crisis B-W kept in close touch with Massey who, according to the diary, was 'all against a world war merely to keep minorities under Czech rule'. The entry continues: 'Canadian Government (Mackenzie King, the feeble creature) forbids him to join consultations at the Dominions Office. He goes all the same to get information but does not advertise his presence there.' Massey kept himself well enough informed to be able to show to B-W on 25 September Hitler's Godesberg proposals the day before Jan Masaryk made them known in London.[2,3]

†'Appeasement in Europe' appears as a news headline in *The Times* on 15 January 1935 to describe the policy planned by Simon after the Saar plebiscite had produced a 90.8 per cent vote for return to Germany.

This being the picture of events since 1936 as B-W sees it, he cannot understand why 'appeasement' is to be represented 'as a sort of criminal undertaking'. Does Ferguson really believe that its supporters are not in favour of a League, of the rule of law, or of anything that the last war was fought to establish?

Why was it wrong or criminal to put Nazi professions to practical proof and to put British good faith (compromised in all German eyes by our part in the 1919 settlement and by much else between 1919 and 1933, to take that period only) beyond all possible question? I think it was right and that it has added enormously to the strength of our present position. The plain fact was that the League had for the time collapsed and that some way back to it had to (and has to) be found. I am frankly staggered when you associate *T.T.* with the view that it was 'necessary to eliminate the League' at one point, or with 'a skilful anti-League campaign'.

B-W now asks the counter-attacking questions which he used so effectively when dealing with critics on his own staff. Was there an alternative policy?

What would you have put in the place of 'appeasement' in the then existing circumstances? Unconditional encirclement? Would you have fought, and would Canada have fought, to prevent the re-occupation of the Rhineland, the *Anschluss,* or the union of the Sudetenland with the Reich? Did we give the Germans at any time the hope and opportunity of accomplishing their aims peacefully? Even Memel was German-speaking territory, grabbed originally by the Lithuanians in a way that was universally condemned at the time.

He ends with a note of impatience and bitterness, not surprising in a man who had seen his judgement so impugned by the events of March. This exchange between the two assistant editors is interesting not only for its account of *The Times*'s view but also because Ferguson's reply reveals the reluctance that still lay at the heart of Canadian policy less than five months before war broke out:

Here in this country there is little doubt that Canada, in the event of war, would participate on a large scale. *The ultimate effects on this country would be disastrous, but there it is.* There is a good case, therefore, for this country, in the absence of any effective League, *to stand aside and practise the refusal to accept commit-*

ments, which was for so long the British policy. I doubt if the people of this country now appreciate that we, here, have also guaranteed Polish, Greek and Rumanian independence. [Author's italics]

It is easier for us, with twenty-five years' experience of the United Nations, to make allowance for the illusion of Liberals (and of many others to their left and right) that the League represented something greater than the sum of its constituent members; something with weapons, forces and a will of its own, the authority of which would make it unnecessary for a country like Canada to entangle herself in alliance and European commitments. In Britain, too, millions of ordinary newspaper readers believed – or had been led to hope – with thousands of more intelligent and better informed people, that 'collective security' was something to be invoked against aggression as the TUC is invoked to settle an inter-union dispute. Indeed, it is difficult to convey the indignant scorn with which criticism of such illusions was treated by believers in the power of the League during the years between Locarno and Munich. The letter columns of *The Times* rang with arguments from Gilbert Murray, L. P. Jacks, Philip Noel-Baker, Lord Allen of Hurtwood, and similar contestants.*

The only other private document explaining B-W's thinking is also addressed to a Canadian, J. A. Stevenson, the paper's correspondent in Ottawa. Its date is earlier – April 1938, five months before Munich and a month after Hitler's *coup* against Austria.[5] Stevenson had been warning London of the strength of isolationist feeling in Canada, sharpened by disappointment with the League and with Britain's apparent return to 'old fashioned power politics'. B-W points out in reply that 'the reluctance of the Empire to accept commitments in Europe and therefore to give the French in good time the assurance which we have now had to give them after all' had been one cause of Laval's abandonment of the League ('with Hoare as accessory after the fact') when Italy attacked Abyssinia. People had credited the League with power it did not possess, and the bluff had been called.

*Dawson, who was always less sanguine than B-W about 'collective security', liked to tell colleagues the story of a Yorkshire plumber who said he distrusted the League because there were so many foreigners in it.

B-W again rejects the charge that British policy is anti-League. The question is how best to organize peace.

Gt Britain is carrying the whole burden at the moment. The United States would probably be 'all right on the night' (though certainly a few nights late) if it came to a clash between the democratic and the fascist countries. But you cannot found your policy upon a presumption, least of all when the pressure is daily and immediate. In these circumstances we must either line up for war along with France and Soviet Russia (of all Powers) in the name of Democracy, or we must try and remove some of the causes of war before it arrives. Wd such a war be a welcome or practicable means of re-establishing the League? And, if not, what can the critics suggest?

What the British Govt has in fact to carry is the odium of being the only responsible factor in international affairs at the moment. Foreign policy here, after all, is controlled by public opinion, and the British public is more League-minded than any in the world and at least as averse from war.[5]

It is unfortunate, B-W complains, that American and Canadian newspapers pay so much attention to the British Press of the left.

'The whole case of the Left is that an anti-Fascist front would frighten the Dictators into compliance without war. But would it? And, if it did not, what then? And are we to commit ourselves to an ideological campaign in the untrustworthy and compromising company of Stalin? There is really nothing but danger in this view.'

NO BLOCKS OR BLUFF

We may remind ourselves that there was as little sympathy in the Dominions for the essentially European notion of forming an ideological bloc (popular front) against Fascism as there was for 'old-fashioned' power politics. Indeed, in South Africa, there was probably as much sympathy for Hitler as for Benes, and in India, Australia and New Zealand eyes were firmly fixed on Japan. Yet it was *The Times*'s determined opposition to such a bloc, and especially its support of non-intervention in Spain, that inspired some of the bitterness against the paper that survives to this day. The sustained propaganda pressure of all Communist parties in Europe – and their sympathizers – for a popular front against Fascism was not relaxed until

Hitler and Stalin came to terms in August 1939, and it was a curious twist of history that made Winston Churchill the hero – if not the leader – of the anti-Fascist campaign. There survives a letter to him from B-W which states the case for seeking peaceful co-existence with totalitarian states. The time was six months after Hitler had moved into the demilitarized Rhineland and offered proposals for a new Locarno. Churchill in September 1936 sent the Editor the draft of a speech on Anglo-French collaboration in defence which he was to make in Paris the following day, with a note saying: 'I should be very glad to know privately how it strikes you.' In Dawson's absence B-W replied:

Like yourself *The Times* attaches great importance both to effective readiness in the defence of democratic civilization and to the maintaining of close relations among like-minded powers. At the same time we have always taken the view that it is the negative, if indispensable, side of national duty. On the positive side *The Times* has always held that this country should most firmly decline to take part in the formation of 'fronts' until or unless the choice of a 'front' is positively forced on us. However alien to our way of thinking may be the governing philosophies of other countries, we feel that the only safe and impartial test to apply to them is whether or not they are ready for practical collaboration, political and economic.

This, chilly and slightly pompous though it is, might be the voice of Khrushchev or Churchill chiding Dulles twenty years later. B-W goes on:

We should, for example, certainly be against premature abandonment of the hope, supported by many authoritative pronouncements on the German side, that Germany is prepared to reach a general understanding and settlement with the British Empire. *The Times* has consistently endeavoured to argue—and I well remember your stating the same case in several speeches some years ago—that there is no other ultimate basis for stability in Europe but an understanding between France, Germany and Britain on lines designed eventually to embrace Europe generally...[6]

Shortly after this exchange with Churchill, B-W received from Basil Liddell Hart a letter in which the Military Correspondent suggested that a recent leading article had hinted at giving Germany a free hand in the East. Emphatically B-W denied this:

The Times has most definitely set its face against the foolish, cynical and short-sighted idea that it is desirable or profitable to purchase a deal with Germany by giving her a free hand in the East. This has been stated already in a number of leaders.[7]

Again, three months later, in another letter to Liddell Hart, British policy was expressed somewhat as follows:

We will not be indifferent to aggression anywhere. Aggression in the Mediterranean or in Western Europe will immediately encounter determined military resistance. As to aggression elsewhere we are not prepared to say in advance precisely what we will do but the aggressor can take it as certain that he will encounter resistance in some form. This is broadly how the gap left by the crash of Article XVI ought to be filled, I think, but it is after all a negative though important fraction of a policy which must be positive if it is going to succeed as a whole.[8]

Feeling, perhaps, that this dodged the question of preventing the gradual swallowing up of Eastern Europe B-W added this postscript.

It seems to be essential for Eastern Europe to find its own equilibrium as far as possible without interested disturbance from the West. The point of our policy must not be to forbid new groupings and agreements in the East but to ensure as far as we can that the attempt is not made to accomplish them by war. The safe and peaceful dissolution of the French 'system' was, after all, the central hope of the original Locarno treaties.[9]

So B-W's policy, if it excluded lining up with the Soviet Union against Germany until the last moment, also excluded lining up with the Germans against the Soviet Union – an intention with which *The Times* has been credited by some critics. The diary mentions a visit by Professor Edward Mead Earle, of Princeton, to whose questions about the alleged anti-Russian slant of British policy B-W replied: 'Our supreme aim in Europe is to prevent the line-up, above all on doctrinal lines, and to keep democracy as a middle term between Fascism and Bolshevism. If Russia would drop the Comintern the whole problem is simplified.'[10]

These extracts from B-W's correspondence – one written at the moment of disillusionment, another at a moment of deep anxiety, another at a time of fair confidence – show more clearly than any leading article the basis of his thinking. What does not appear in them is the belief, which his son Mark in later years heard him assert with the utmost confidence, that the time gained, and the feelings aroused by the policy of 'appeasement' and Hitler's contempt for it, brought the Empire and the British public into the war united. Nor was he more penitent than Lord Halifax showed himself in 1951 when writing to W. F. Casey, who had succeeded B-W as Editor. Halifax had read in the *Manchester Guardian* a review of a volume of British Foreign Office Documents which seemed to him 'grossly unfair' to Chamberlain. He said he felt impelled 'to get out on paper the short argument justifying his policy at the time'.

I do not here argue about Munich; on that, those who had responsibility will be well content to let history judge. But it is worth while remembering that in the event of war in 1938 South Africa had decided to remain neutral, a powerful opposition in Australia had declared against participation, and the attitude of Canada was uncertain. So the British Commonwealth, which was unanimously behind war in September 1939, would certainly not have been united for war in 1938.

After Hitler's rape of Czechoslovakia in March 1939, Halifax continued, German policy 'could no longer make any pretence of being directed to the reunion of scattered elements of the German people – the purpose of dominating Europe was exposed'.[11]

Neither members of his family, nor his intimate friend Stanley Morison (responsible for the chapters in the *History of The Times* which deal with the appeasement policy), nor the new post-war generation of colleagues remember B-W expressing regret or second thoughts about this policy. Appeasement to him meant exhausting every possibility of negotiation before accepting the inevitability of war as the basis of national policy. Even if he had admitted to himself that the Nazis were greater villains than he had believed, there would have remained the question of what precisely was to be done against each act of aggression. He did not believe in bluff. No democracy, he said, could bluff convincingly and the particular bluff of League of Nations sanctions was called by Mussolini. 'Resistance to aggression' meant in fact readiness for war; and readiness for war meant the ability to defend Britain against German air attack and a public opinion convinced that there was no alternative.

Most of the arguments here set out would have had Dawson's approval, even if his own approach was simpler and his emphasis different. Dermot Morrah,* who was briefed to write leaders by both men, says that Editor and Deputy Editor saw eye to eye but with this distinction: B-W was inspired by a passionate determination to do all he could to prevent a repetition of the war in which he had fought, whereas Dawson feared above all that such a conflict would find the Empire divided and leave it, whatever the result, in ruins. Dawson's particular attitude to Germans was perhaps set out best – he expressed it only rarely – in the leader that he wrote about the expulsion of his correspondent Norman Ebbutt from Berlin in August 1937.

There has never been any illusion on the part of *The Times* either about the strength of the present German regime in the eyes of its followers or about their absolute right to have the kind of constitution they prefer. The notion that there can be no dealing with National Socialism (or for that matter with Bolshevism) has found no countenance in these columns. . . . The distinction which it has always drawn is between the internal affairs of Germany (which are her own concern) and those national activities – due to some extent no doubt to the character of her rulers – which may threaten the peace and security of other countries or strike at the world-wide freedom of religious belief . . .

---

*Dermot Morrah, Winchester and New College, had served in the first war and was elected Fellow of All Souls in 1922. After five years as a civil servant he asked for a job on *The Times*, but Dawson advised him to get general experience elsewhere first. For three years he wrote leaders for the *Daily Mail* before coming to Printing House Square in 1932 to assist with the History. By 1936 he was writing every kind of leader and was chief representative of the paper at the Coronation of King George VI. B-W thought highly of him as an all-round writer who would follow brilliantly the Editor's brief.

12

Three Fruitless Years

I have resisted the impulse to telephone a word of
admiration for the line and language of the first
leaders of Friday's and to-day's dates. Their sturdi-
ness and clarity of statement, their dialectical
power, and – equally supreme virtue at such a
crisis – their up-to-the-moment factual basis, place
them on a level, at least, with the very finest that
have ever appeared in the journal. They are
Barnes-worthy.

Stanley Morison to B-W, March 1936

It was in 1936 that B-W first had the opportunity to set *The
Times* firmly on a course of policy towards Germany from
which it scarcely veered until the spring of 1939, when Hitler's
seizure of Czechoslovakia convinced him that the Nazi plan
was to dominate all central and eastern Europe by force. These
three years were in one sense for him a chapter of failures: his
judgement of the Nazis' hold on the Germans, and of the possibility of doing business with them in normal diplomatic ways,
was proved wrong. He had found it impossible to believe – as
did 'Pug' Ismay in Whitehall up to the very last moment – that
Hitler was ready to risk general war. Yet those years were also
a chapter of success, of maturing powers and growing authority
in the office. Those who disagreed bitterly with B-W never
questioned his motives. The more he was criticized the more
formidable he became in his determination. His war record
made his peace-efforts, if not admirable, at least respectable.

To go over the whole 'appeasement' issue from 1936 to the
outbreak of war would entirely unbalance a biography. The
most that can be attempted is to show B-W's mind at work and
to examine the evidence of those who worked with him at the
time. Because the earlier policy decisions led to the later ones,
it seems appropriate to narrate the facts in less and less detail
as the climax of March, 1939 comes nearer; to spend more
time, for example, on *The Times*'s reaction to the Rhineland

episode of March 1936 than on the invasion of Austria two years later. The Munich episode has not been treated at greater length because so much has been written elsewhere about it and about the role of the paper at the time. What is included is by way of correction of misunderstandings.

THE RHINELAND – 1936

To believe, as a few did at the time and many still do, that a decisive check could have been inflicted on Hitler by France and Britain during the weekend of 7 March 1936, when 25,000 German troops were sent into the demilitarized Rhineland in defiance of the Versailles Treaty and in flagrant disregard of the Locarno Treaties, is becoming increasingly difficult. Now that more is known of the thinking and dispositions of the French General Staff and of the true state of potential resistance to Hitler in its German counterpart, it is not easy to decide which was the more unlikely feature in the case for retaliation: a swift, efficient and decisive counterstroke by a small French force without risk of general war, or the seizure of power by German generals from a humiliated Führer which, it is suggested, would have followed it. Tempting as it is, however, to transfer our present knowledge back into the mind of a British editor at the time and to say that he swallowed the Nazi smack in the face because of it, to do so would be quite wrong.

Dawson and Barrington-Ward were against retaliation for two quite different reasons: because they had long considered that the Germans had a good case against the restrictions of the Versailles Treaty; and because they judged public opinion quite unready and unwilling to support the use of force by the French. The issue was not in their view a good one, especially when compared with that presented in the previous year by the Italians in Abyssinia. The moral indignation that had been roused against Mussolini could not be roused against Hitler – yet. Hugh Dalton, though speaking for the Labour Party, expressed a view held on both sides of the House of Commons when he opposed the taking of military or even economic sanctions against Germany.*

*It is appropriate to record here the opinion of French military intelligence that the choice for France was all-out war against Germany or to maintain her legal position after protest. 'Nothing serious could be tried without mobili-

Public opinion here does, I think, draw a clear distinction between the act of Signor Mussolini in resorting to aggressive war and waging it beyond his own frontiers and the actions, up-to-date at any rate, of Herr Hitler, which much as we may regard them as reprehensible, have taken place within the frontiers of the German Reich.[1]

There were at work in Printing House Square two other influences: Dawson's dismay at the practical difficulties that had revealed themselves for Britain when planning sanctions against Italy in the Mediterranean, and B-W's knowledge that further concessions over the Rhineland and a limited acceptance of German rearmament as an accomplished fact had already been officially considered in London and Paris – as was well known in Berlin.

Only the actual date of the German move was a surprise. To B-W, with his sense of fairness and distrust of French policy towards Germany, much of Hitler's behaviour was the predictable result of grudging and delaying the revision of Versailles and the reorganization of European security, with Germany as equal partner, which the Locarno policy of ten years earlier had envisaged. When the Germans had protested in May 1935 against the Franco-Soviet Pact (which promised mutual help if either party were attacked in Europe) B-W had noted that encirclement would merely strengthen Hitler's hold on his people.

To see the Rhineland *coup* and its aftermath in the perspective of a daily newspaper, it has to be remembered that it was not possible for *The Times,* any more than for the Cabinet or the Foreign Office, to concentrate attention during 1936 on Germany. For it was the year of the death of King George V and national mourning; of the abdication crisis and national bewilderment; of the collapse of Abyssinia and the flight of its Emperor in a British cruiser; of the outbreak of the Spanish civil war; of the great purges in the Soviet Union. It was a year in which pacifism gained ground: many Labour intellectuals, disillusioned with the League and disinclined to support 'national' rearmament, sought refuge in absolute pacifism. The Peace Pledge Union was formed. Those were the days when

zation. . . . I must destroy the stubborn belief . . . that in 1936 a simple threat would have been sufficient to make the Germans leave the Rhineland. The Deuxième Bureau never wrote or spoke anything which could have authorized such an opinion'.[2]

113

Canon Dick Sheppard was a household word. *The Times,* like other newspapers, was not aware of how fast Germany was rearming.

Neither Printing House Square nor the Berlin office was taken completely by surprise by Hitler's move; but it was made at the weekend, as became his habit, and the first news found Dawson on Saturday morning at Eton and B-W visiting his brother John at Christ Church. They had thirty-six hours to think about the line to be taken by the paper and the benefit of some intelligent if not representative advice from scholars and historians. They agreed that both should go into the office on Sunday, Dawson to edit and collect news, his Deputy to write the leading article. Their diaries show this formidable pair, generally separated at the weekend, dealing together with a major event. Dawson wrote:

I took train for London directly after lunch and plunged into a desperate day's work. There was great hubbub in Europe and the French were growing more and more excited. Masses of news from everywhere.... Our correspondents in Paris and (oddly enough) in Berlin were inclined to be a bit wild. I went down to the Foreign Office at 6 for a talk with Anthony Eden and found him in very good form, as he reported Stanley Baldwin also, and determined to bring good out of evil.*[3]

There was no time or need for B-W to worry about office matters or take soundings – Dawson was doing that – so he lunched at home and wrote in peace, also determined to 'bring good out of evil'.

Wrote and enjoyed writing a difficult leader trying to ensure, while condemning her breach of the treaty [of Locarno] that her offer to negotiate a full settlement should not be rejected.... The leader was telegraphed in full to Litvinov in Moscow at his request at midnight. Which shows how anxiously Russia is watching British opinion and what finger they now have in the European pie.[4]

But before that leader was published he had to run the gauntlet of indignant colleagues who wanted Britain to 'stand up to Hitler'. There was a spontaneous gathering in his room, in which Casey (the assistant editor who scrutinized the proofs

---

*Copious extracts from the Dawson Diaries, to which the author has had access, are to be found in *Geoffrey Dawson and Our Times* by John Evelyn Wrench (Hutchinson, 1955). This passage is on p. 331.

of foreign news at night), Arthur Barker, the newly appointed diplomatic correspondent, and the leader-writers Braham and Coote took part.* Barker has described the scene:

We did not start with a sense of issues being pre-determined. Indeed, we went into the discussion with zest and eagerness, which we should not have done had we felt it was going to be useless to talk to B-W in the way we did. By the end of the day recognition had begun to dawn that the paper was set on a 'no collision' course in its German policy.

On that Sunday morning we argued to B-W that this was the one time for stopping Hitler. Whatever might have been the reaction to earlier unilateral treaty revision by Germany, here were Hitler's troops and armaments put across a prohibited line; one, moreover, which Britain had guaranteed in the Locarno Pact. France could claim British assistance in ejecting those troops.

Acquiescence would give Hitler a resounding success, so that he would be virtually unassailable in Germany; whereas, if he were compelled to withdraw now, the reaction at home might well be fatal for him.

Now, we maintained, was going to be the crucial test. *The Times* still had the chance for a few hours more to give the lead that had been lacking so far. Let there be no excuses in the next morning's paper for Hitler's action, no suggestions of settling for verbal assurances while accepting a *fait accompli*. If the French (as it seemed then) thought it necessary to put the Germans out, Britain should be ready to fulfil her promises.

B-W agreed in condemning Hitler's choice of method. He considered this to be the worst sort of prelude for the sort of negotiated settlement of which he was a forthright advocate; but while condemning the method B-W endorsed the objective, arguing that the moral issue presented by Germany's one-sided treatment at Versailles, as he saw it, had not been disposed of by Stresemann's signature of the Locarno Pact. If the Germans under Hitler's leadership felt the Rhineland demilitarization to be discriminatory, this was a point of view he could well understand, and one that would come up under any leadership.

*The incident is referred to in Sir Colin Coote's *Editorial* (1965). The suggestion that B-W was ill at the time or suffering from the disease that killed him twelve years later is without foundation.

Arthur Barker, son of Sir Ernest Barker, the historian, had joined *The Times* in 1926 had served as a correspondent in Vienna, Poland and Geneva and was made diplomatic correspondent in the circumstances described on p. 128. He left *The Times* in 1937 to become Foreign News Editor of the BBC. He had seen Germany revisionist claims from a standpoint very different from B-W's – that of Germany's neighbours.

As the talk went on, it became more and more clear that the one thing B-W just would not contemplate in dealing with Hitler was a head-on clash of wills. Not to be in contact with the German Government about the terms on which they might join in maintaining peace would be to permit a situation in which Germany might find it possible to resort to war. He also made it clear to us that he did not share our view of Hitler, from whom, like many others at this period, he still professed hopes of evoking constructive statesmanship. Even if Hitler were what we thought him to be, and if his fall—with whatever attendant risks—could be brought about, Germany's neighbours would still have the problems of German grievances.[5]

So B-W was not to be shifted from his conviction that the German plan for a new security system in Europe, offered independently by Hitler in the act of destroying the old one, must be examined patiently. Such ideas had been talked about in Paris and London for four or five years, but nothing had come of them. Now they had to be examined seriously to see if there was a 'chance to rebuild'. That, indeed, was the title of the piece.*

Let us look closely at this much criticized article of 9 March 1936 which brought the author 'letters and congratulations and thanks from friends and colleagues . . . people are grateful for having been relieved and steadied'.[6] There had been plenty of angry and brave comment in the Sunday papers. For Monday morning it was a matter of offering second thoughts rather than spirited reactions. So the ingredient of rebuke was sparingly used: 'a breach of a treaty is not to be condoned or explained away. . . . France and Britain alike have reason for indignation and food for suspicions.'

Locarno, the argument ran, had been intended ten years earlier to make possible a negotiated revision of the penal clauses of the Versailles Treaty by creating Franco-German understanding, 'the first essential of European stability'. But it embodied those clauses of the treaty which imposed demili-

---

*The author recalls reading this article with disappointment, having been in the Berlin office six months before. When he discussed it with the form of 17–18 year old boys he was then teaching at Winchester College, he found them unanimous that this was not an issue to fight about. (A quarter of them died in the war that came three years later.) Views in the common room were divided: only the younger men were in favour of action. Nobody had clear ideas about the form it should take, least of all the survivors of Mons, Ypres and the Somme.

tarization on the German side only of the common frontier. So it guaranteed not only the common frontier but also one of the 'inequalities in which the Nazi movement of resurgence and revolt had its birth'. The concession made by Germany in accepting this had proved after ten years futile, for the French still did not relent. Hitler's action 'thus strikes the Locarno arrangement at its weakest joint'.

As Hitler had said to the Reichstag on Saturday, he was aiming not so much at the Locarno Treaty as at the 'particular servitude which it borrowed from the Versailles Treaty'. Some had called it an act of aggression, but 'there is still a distinction to be drawn between the march of detachments of German troops, to reoccupy territory indisputably under German sovereignty, and an act which carries fire and sword into a neighbour's territory.' None the less the Locarno treaty would be invoked and the parties to it must 'examine jointly and dispassionately the whole meaning of the move which confronts them'.

The occasion and excuse for Hitler's 'long-meditated departure' were the Franco-Soviet pact. It was, admittedly, purely defensive but it pointed to Germany as the potential aggressor. But Germany had her own fears of encirclement. The demilitarized zone was now a source of military weakness 'to a power which might one day become involved in war on two fronts again'. Is France, B-W asked, ever to be satisfied? Is Germany ever to be trusted? Statesmanship must break this vicious circle, and 'the statesman as well as the judge must be heard' when British and French statesmen meet in Paris. Hitler's ideas must be examined.

Then came a long rhetorical question. Would the Franco-Soviet pact ever have been found necessary if Germany had had no 'inequality' on her western border to complain of? Suppose Hitler had given a fresh guarantee of the French and Belgian frontiers, and that Britain and France had done the same – and Holland. Suppose the increase and use of air forces controlled by a western air pact; the frontiers of the eastern states secured by non-aggression pacts with Germany; and Germany back in the League – would the French then have sought the Communist Russian alliance? Yet these were precisely the offers made by Hitler on Saturday as his price of armed re-entry to the Rhineland.

British opinion 'would be nearly unanimous in its desire to turn an untoward proceeding to account ... and to seize the opportunity of broadening and strengthening the collective system, which opens with the German offer of re-entry'. Britain was vitally interested in French security; and any threat to French and Belgian territory engaged Britain, which had shown its belief in collective security by leading the League against Italy. Then the peroration:

France and Britain alike have reasons for indignation and food for suspicions. But, since neither stands alone, they have the more power even while they are faced with an admitted offence against the law of Europe, to take a steady measure of the undertakings which Germany has offered in extenuation. The old structure of European peace, one-sided and unbalanced, is nearly in ruins. It is the moment, not to despair, but to rebuild.[7]

The following day a second article went over the same ground commenting on Eden's House of Commons statements and making two fresh and critical points: first,

At the very moment of suggesting negotiations for fresh agreements, Germany has torn up an existing agreement to which she had freely subscribed and which she had repeatedly reaffirmed. It is hard to see what assurance she can now give which can be accepted as a guarantee of good faith.[8]

This was franker talking, perhaps reflecting advice and criticism of the earlier article. The second was a reminder of Austen Chamberlain's demand in the House that the Government would bear in mind 'the interest of this country in the independence and integrity of Austria as part of the system of European peace'.

Except in the understanding shown for German resentment of inferior status – constantly played on by Hitler – B-W's line is not different from that of Eden. Indeed, it probably reflects the inside knowledge that Dawson had gained on that Sunday. It would hardly have been adopted unless it was certain that neither in London, nor in Paris were 'sanctions' against Germany being considered. Whatever one might think of the argument and the style – 'untoward proceeding' is a phrase which cries out for a cartoonist – The Times was accurately anticipating and preparing the way for the official view, as well as reflecting majority opinion.

Leo Kennedy, who was acting for Ebbutt in Berlin, wrote to B-W that his first article (the one analysed above) seemed to 'abandon Locarno rather too readily' and 'to jump at the new proposals'. This would strengthen the hands of those who originated Hitler's action, whereas a very firm stand at this moment might have transferred control to the proper hands. 'However,' Kennedy added, 'I will frankly say this, that had I had to write the leader before I came here, I should have written on exactly the same lines but not so brilliantly.' 'Before I came here' are the crucial words. In B-W's reply to this generous tribute there is this significant passage:

I am impressed by the fact that Germans of various opinions, none of whom has any reason to love the present regime, have told me that they think the line which *T.T.* has taken to be helpful on the whole to the cause of a more tranquil and civilized Germany. And you know the pitfalls of a foreign policy which aims directly at influencing the internal politics of another country.

I think that the welcome that was given to the first leader here was largely due to the effort which it made . . . to put the event into perspective and *to distinguish between the illegal and the catastrophic.* As to British opinion generally, our difficulty has been to find enough letters stating what might be crudely called the anti-German view to balance the correspondence.[9]

Kennedy replied that as a result of living in Germany he understood the French feeling about the Nazis. His instinct had been to say to them:

This simply won't do. We can't deal with you—though we sympathize heartily with both your immediate and your ultimate aims—until you acknowledge that a treaty cannot be and is not abrogated by this sort of action.

B-W was at once busy with one of his kite-flying plans. The day after the 'Time to Rebuild' leader he was suggesting to Dawson that the French might be compensated and reassured by an offer of a complete British guarantee for the French and Belgian frontier. 'We shall,' he noted in his diary, 'have to come to their aid in time of trouble in any case – it has always been so and is still truer now – and may as well have the advantage of saying so. Dawson is, and has been, of the same opinion.'[10]

The next day he called on Leeper to try the suggestion on him.

The more he thought of it the more he liked it. If it is the means of strengthening the League by bringing Germany in, and if it is clearly not a part of the encirclement but the contrary, we may as well give it military definition and allow the staffs to converse. He went off to put it to Vansittart, who liked it equally. But both may like it for other reasons—i.e. anti-German reasons—than mine.[11]

He then advanced some of his arguments in the paper, with Dawson's approval, and on 13 March Leeper rang up to say the idea was being pressed, asking the paper to take it a step further. It appeared among the proposals for repairing Locarno mentioned in Eden's speech on the 20th about which B-W wrote yet another article. That evening he proudly noted:

Thus I have had a leader in each of the six consecutive issues of *The Times*—five first leaders and one second, five of them written on the day. I don't think it can have been done often.*[12]

During the next three months, alternating with Dawson, he went on with his foreign policy offensive. He worked at the Hitler peace plan given to Eden by Ribbentrop, found the French counterplan 'hopelessly elaborate and very French', and the Foreign Office dilatory, kept in regular touch with Eden. But Abyssinia, with Mussolini pledging the annihilation of the Emperor's armies, demanded more and more attention in the leader columns. On 7 April B-W called on Eden:

I found him tired but not dismayed. Never has a Foreign Secretary had so gruelling a time. The difficulties and the pressure are unrelenting. He told me he was going to stick to his guns. If the Italians break an agreement in order to use gas in war, what agreement is safe? Nor can they go on using the League offer of conciliation as a means of delay and prolonging the war. If they won't come to terms then oil sanctions must follow. He is right and most of public opinion will be with him.[13]

But ten days later he was 'feeling so indignant and exasperated over the tolerated destruction of the Abyssinians by

*He had presumably forgotten – though he must have known about it at the time – how in 1914 Flanagan wrote ten crucial leaders, most of them firsts, about the crisis in Europe leading up to the outbreak of war on 4 August. That must be one of the greatest and most decisive feats of advocacy ever achieved in newspapers.

these wanton Italians and over the League's failure to stop it that it took me a couple of hours to cool off for sleep'.* Then the end came and the Emperor left his country: 'The League has failed – a failure of will rather than of capacity,' says the diary. 'Mussolini has won a victory of ruthlessness. Will it prove a victory in the end?'[14] That same evening Dawson was down at Cliveden, heard the BBC news, and spent the evening 'wrangling about British policy and sanctions and the future of the League'. This time the Monday leader was written by the Editor himself 'lunching off a tray', a sign of emergency.

It was a sad piece, reflecting Dawson's depression at the state of the world; but its argument was realistic and hit hard at those who would pin all the blame for the Abyssinian disaster on the present Government:

The critics would be on stronger ground if they were to argue that there was once a period, long before the Geneva speech so signally confirmed our policy, when Great Britain should have revised her commitments in the prospect of some such an event as has since occurred; that in the light of these commitments she should have looked sooner to her military strength; and above all that she should have made more certain betimes that her neighbours shared her own conviction of the sanctity of pledges.... In the most conspicuous case of aggression that it is possible to imagine, she has tried out the whole present capacity of the League for effective common action. She has found it wanting...[15]

In other words Britain had done all that could be expected of her, and the blame for the League's failure to check Mussolini lay in the reluctance of others (notably the French) to supplement British forces which were too weak for all the potential enemies they had to face.†

---

*B-W's views on the Abyssinian episode are further explained in Chapter 15.
†A leader page article on the French view of the Abyssinian affair sent by the Paris office on 9 October 1935 was accompanied by a message from Thomas Cadett. It said that Hoare (the Foreign Secretary) had told the French that they had shown reluctance to agree to even the mildest sanctions in a blatant and flagrant case of aggression. 'If this continued the British would conclude that the League was an anti-German combination and nothing but a sham and a delusion.' Cadett added that the French Ministers were afraid of the Right starting a civil war in case of hostilities over Abyssinia and warned the office that Laval's position was in danger.[16]

VISIT TO BERLIN – 1936

In June B-W, still interested in Hitler's new Locarno, spent four days in Berlin. The original purpose was that he should talk with Hitler; instead he was seen by the Führer's deputy, Rudolf Hess, accompanied by Paul Schmidt, the interpreter – but to no good purpose. Hess would not answer the question addressed recently by Eden to Berlin: whether Germany recognized and respected the territorial position in Europe except in so far as it might be modified by free negotiation and agreement.

It was rather solemn and absurd. A round table.... I tried to get Hess to speak of German intentions in the matter of the British questionnaire (recently addressed to Hitler) but in vain. The usual generalizations of goodwill towards us. I put my well-worn point that we were now, as 40 years ago in the days of Chamberlain's offer, facing a chance of real collaboration which, if lost, might not recur.*[17]

From his disappointing interview with Hess he drove straight to lunch with Kurt Hahn's brother Rudo at the family home in Wannsee, where he heard from this distinguished Berliner, not for the first time, what he and other Jews were suffering.

From the top dog to the under dog. Hahn had been taken from his office by the Gestapo, without charge or warning, and kept a night in a detention cell. Wife not allowed to be informed. She did not know where he was. Three Gestapo men visited her and ran-sacked his books and papers, threatening her at the time.
In the prison Rudo was made to undress and lie on a dirty bed. At intervals during the night a warden flashed a torch in his eyes and called him *Schweinhund*, etc. About 11 a.m. he was let go.
Rudo's wife's morale is quite unbroken, though the nerve strain is terrible.... She could leave but she stays to help her compatriots. Hundreds of Jews in the arts and the professions have lost every-thing. The plan is to keep one of their houses going there and to provide a good midday meal and a meeting place to keep body and soul together. Otherwise men of education would sink, isolated and destitute, into sheer despair and annihilation ...[18]

He was to hear in Hamburg the following year from his friends the Warburgs a similar story, and it is absurd to allege

*Two months earlier B-W exclaimed in his diary, after reading *Inside Europe* by John Gunther: 'What thugs the Nazis are!'

— as some critics have — that he had neither knowledge of nor sympathy with the plight of Jews in Germany. He knew well what was going on and wrote three or four outspoken leaders in their defence; but he refused to jeopardize the influence he believed *The Times* to have in Berlin by letting it join the violent anti-Nazi propaganda chorus of London, Paris and New York.

B-W had talks during his visit with Phipps, the British Ambassador, who invited Schacht to lunch to meet him. He asked the Economics Minister why he was pressing so hard for restoration of Germany's former colonies. Why not talk with Britain in terms of general trade?

Schacht denied that he was emphasizing the need for colonies and would willingly talk about trade; but B-W had seen a memorandum by Kennedy (then acting as *locum* in Berlin) of a talk with Schacht in which he had insisted on the return of colonies as vital and urgent. The diary commented:

A cool old humbug but very able. I think his line on colonies is taken to give him a good standing with the Nazis, whom he has to try and restrain in other directions.[19]

He disapproved of Phipps, 'a small dapper man with a monocle. Not the man for Berlin, where weight and dignity, physical as well, are wanted rather than cleverness. P's smart sayings about the Nazis will go back to them.' As an ambassador the Frenchman François-Poncet impressed him more. After a cool and dispassionate survey of the situation he said: 'We must press these people to an arrangement and find out where they stand' — which was exactly what *The Times* was recommending.

He recalled how the German Foreign Office had assured him on 5 March that nothing was contemplated in the Rhineland, barely a day before it was occupied early on March 7 — and now he had since proved that the F.O. had deceived him because it had been deceived, or left uninformed itself.[20]

B-W noted how much nearer the Slav world, powerful and mysterious, felt in Berlin. In London it was merely an abstraction. While he thought it absurd to consider Russia as an aggressive power in the military sense, he perceived that 'anti-Bolshevism was of course the law of the Nazi being, the only excuse for it as it were'. As he left Berlin he asked himself once again the crucial question – whether peaceful co-existence between free and unfree was possible. Of the Germans he wrote:

A splendidly vigorous, magnificently capable people but flawed with the odd strain of atavistic emotionalism. The forest tribes. Mentally enclosed. All their best and worst qualities evoked and stiffened by the stupidities of the victors after the war. They seem set in thought and deed, collectively, for war again. But, individually, as everywhere, few or none want it. We can only go on trying to make civilization prevail. But can democracy and these regimes co-exist successfully?[21]

The morning of his first day in Berlin there had appeared in the paper a leader by himself stating its views on British policy for Europe. It was obviously composed as an anthem for the visit of the Deputy Editor of *The Times*. It demanded:

A plain declaration to the world of the commitments by which we stand, a firm grasp of the negotiations with Germany, and the most rapid possible execution of an imperial defence plan.

Starting from the deep divergences of view about sanctions against Italy which were then filling the letter columns day after day, the argument moves on to suggest that the League may have to reorganize its peace-keeping function on a regional basis. The start with a new system must be made in Western Europe, where Germany for the first time since 1918 'has come into a position to claim her full international right and to take her own part, from the beginning in redesigning the foundations of peace'. Britain should help by defining her policy publicly. She must offer 'immediate and unlimited resistance' to any attempt upon the territorial integrity of France and Belgium; the Mediterranean powers should be told that any interference with the freedom of transit on the short sea-route to the East would 'encounter the full and unhesitating employment of British resources'. The British interest in these cases coincides with larger interests of liberty and stability.

As for German intentions, Britain must be the pacemaker in getting a plain understanding about a settlement, although Germany at the moment is waiting to see what happens in France. Meanwhile there must be the 'speediest possible completion of our defence arrangements'. Foreigners must not be misled by the arguments going on in Britain about rearmament. Napoleon made the mistake of seeing only a nation of shop-keepers: 'in present circumstances an adequate level of British armament is paradoxically indispensable if the advance to agreement and disarmament is to be resumed.'

BACK IN LONDON

But back in London there seemed to be too little steam behind the British inquiry for details of the Hitler plan. On 8 July the diary remarks: 'Eden has now been swallowed up by the F.O. . . . The Government have no foreign policy at all.' Vansittart was concentrating everything against Germany and the withdrawal of sanctions against Italy was partly the victim of that policy.* At the War Office, however, the anti-German obsession of the Foreign Office was being resisted. Generals Dill and Paget told B-W over lunch that the Government had no policy to put in the place of *rapprochement* with Germany and that 'its technical advisers lacked any strategy or guide to strategic requirements' from Ministers.[22]

This was merely the sequel to what Paget had told him a year earlier, when the generals felt that the F.O. was 'practically inviting an unwanted war in time' and met all their representations 'with a brandishing of the Eyre Crowe memorandum of 1907'. They were 'entirely in agreement with and grateful for the line that *The Times* had taken'. However, this evidence of unreadiness for continental war was not of a kind that could be frankly presented in the paper, useful though it might be for guiding editorial policy.[23]

Also recorded in the diary at that time are a couple of talks with the Military Attaché at the German Embassy, Geyr von Schweppenburg, an honourable and much-respected officer.† B-W had it pointed out to him by this friend that

---

*Compare the letter sent on 20 May 1935 to Ebbutt in Berlin by Kennedy, then in daily touch with the Foreign Office: 'I have never seen Vansittart's memorandum but it exists alright. I understand that he has mapped out the German programme step by step showing how Germany will ultimately dominate Europe. The worst of this is, that he cannot bear to allow it to appear that he is wrong, and therefore Germany has to be the villain of the piece whatever she does. We have proof of rather outrageous attempts by the F.O. under his direction to rush the public into forming unfavourable opinions of German official utterances.'[24]

†It was about this time that Ribbentrop, despite the cool welcome given to his appointment to London as Ambassador in July 1936, asked through Tom Jones –

Britain was greatly dependent on France strategically, for example, for communications, especially by air, to Africa and the East. 'France will not meet German claims, sticks to encirclement. What shall we do to put pressure on France to come into the much-needed understanding with Germany?' To which B-W replied that France was also dependent on Britain; if Germany were reasonable London could put much pressure on Paris. Two months later they lunched together again:

> I insisted, Russia no military menace at present. 'Yes', he said, 'and Germany is no military menace to you but you are determined not to be outstripped by Germany in the air.' He declares the Reichswehr is peaceable.[25]

While *The Times* continued to hope that Germany would state her aims and terms, so that the Locarno system might be reconstructed, Hitler, as was his way, preferred to wait on events and not to tie his hands.* His 'volunteers' and those of Italy were now getting more deeply involved in the Spanish Civil War, over which British public opinion, with right and left taking sides, was getting almost as indignant as it had been about Abyssinia – but much more divided. At this time Churchill rang up B-W to thank him for the comment on his draft speech mentioned earlier (p. 107) and explained that he wanted:

> A 'front' with France not for warlike purposes but to bring Germany to a deal. Does not think Germany will come to a deal otherwise. Must be compelled. Pleased with the reception of his speech by the Left here. Maintains the broad national agreement in support of rearmament. Says French General Staff don't like the

---

who had gone with Lloyd George to visit Hitler – for Dawson's help in getting his son Rudolph into Eton. Jones, in a letter from Berchtesgaden, reports Rudolph's mother as saying that he would 'see how English boys live and will be able to teach the Hitler Youth'. Three weeks later Dawson replied cautiously that he had talked with the headmaster, but that there were 'grave difficulties' in the way, due partly to the boy's age (he was fifteen) and partly due to the congestion in the school.[26]

*During September B-W wrote to Dawson, on holiday in Yorkshire, about a talk with the Foreign Secretary:

'Eden is not apparently very hopeful of bringing off the Locarno conference at the moment, though he thinks that it will probably come off later. He is not a believer – rightly I think – in imminent war. The Government are pleased with the way in which things have gone for them; they feel that they have – thanks to Hitler and Stalin between them – got a large concentration of public opinion behind them at home. It will be the Germans' own fault if they now hang back.'[28]

Soviet Pact. Would gladly be rid of it, but recognize that it has turned the French Communists into patriots.[27]

There was no lack of voices to play on a mind which was worrying about the possibility of being wrong. For example, his old Balliol friend Namier, the historian, a Pole by birth, thought the Franco-Russian pact good: 'a German-Russian alliance would dominate the world,' he said; 'what a mug Hitler is.'[29] General Haining, the Director of Military Operations argued with him at lunch over Liddell Hart's view, strongly supported by the paper, that Britain must not plan for extensive participation by land in a next war. B-W maintained that 'it was a doubtful strategy and fatal to British power in the end, win or lose. No perfunctory pledging of a million lives again.' British support to France in the form of troops must be only limited, whatever might be required in the air.

Then from October onwards the 'King's business' and Mrs Simpson entirely engaged the Government's attention for some weeks. During that time B-W was invited by the Chairman to Hever Castle for a weekend of the kind of highly organized pheasant shooting of which he silently disapproved. One man with a dog was more his style of sport, but such weekends brought other opportunities. Eden came to dinner and, while the others played card games, minister and journalist went aside to talk. They discussed the Simpson case, which Eden said was 'paralysing foreign policy', and then came to the problem of guaranteeing and protecting Belgium, an essential part of any new Locarno such as he was still seeking. Van Zeeland, he said, was proposing neutrality for his country. B-W suggested it might be the Swiss kind of neutrality. Eden replied: 'The Chiefs of Staff agree with you. It is strategically sound but politically difficult.' He would meanwhile go on trying for a new Locarno; at worst 'Germany must be made to bear the responsibility of refusal'.

By the end of the year there are signs of disillusionment with Germany in the leaders he wrote on 21 December and New Year's Eve. Thanks largely to Britain, the march into the Rhineland had been met with no counter-action more provocative than the questionnaire about intentions, which had been ignored in Berlin. In return Britain was entitled to expect Hitler to make possible the conference he had proposed in March; instead 'the policy of the Reich had been obscure and mystifying'. Britain had been ready to sympathize with German objections to the Franco-Soviet pact and with the demand for access to raw materials, whether with the return of colonies or not. But the Germans had been repeating and exaggerating their objections in a way which was making negotiation more difficult. Lately Hitler's attention had turned to Spain, to Czechoslovakia and even to a 'grandiose agreement with Japan'.

The way to fight Bolshevism was by economic means, as the British themselves had shown. To fight it by war, B-W argued, would merely lead to more Bolshevism. But the economic concessions now being demanded by Hitler were one-sided and intended to build up German rearmament and self-sufficiency. That was not acceptable. Germany must choose between cooperation, which was being offered to her, and the isolation of 'an armed and irresponsible opportunism'. When a visitor from the German Embassy called at the office on 18 December and complained of a growing fear of Germany in Britain the Deputy Editor replied:

It was because she persisted in keeping us uncertain of her intentions and unwilling to register them in an agreement. A vacuum in international relations was naturally dangerous. He tried to put the anti-Communist formula over me but I wouldn't have it.[30]

The evidence is quite clear: the year 1937 opens with *The Times* becoming deeply sceptical of any rational deal with the Nazis. During this year of anxiety and regular leader-writing B-W had found time to arrange with the Foreign Office that the paper should have a regular diplomatic correspondent who would collect news and views every day. The News Department under Rex Leeper was growing in importance and *The Times*, with its semi-official status in the eyes of foreigners, was likely to get there most-favoured paper treatment. The proposal was discussed over lunch at the Athenaeum:

Leeper wishes *The Times* would have a diplomatic correspondent to see him regularly on broad policy and get the mind of the Government as *news*. Kennedy, he said, merely argues with him and reports not the news but his own views. This I believe to be largely true. . . . L. much disposed to warm up the rather cool relations that have subsisted between his office and ours.[31]

Arthur Barker was the first to take the job on, and after less than two years it was taken over by Iverach McDonald, who turned the daily diplomatic column into one of the most distinguished features of London journalism, while maintaining anonymity before the general public. Leeper doubtless hoped that by feeding *The Times* with official view-points in the form of news, it would become possible for foreigners and others to distinguish clearly between the paper's policy as declared in leading articles and that of the Government as reported in the news columns.

It has been alleged that Dawson and B-W were in those days at the beck and call of the Foreign Office and unduly influenced by ministers. The relationship can be recorded here as it was seen by the Diplomatic Correspondent. Arthur Barker writes:

I had to take the day's news from the F.O. and Embassies to B-W whenever he was editing the paper, or in action himself as leader-writer. I also made a point of calling on him when he was restricting himself to the Deputy Editor's normal day duties. On evenings when he was editing or leader-writing he was usually under strain. On days of the other sort he would sometimes be quite relaxed, appreciative that one had sought him out and ready for a few minutes of quiet conversation.

Whatever the circumstances he would assume his quizzical expression, with the querying twinkle and downward twist of the mouth, as he sat forward shoulders hunched to hear my recital of news. His view of affairs, more often than not, was sharply opposed to the official one, which moved him now and then to interject a single terse dissentient sentence.

He very much gave the impression of treating these communications, as from the Foreign Office to *The Times,* with a certain sense of occasion and protocol. Even when time might have allowed, he would not let himself go, as he did at other opportunities, controversially. Impatience and irritability might begin to show, but were always controlled. One took them for what they were—marks of overwork.*[32]

What is to be said about the charge that the paper, as part of its policy of bringing Hitler to the conference table, played down its treatment of Jews and political prisoners? In this charge there is some substance. So far as news was conerned, although B-W wrote vigorously against Nazi persecution,

---

*The author's recollection of B-W's attitude to the Foreign Office ten years later is described on p. 250.

129

probably he believed, as Philip Lothian said he believed when asked to take up the case of Hans Litten,* that the power to avert war by influencing and dividing German opinion must not be weakened by intervening between the Nazis and their political enemies. Perhaps he believed the position of the Berlin office and its sources of information must be protected. However, readers were reminded in other ways of persecution in Germany. In the letter columns especially there were such continuous references as the attacks by readers on the holding of the Olympic Games in Berlin because of Nazi race discrimination; or the thanks from scientists like Einstein and Schroedinger for what had been done to help Jewish scholars; or the long and distinguished argument between academics for and against attending historic celebrations at the university of Heidelberg; or the debate on the nature of race in which Keith and Huxley took part. In January 1936 the paper was confiscated in Germany because of news reports about the persecution of Jews and Catholics and about Goering's views on the teaching of history. Indeed, its unpopularity with the German Government was to culminate the following year in the expulsion of its distinguished correspondent, Norman Ebbutt, who had been in Berlin for ten years.

*Hans Litten was a thirty-one year old German lawyer who had incurred Hitler's personal hatred by cross-examining him severely in a law case, in which Nazis were accused of violence against Communists and Socialists. Litten was sent to Sonnenburg concentration camp in April 1933 and during the next years barbarously treated. Ninety-eight British lawyers appealed on his behalf to Hitler in October 1935. Ribbentrop's almost incredible reply is to be read in Martin Gilbert's biography of Lord Allen of Hurtwood. (*Plough My Own Furrow*, Longman, 1965, pp. 367ff.)

13

1937 - Berlin Unappeased

Before picking up again the threads of policy-making in B-W's leading articles it is helpful to pause and consider what rights of killing and cutting an editor can and should exercise. By now he was regularly taking the chair and, more often than not, writing the main leaders on foreign policy in Europe. Whatever blame attaches to Dawson for their argument and tone must be shared by his deputy; whatever credit is due for their interpretation of Britain's duty and capacity to resist Hitler should go to both.

This was the year of the famous sentence so often quoted against Dawson. It occurred in a letter written by him on 23 May to H. G. Daniels, his senior correspondent in Europe, who had been sent from Paris to Berlin for a brief spell to take the temperature of the Germans, while Ebbutt (who had succeeded Daniels there in 1927) visited London.

... it really would interest me to know precisely what it is in *The Times* that has produced this new antagonism in Germany. I do my utmost, night after night to keep out of the paper anything that might hurt their susceptibilities. I can really think of nothing that has been printed now for many months past to which they could possibly take exception as unfair comment.[1]

These sentences, charitably interpreted, can be read to mean that he and B-W had been taking special pains – at a time when they still hoped for a European settlement, in spite of events in Abyssinia and Spain – to exclude news and comment which would play into the hands of Nazi extremists who wanted no understanding with Britain. For they believed – as did Ebbutt, but less confidently – that there were moderate elements in Berlin which might still prevail if good temper could be maintained. The sterner and more familiar interpretation has been that Dawson would stop at nothing to appease Berlin. Obviously the context calls for closer scrutiny. A week earlier, on 16 May, Daniels had reported to Dawson:

The German Press has been savage about *The Times*, in fact worse than at any period I remember. The latest discovery is that if you spell it backwards it spells SEMIT, which leads them to deduce that we are a Jewish-Marxist organization and that nothing else can be expected of us. Such are the childish results of a sheltered public opinion. The worst of it is that it renders honest efforts hopeless.[2]

That Ebbutt's quiet, authoritative reporting of the successful resistance to Nazi influences in the Protestant Church and his diagnosis of strained relations between Army and Party had disturbed the regime was well known. It was to lead three months later to his expulsion from Berlin 'on account of dissatisfaction with his published record of affairs in Germany'. But there had been nothing in his correspondence around this date to produce sudden tantrums in Dr Goebbels. Scrutiny of the files reveals that the explanation was probably to be found elsewhere – in recent reports from Spain about the German military role in the civil war. On 3 May, for example, there was published a Basque priest's eye-witness account of the Nationalists' bombing of Guernica on 26 April, the reporting of which by the special correspondent, G. L. Steer,* had caused an international sensation. 'The sky was black,' he wrote, 'with German aeroplanes . . . firing their machine-guns at 600 feet.' This provoked from the official German News Service a furious commentary entitled '*The Times* Bombs Guernica', which said that the newspaper's behaviour 'presents a picture of the British people combining stupidity with Machiavellian craftiness in a manner not altogether convincing'. That ardent Nazi, Dr Goebbels, resented and feared above all the charge of 'frightfulness' because he knew that British propaganda had had twenty years earlier no more deadly theme.

The next day (5 May) there was published prominently a

---

*Working with the Nationalists at this time as special correspondent of the paper was 'Kim' Philby, who later worked in the British Secret Service as a spy for Russia. Philby was already a Communist agent. He was appointed by B-W, doubtless on the strength of being an Old Westminster, at the suggestion of his father, St John Philby, known to *The Times* as a famous Arabist and occasional contributor of articles.

letter from Communist sympathizer Dr Hewlett Johnson, the 'Red Dean' of Canterbury – not one of Dawson's favourite churchmen – which praised the reporting from Spain and said that he, too, had been in Guernica. For good measure, there appeared on the same page a leader stoutly answering German official attacks, asserting that *The Times*'s reports were authentic, while admitting the possibility (as alleged by Nationalists) of some incendiarism in Guernica by Republicans after the air raids. The comment shows little regard for Nazi 'susceptibilities':

Where is the wisdom, from Germany's point of view, in allowing her embarrassment to inspire a press campaign which is calculated to damage her relations with Great Britain, and which, consisting as it does of a series of chimerical accusations intemperately made, can only discredit her powers of self-control and, incidentally, arouse suspicion of her complicity in the bombardment.

'Chimerical accusations intemperately made' was good 'Auntie *Times*' language, and on 6 May Ambassador Ribbentrop protested to Eden about Press reports from Spain. They included a message from the paper's special correspondent in Bilbao saying that he had himself been machine-gunned near Guernica and had identified six Heinkel fighters and some Ju 52 and He 111 bombers. (This was published on the very day that Dawson's friend Lothian – as the Editor well knew – was seeing Hitler on one of his 'appeasement' missions.) Unabashed *The Times* went on publishing reports about German pilots captured in Spain and held for trial by the Government forces.

Whatever may be said generally of the restrained editorial attitude towards Germany, neither Dawson nor B-W was taking pains to suppress news offensive to Berlin for some time before and after the date of the letter to Daniels. Indeed, to report German bombing in Spain and to defend the reports in a leader was about the most provocative thing the paper could do – short of attacking Hitler personally. There are two points, therefore, to be made about this episode, which over the weeks and months involved B-W just as much as Dawson. First, whoever was in the chair had a right to suppress or limit publication of emotional, sarcastic and sometimes violent letters about the Nazis and German internal conditions (of which there were plenty) so long as he believed a general settlement to be possible.

To extend Dawson's single sentence of 1937 to cover the whole German policy of the office from 1933 to 1939 is manifestly absurd. There was much in the paper between 1933 and 1937 that criticized and exposed National Socialism, for example Douglas Reed's remarkable reporting of the Reichstag Fire trial.*

Some criticism that has been heard ignores the paper's detailed exposure of Nazi treatment of the Churches and makes inexplicable the expulsion of Ebbutt even if it was partly intended as a reprisal for the expulsion from London of Nazi correspondents, who had been playing politics in the German colony there.

Second, Dawson and B-W were more interested in the control of letters and leaders, which came daily under their hand, than in the detailed control of the copious foreign news. It is likely, therefore, that Dawson's letter had nothing to do with news. For in the month that it was written the news columns contained matter about the Germans which did indeed deeply 'hurt their susceptibilities'. It was not left out, because no newspaper can suppress important news. What could be done was to temper the tone in which news was reported and avoid the sensationalism with which some newspapers covered the Spanish civil war.†

Correspondents well understood this, and realized that they

---

*A special article from Berlin of 31 January 1934 said:

'To reject obstinately everything in the Third Reich because features of its beginnings shocked public opinion in many countries is not going to help the world to understand the new Germany and adjust itself to the changes. But it is no more helpful to accept everything uncritically as presented by the fanatical pioneers of the Nazi regime. The brutalities and stupidities, the cynical evasions of promises and withdrawals of concessions which have accompanied the change are established facts which cannot be forgotten. Nor, as long as they continue, can the world be expected, or afford, to close its eyes to them.'

†Had Stanley Morison felt less uncharitable towards Dawson's editing he could have referred back to instances of cutting mentioned in earlier volumes of his own *History*. On p. 231 of Volume IV we read that Dawson's cutting of Repington, the military correspondent during the First World War, helped to maintain 'consistency and good sense'. In 1918 Repington moved to the *Morning Post*. 'There,' says the historian, 'he spent the rest of the war industriously destroying the reputation for intelligence which Dawson had preserved for him by judicious deletions while he worked for *The Times*.' On p. 373 of Volume III we read that Valentine Chirol (as head of the Foreign Department) altered the text of G. B. Morrison's despatches from China 'because he thought their publication impolitic'. Yet Morrison was one of the giants. Mackenzie Wallace, too, restrained the sensationalism of the notorious Blowitz, who regularly complained of 'the brutality of the alterations in my telegrams'.

must do their best – compatible with self-respect – not to get expelled. If Dawson believed that extensive reporting of extremist activity in India would jeopardize in the House of Commons the chances of Indian reforms, his correspondent in New Delhi would be expected to bear this in mind. Ebbutt, a very shrewd and experienced reporter who had been a sub-editor himself, found his way around the difficulty of depicting the ways of Nazi Germany by giving detailed day-to-day news of the dispute within the Protestant Church and by watching carefully the role of the Army. It was only from those two bodies that any effective resistance to Hitler was to be expected and that reliable inside information was volunteered.*

The plain fact is that an editor's right to kill, cut and improve is beyond question, especially with anonymous copy. The processes to which news and views are submitted in a news-paper office may be compared to the work of a good kitchen. It is the selecting, preparing, reducing, rearranging and present-ing (with headlines) which gives the product the special style which distinguishes news in, say the *Daily Mirror,* the *Daily Telegraph, The Times* and the *Daily Express.* The editor's rights in this regard are, it is true, not absolute; he will alter copy only as much as his writers will tolerate. But laymen who criticize this process as distortion or censorship seem often to confuse their objections to the editorial view that is being enforced with objections to editing as such. That is to say, those who have criticized B-W's restraint towards Hitler do not – as they should do, for consistency's sake – also criticize his later restraint towards Stalin. If it was wrong to 'edit' news and com-ment about Nazi treatment of Jews it was also wrong to 'edit' news and comment about Soviet treatment of Poles.

The *History* points out that Dawson, who had been himself

---

*In a letter to the Foreign News Editor written in May 1946 Ebbutt acknow-ledged his debt to one particular German, who 'was the only German contact I ever had worth the name'. This man, who was to help Ebbutt's successors in the very difficult days of 1938 and 1939, seems to have enjoyed some kind of immunity from Gestapo inquisition. For he maintained contact with *The Times*'s men in Berlin, sometimes three or four times a week, through meetings in the under-ground railway and at other rendezvous. He had special sources on the Church conflict but was also able to give inside information about the General Staff and leading Party figures. James Holburn, who was in Berlin after Ebbutt, now believes that this man may have been briefed by the anti-Nazi group in Admiral Canaris's counter-intelligence organization, but no documentary evidence of this has been found.[3]

a foreign correspondent, disliked 'viewiness' in news-writing; and it was to this and other aspects of foreign news that an assistant editor devoted his attention in the evenings. Fresh of face and silvery-grey of hair, Casey would walk into the foreign sub-editors' room in his relaxed, quiet way, carrying a proof, or the flimsy (carbon copy) of a telephoned message, lean over the chief-sub's chair, and murmur, 'Pearson, I don't think we want this, do you?' 'This' would be some flash of individual opinion in a report, some extravagance of style or unusual verbosity. Sometimes he would say, 'I expect you've already dealt with that one', handing him a marked proof. This, G. L. Pearson (chief foreign sub-editor) insists, was the only correction of news for policy reasons that he ever saw being made; and his evidence is supported, so far as copy from Germany is concerned by James Holburn, Iverach McDonald and Euan Butler all of whom worked in Berlin after Ebbutt had been expelled, that is to say when 'appeasement' was at its height.* How far Ebbutt himself was unfairly treated it is difficult to say with confidence. He regularly wrote more in major despatches than he forecast in the five o'clock message to the office; and he was quite often late with his copy, for reasons which had only partly to do with the special difficulties of news-gathering in Berlin. The result was that he was often cut for excess length, and that the first edition version of his main despatch had to be rearranged for the final edition in order to get in later – and probably more important – paragraphs.†

The theory and practice of this killing and cutting are illustrated by what Dawson wrote in 1912 when remonstrating with that formidable and famous Vienna correspondent, Wickham Steed. He had been Editor for only three weeks when he decided to put his foot down with this diplomatic pundit. He is explaining why a sentence which Steed has especially asked to have left in had been taken out.

*See Appendix, p. 282.
†At intervals over two and a half years the author sub-edited messages from Germany, unless he was in Berlin, when they were done by J. D. L. Hood, who agrees with the views here expressed. He has no recollection of his own contributions being distorted for policy reasons, but does recall occasional grumbles from Ebbutt, and more frequent protests from Douglas Reed, at the way messages were handled in London. For a foreign correspondent to find fault with sub-editors is normal. What may be done for technical reasons, or because of a particular situation, is sometimes put down to policy or prejudice.

It may seem to you to be a pedantic view of my business, but I can't believe it is in the interests of the paper that it should speak with one voice in its editorial columns and with another in the messages of its most distinguished correspondents abroad, on a fundamental question of foreign policy. That is in fact what the publication of this particular message would mean.

Whether it is right or wrong, my point now is that it is fatal that the paper should, so to speak print leading articles taking opposite sides in different parts of the paper...

I have always felt that their [correspondents'] business is to be chroniclers first and foremost—no doubt with a general bias in favour of the views of the country where they are stationed—and diplomatists and leader-writers afterwards; and that in a vital question, as this is, of British policy, the best way of influencing the attitude of the paper is by private letter, of which I would welcome more from you.[4]

This ruling is as valid today as it was then, even if the disappearance of anonymity makes it harder to apply. The editor and his representative, the sub-editor, are still indispensable as mediators between the specialist and the ordinary reader: explaining what is not obvious, maintaining continuity, deleting what is repetitive and providing the impetus of a good headline.

This year 1937 brought Neville Chamberlain into 10 Downing Street, in place of the weary Baldwin. B-W was to see him only seldom and the office contact was maintained by Dawson himself, the intimacy of whose friendship with the new Prime Minister has been exaggerated. Colin Davidson, Baldwin's adviser, called at *The Times* on the day of the change and B-W recorded what he heard.

Neville has no committed confidant, no outside contact. Either must act wholly on his own without reconnaissance, which is bad, or must consult colleagues, which, for a P.M., is fatal. S.B. [Baldwin] always had Colin to take soundings for him, or saw G.D. or some other neutral friend. A P.M. must be a little aloof from his Cabinet to run it successfully and without fussiness.... Neville is too shut up and solitary, but we shall see.[5]

August saw B-W spending three weeks, most unwillingly, in the German spa of Schwalbach, where he tried by drastic mud-bath treatment to relieve the pains in neck and shoulder which had been worrying him for some years. Recently a specialist had diagnosed rheumatoid arthritis at an early stage. 'If nothing arrests it,' he wrote, 'I shall in time be done for. But trees need not grow into the sky, do not in fact.' This costly experiment, which took him away from wife and children in the August holiday season, did little good; but it did allow him to see something of Germany in the year which opened with Hitler's assuring the world that 'the time of so-called surprises is over' – the year which Churchill called 'the loaded pause'. B-W realized that a spa was no good vantage point for general observations on the Nazis but he allowed himself some none the less.

There is a great deal of dissatisfaction but it will never come to anything. The Nazi regime is founded on more than compulsion. . . . But there is something oppressive in the monotony of the pervasive Nazi dope – the same thoughts and even phrases all round – and in the sense of restriction.

He brushed up his German with a teacher, and made a couple of visits to a Protestant church. He noted the silence in which the forty minute address was listened to. It had some special quality, even though there were no references to the struggle between Church and Party.

The whole service becomes topical and real. In its present German setting every sentence has its full meaning. Civilization, I concluded, in the free countries blunts the edge of Christianity. We are able to be 'light half-believers of our casual creeds'. Paganism and persecution give it new force and truth. Will pagan Germany succeed in stifling it by law and propaganda?[6]

14

Year of Munich

We can lay down the proposition that the Angel
of Peace is unsnubbable.
*Churchill in the House of Commons,
21 December 1937. Volume 330, Col. 1832*

Hard things have been said about consistency in politics,
mostly by politicians. Whether in a journalist dealing with
public affairs the quality is to be regarded as strength or weakness, there is no doubt that B-W had it. The main strategy of
his thinking about relations with Germany does not change
between 1934 and 1939; and the emotions and motives which
it rationalizes can be traced back to his *Observer* days and
earlier. As for the tactics of the argument, confronted by
successive crises in Austria, Czechoslovakia and Poland,
examples will be given of the brilliant and fervid pleading of
his leading articles as well as extracts from the diaries throwing
light on his moods and contacts in the time of Munich and after.

Eden's resignation from the Foreign Office in February 1938,
because of Chamberlain's independent dealings with the Duce,
caused him no regrets, close though their contacts had been.
Eden was now regarded as an obstacle to real negotiations
with the Germans and Italians, in the form of what were later
called 'summit meetings'.

He really had no heart for any kind of direct talks with the
dictatorial powers. This policy restricts diplomacy to a gamble
on their collapse or to waiting for the next war. Pity is that he
goes just after Hitler's speech. Pity too that British diplomacy was
not liberated for active negotiation two years ago or more.[1]

Where some might have been deterred, B-W was encouraged
in his recognition of Germany's special role in Eastern Europe
by meeting, at lunch with Arnold Toynbee, von Rheinbaben
who said that.

Britain, by being too magisterial and Edenesque, had missed

the big opportunity with Hitler. At the same time the real difficulty, as he sees it, is that the two countries have no common
ground for collaboration, no problems they can tackle together.
I suggested Africa and the economic field. But even the chances
there have been lost by this time. The Germans' case for a full
share in the reshaping of Eastern Europe, as stated by a non-Nazi,
is v. convincing.[2]

Though B-W was still regretting the opportunity of a new
Locarno missed in 1936, the diary shows his attitude hardening.
He met a Toronto industrialist who claimed that Canada,
properly organized, could quickly equal German airframe production and he noted, 'We must show the Germans that they
cannot outbuild us.' He told a German correspondent, Baron
von Studnitz, that the Nazi method of forcible seizure and *fait
accompli* 'required us to take no chances'. The British did not
want to thwart Germany's lawful economic expansion and
reasonable treaty revision, but they asked, what did she really
want? Studnitz declared – with what authority is not clear –
that Hitler would accept a federalized and neutralized Czechoslovakia which had shed its French and Russian treaties and
would have its integrity guaranteed – B-W's own favoured
solution.[3]

That was in May. Four months later, on the day that
Chamberlain set off on his first journey to meet Hitler at
Berchtesgaden, B-W dined with his old friend Kurt Hahn, now
headmaster of Gordonstoun, who was greatly worried by *The
Times*'s attitude. 'He is fearful of a peaceful success for Hitler's
method,' the diary records, 'which would make him the Prince
of Peace in Berlin and a victorious gangster': characteristic
and penetrating Hahn phrases, on which B-W comments: 'Can
we shape our foreign policy solely to the dethronement of
Hitler and his detestable creed?' 'No,' was the answer, 'even if
Britain were strong enough.'

There followed the three weeks' crisis of Chamberlain's
visits to Godesberg and Munich, with the threat of war very
near, the paper's staff divided, the public bewildered: 'I don't
know when I have lived through a time of heavier or more
continuous pressure ... leader-writing, editing, administrating,
interviewing, discussing, speculating.' One wishes there was
here a note of self-criticism, asking whether this was the way
for the Deputy Editor to organize his work amid intense crisis,

whether his own pen was in fact indispensable to each leader, whether it would not be wiser to sit back and think instead of going off to talk tête-à-tête with Sam Hoare – who told him that French ministers 'were abject in their anxiety that no *casus foederis* should arise over Czechoslovakia and must not later be allowed to put all responsibility on us'. But such situations are stimulating and absorbing; the writer feels he is taking part in government; the temptation to do it all oneself is overwhelming; and Dawson was kind and spoke 'very approvingly of my leaders. We see entirely eye to eye.'

B-W did take time off from the office to attend that extraordinary debate of 28 September, when Chamberlain gave an account of his negotiations with Hitler and announced at its very end the invitation to a final peacemaking effort in Munich. For that night there is a long diary entry: B-W is relieved that he can cancel the children's departure to country quarters; convinced that the air raid trenches dug in Regent's Park under his windows would no longer be needed; hopeful that negotiation may after all lead somewhere; speculating that the Nazi extremists may have suffered 'their first setback' because the German people did not want Nazi war. That scene in the House, often described since, had been electrifying. To. B-W it was Edward Grey's speech (of 1914) all over again with a different ending. He had noticed 'Winston full of notes and taking more; the news torpedoed him'; and Dawson reported that when Churchill 'shook hands, like the others, with the P.M. he said "You have all the luck," a saying which is as good as a biography'.[4]

How long a respite B-W believed Chamberlain to have gained is not clear.* But his belief that something happening in Ger-

---

*Presumably he shared the view of Dawson, who wrote just after the Munich agreement a reply to a critical letter from his friend Bob Brand:

'I entirely agree with all you say about the Nazi regime and am not in the least 'carried away' by the Hitler–Chamberlain declaration. . . . Where I probably differ from you is on the method of getting rid of the Nazi regime. I regard it as largely the creation of ourselves and the French in the past. I am sure that it would have been immensely strengthened by a war – particularly at a moment when we are insufficiently prepared, the Russians immobilised by the murder of their leading generals and admirals, and the French positively squealing to be saved by any means from the obligations to the Czechs. (You should see some of their telegrams to our Government.) On the other hand I am convinced that Hitler has been impressed for the first time during the last few days by the hostility of the whole world to his methods and particularly by the obvious sentiments of the German people.[6]

many might hold Hitler in check was to wane quickly. He noted a long talk with Kurt Hahn's brother Rudo, with whom he had stayed three years before, and who had finally decided to get out of Berlin by letting his house free to State Secretary Brinckmann in return for a passport. He was horrified by the stories he heard of Jewish sufferings:

The name of the Nazis will reek in history. Agreed that the Reichswehr will do nothing to assert itself unless there is mobilization for war or war itself, and I wouldn't be too sure of their doing much even then until and unless reverses come.[5]

He found this growing scepticism shared by Rab Butler, then a Junior Minister at the Foreign Office who doubted that anything could be done with Hitler and thought all pressure should be directed at Mussolini.

Cool, detached, mature as ever. Would like a small Cabinet as a more discreet and coherent originator of foreign policy. Weary of arguing with dissident colleagues (including Buck de la Warr) and controlling disloyal subordinates in the F.O. Agrees with me that if Neville went Halifax should be P.M.[7]

To go back a month to the Munich crisis: what were they like, these leading articles which brought such welcome compliments from some colleagues and such expressions of disgust from those who disagreed with them? Were they lacking in dignity and in strength? Did they make Britain look craven and bemused? Is the selection and summarizing of them, as done in Morison's last volume of the *History,* quite fair? To answer the last point first: it is not difficult to find a number of cases where what may be described as 'tough' or militant sentences and paragraphs were omitted from passages chosen by the historian to illustrate his attack on 'appeasement'. Most remarkable is the instance of the leading article of 24 September when Chamberlain returned from Godesberg. This contains passages highly critical of Hitler which are not mentioned by Morison:

The demand for a military invasion of the Sudetenland supported by rancorous abuse of Czechoslovakia and the Czechs, some of it in terms which almost deny the existence of civilization in official Germany, is accompanied by an agitation to secure that Czechoslovakia, meaning the genuine homeland of the Czechs and Slovaks, shall be dismembered and in a political sense destroyed. These claims have made their appearance fortified—though enfeebled would be the better word—with sudden and incredible absurdities and inventions about the emergence of Bolshevism in Prague.

With negotiations actually in train, *The Times* could hardly 'speak for England' more clearly than that. That Britain would fight against invasion had been made clear in another remarkable article the previous morning. It declared that if the Godesberg meeting failed 'there cannot be a doubt in anyone's mind in this country – there should not be a doubt anywhere – that the British people would answer with instant, unhesitating and united resolution any call that might be made upon them.' This passage the *History* also omits.

If the paper was often militant towards the Nazis in this crisis, it was hardly less militant towards Chamberlain's critics: Attlee leading Labour, Sinclair leading the Liberals and Churchill fighting his own battle. B-W had a useful memory of Churchill's histories of the war in which he had fought.

He was one of the first to propound, as he is now one of the last to remember, the dilemma responsible for all the bitter and tragic complexities with which peacemaking has been beset. 'To exclude the German-speaking population (of Czechoslovakia) was deeply and perhaps fatally to weaken the new state; to include them was to affront the principle of self-determination.' So Mr Churchill wrote in the *World Crisis* ...

Mr Churchill preaches preventive war while the Prime Minister preaches preventive diplomacy.[8]

Against the critics in general B-W turned the memory of what they, too, had said should be offered to Bruening when he was Germany's Chancellor:

It has been held to be axiomatic truth by every student of Europe that there can be no peace without revision. Year after year from 1919 that truth boomed from the lips of every Liberal and Labour orator in the country. It is preserved in one Labour resolution after another.... It is more than incontestably valid to-day; it is proved; and the proof is that Czechoslovakia has been faced in the last week with the alternatives of destruction by war or of disintegration without it. No pressure could have had this result on a truly cohesive country.

About the point of it all – the clarification of the issue, the

143

demonstration of Hitler's Napoleonic ambitions – the articles, one after the other, are consistent:

It is a novel cause for offence in a British Prime Minister that he has spent himself in the quest for the constructive prevention of war and, by consequence, for the clear line of principle upon which, if war should come after all, his fellow-citizens could stand as one man and stand to the last.

Revision by agreement in the East: Yes. German domination by force in the East: No. Those were *The Times*'s terms in 1938–9, whatever ideas might have been toyed with for allowing the Germans to make Eastern Europe their economic empire. Had Dawson and B-W been genuine *Realpolitiker,* had the 'Cliveden set' and the fraternity of Round Tables possessed a compact, cynical, well thought-out stategy for a new power balance, they would have frankly advocated the bargain which Hitler must always have hoped for: a German deal with the British Empire in Eastern Europe at the expense of the Soviet Union. But there is no doubt that *The Times,* whatever is true of the months after September 1938, had ascertained and was truly expressing national opinion at the time of Munich. This was the burden of the article written by B-W on the eve of Chamberlain's journey:

... with every move in his long and ceaselessly renewed campaign for the triumph of diplomacy over force, he [the Prime Minister] has rightly interpreted and anticipated public opinion. If it were ever possible to question the national mandate behind his mission, it is open to no one now.[9]

And straight from the heart came the parallel with July 1914, the crisis which he had watched from close to the Editor's desk as a young secretary, expecting to have to fight.

A few days' delay in 1914 would have saved eight million lives. England then had lost control of its policies. One country carried another, like climbers roped together, into the abyss. The same rope binds nations to-day but it is choice and not blind necessity that governs possible catastrophe.

This, surely, was the moment to which B-W's career had been directed: to be in a position as a journalist to influence the decision for peace or war against war. The excitement of the moment must have been intense.

As he saw it Chamberlain had done Hitler out of his war, a judgement which some German generals endorsed, then and later. B-W turned bitterly on Duff Cooper and other critics of the Munich settlement, who cherished the old illusion that 'Europe could get along by ignoring what was just and permanent in the German case and maintaining the discipline and vigilance of an armed ascendancy keeping the Versailles Peace'. This was the climactic leader of the series, with the title 'Impregnable Case', which appeared on 4 October:

The charge against the Prime Minister is that he ought to have offered blind resistance to Nazi Germany, right or wrong. He and his country are represented by some of his critics as having callously sacrificed a small and democratic people to the overbearing might of undemocratic Germany. That has become the staple of self-righteous indignation against him. No Opposition speeches omitted it yesterday, nor were they likely to. It has the valuable property of stirring emotion without invoking thought. It is facile and false.

But that is precisely how it looked – and still looks – to millions. How does B-W answer this indignant, apparently realistic, appraisal of what had happened?

The first Czechoslovak state could never have survived a war, and its failure, without a war, has been automatic. It was doomed as soon as its largest minority found sufficient backing from outside. It had no counter to centrifugal force. Beginning as an essay in *Realpolitik* it incorporated impossibly large minorities upon military considerations only. It was to be the armed guardian of the *status quo* upon which its existence was staked. It was an active and integral part of the system which broke the League and the German Republic alike by refusing at every turn the power of revision.

B-W was arguing, even at this late hour, that it was years of injustice that had brought to power in Germany an evil regime. Cure the injustice and the regime would lose its roots. Something better would then grow in its place. It was a judgement that made too little allowance for the impatience of Hitler and for the compulsion a demagogue feels to produce quick results for the people he has roused. Its real justification was that Britain was still too weak and the Empire too divided to challenge Hitler successfully – or so those at Printing House

Square with inside information believed.* But this was what the paper could not, dared not, say either when appeasing Hitler or defying him.

What, the reader may ask, did B-W think of the notorious leading article of 6 September 1938 (not by him) which – in the view of some – led to the collapse of Czech confidence that Hitler's demands could be resisted? Without dissociating himself from Dawson's part in it, B-W approved of its message but disapproved quite strongly of its timing and style. His diary throws some fresh light on an episode which is dramatically described in *The Times* History (Volume IV, pp. 926–7) and so the Munich crisis must hold our attention for a few pages more.

The Barrington-Wards had not long returned from what they all felt was the best seaside holiday they had ever had, in Pembrokeshire. The diary for those days, six weeks before the world faced war, has rare notes of relaxation:

> Delicious moonlight night. Fresh and still and full of nostalgia. Remembrance of things past and of beloved people gone. Mater and I used to walk about after dinner two years ago.... By special dispensation of the Haverford West postmaster *T.T.* now reaches me on the day of publication. I feel a little safer for it in these chancy days but I grudge the hour or two spent on a daily paper, even *T.T.*[10]

It was against his better judgement that on 3 September he went off to Scotland for a brief visit, leaving the Assistant Editor Brodribb in the chair for the weekend. Leo Kennedy was to write a leader about the Czech crisis on Sunday the 4th, and Dawson would be back from holiday to deal with it on the 6th. He would then return to Yorkshire, after his correspondence and any problems left for him had been dealt with. It seemed a safe arrangement. Brodribb was an experienced *locum;* Kennedy knew the mind of his Editor and Deputy Editor; the Berlin–Prague negotiations were, it is true, at a difficult stage and the tension in the Sudetenland was high; but the telephone had now been installed at Langcliffe Hall. The worst that could be said of it was that Dawson, after three weeks' absence, would return somewhat out of touch.

*This view was confirmed in conversation in February 1970 by Lord Butler, then a Junior Minister and in contact with *The Times*.

The first that B-W knew about the leader was from the wireless, on the day that it appeared.

T.T. has made the suggestion publicly that C-S should cede the SD [Sudetendeutsche] and other minority areas. Heard later on the wireless that this caused the expected sensation. But it is quite right. It would disarm Hitler, whose main object is to get rid of the French and Russian alliances with the Czechs.[11]

B-W had planned to drive back to London by way of Langcliffe Hall where Dawson had promised to find him 'something to shoot', but before he left a letter arrived from the Editor, who sounded slightly apologetic:

I have had Edward Halifax lunching with me. He reported, as I expected, that the last paragraph of Kennedy's leader this morning has disturbed the office, though he did not seem to dissent from it himself. I feel more and more that it is important to cut the ground from under Hitler's feet by reiterating that the whole situation is fluid and that any permanent solution will be considered—except indeed force or the threat of force. But I should have done it a little differently myself if I had had the time. As a matter of fact I had to get Kennedy to rewrite about half the article at the last minute—so late it could not even be typed—and went to bed pretty tired after my journey and a mass of interviews.[12]

Dawson's own diary for 7 September refers to a 'hubbub — which I fully expected':

Reaction in Prague and Berlin, and the Foreign Office went up through the roof. Not so, however, the Foreign Secretary, who came and lunched with me at the Travellers and had a long talk. He is as much in the dark as everyone as to what is likely to happen next.

And on the next day.

Office morning, noon and night. Practically all our contemporaries had broken out into a volley of abuse of *T.T.* for its suggestion that a revision of frontiers in C-S should not be ruled out of discussion—a mild suggestion, often made before ...

Characteristically, Dawson did not allow the uproar to prevent him from keeping his appointment in Yorkshire with B-W and his wife, who arrived at Langcliffe Hall on the 9th, to find a pony club paper-chase over the moors just ended and a large children's tea in progress. The greatest controversy to hit the office since the abdication seemed a long way off as Editor and Deputy strode off across the moors which merge with the gardens of the seventeenth century manor house. They settled office plans and agreed that the critical event ahead was Hitler's oration for the Party rally at Nuremberg from which, they hoped, *The Times* had now stolen if not the thunder at least any element of surprise. If the Führer asked for more than it had suggested might have to be given to him, then the issue would be clear and unite the nation. Before going to bed that night B-W wrote:

G.D. tells me that Halifax does not dissent, privately, from the suggestion that any solution, even the secession of the German minority, should be brought into free negotiation at Prague, though the F.O. is in a high state of indignation about it. Claud Cockburn has produced a special number of his semi-clandestine journal *The Week* with a silly melodramatic account of how the proposal came to appear in *T.T.* A large garbling of a few accurate details. How are these details obtained? Probably from some innocent chatterbox in the office. Outsiders always see some elaborate Machiavellian process at work. We don't!

It seems, however, that Dawson was a little rushed into this leader. It was on the day on which he came back from Yorkshire. Before he and Kennedy came back I had been putting to them the idea of the Czechs letting their Germans go. A.L.K. always impulsive, and not a good or sensitive judge of a situation, wrote a leader on this theme exclusively. G.D. got him to rewrite it hurriedly, toned it down a bit more and let it go. He would have presented it differently himself. So should I. It was abrupt and a little naif in its timing. But essentially the thing is right and *helps to prevent our having to fight on a false issue by putting public opinion face to face with the true one. That is the simple story of what happened.*[13]

What had been written by Kennedy and added to by Dawson was, therefore, no sudden brain-wave.* B-W had been long seeking some solution to the Czech problem, which had haunted him since he had met Benes in 1919. In March he had put up a scheme to neutralize Czechoslovakia – under guarantee from France, Britain, Germany, Italy and Poland – in return for

---

*In his autobiography (*Editor*, Hutchinson, 1968) Kingsley Martin recalls how he wrote in the *New Statesman* on 27 August – a week before Dawson's kite – that if the Czechs and Sudeten Germans could not find a new relationship then 'the question of frontier revision, difficult though it is, should be tackled. The strategical value of the Bohemian frontier should not be made the occasion of a world war. We should not guarantee the *status quo*.'

which Benes would agree to grant federal status to all minorities and give up the Soviet and French alliances. To break the French encirclement system was, B-W believed, the main purpose of Hitler's policy, and he should be helped to achieve that if thereby the general European settlement on new Locarno lines which Britain had been offering since 1936 could be brought closer. He had discussed the general idea with von Scherpenberg, son-in-law of Schacht, who was very active politically at this time.

Like other Germans I have asked he thinks Hitler more anxious to get rid of the Czech–Russian and Franco–Czech alliances than to incorporate the Sudeten–Deutsche. At least thinks that the disappearance of the alliances would make more latitude for the Germans dealing with Prague over the minorities. Von S. anxious to know whether it was worth while continuing to hope for an understanding with England. I told him it was, but Germany must refrain from action which would precipitate war. If she goes slowly she will get all she wants in any case.[14]

There is, unfortunately, nothing in his writing either private or published to show just what B-W meant by this last throw-away sentence. Was he thinking of the destruction of the Versailles 'system'? Or of a free hand for Germany in Eastern Europe? Yet the one thing Hitler could not do was go slowly. From a regime like his, under constant propaganda pressure, the Germans expected *quick* results. The pace at which the two foreign offices of London and Paris worked could never satisfy the Führer. If B-W did not understand this, it was a serious error of judgement.

Four days later Dawson went to see the Prime Minister and put B-W's federal idea to him: according to the diary Chamberlain 'thought it not impossible'. But by June more drastic ideas were seeing the light: on the 3rd a leader backed up a letter from the Dean of St Paul's who supported a plebiscite, as an 'effective expression of the view that the Germans of Czechoslovakia ought to be allowed to decide their own future, even if it should mean their secession from Czechoslovakia to the Reich'. With this, it was said, 'the majority of Englishmen probably agree'. Again on the 14th the paper asked: 'Do they [the Sudeten] really wish to remain where they are? Or have they the wish to be anywhere else? What remains to be done is to rectify the errors of 1919 and to allow the Sudeten Germans peacefully to express their view as to their future.'

If this idea of a smooth and orderly plebiscite now looks utterly unrealistic, it has to be recalled that eighteen months earlier the plebiscite in the Saar, under international armed supervision, had gone off peacefully. On the other hand, Hitler's brutal invasion of Schuschnigg's Austria was only three months past and had provoked from B-W a snort of helpless indignation:

> Shocking display of force in the worst German manner. I have always thought the *Anschluss* inevitable but the manner of it is inexcusable and monstrous.[15]

His leader on that occasion said bluntly that 'this latest and worst demonstration of the methods of German foreign policy' was a blow to the policy of appeasement 'by leaving it more than doubtful whether appeasement is possible in a continent exposed to the visitations of arbitrary force'. But *The Times* was unwilling that a British pledge of protection should be given to the next likely victim.

> Many pressing for a British pledge to C-S. We must give no such pledge as things are. The country will never fight to keep Germans or Hungarians under Czech domination.[16]

Chamberlain's firm but cautious speech of 24 March in the Commons, which remained right up to the Munich Agreement the definitive statement of British policy, brought Downing Street and Printing House Square virtually into line. B-W, writing the leader, found it a 'rough night'.*

As the article is typical of his style and thinking it is analysed at some length.

The Prime Minister's speech, he said, contained no surprises, for radical revision of foreign policy is not possible. But there were some changes of emphasis, and here comes B-W's definition of policy:

> The Covenant has never been understood to impose a simultaneous and identical duty of action, irrespective of place and

---

*Only the previous day he had met at lunch Jan Masaryk, the Czech Ambassador in London, 'highly wrought', saying that 'if his country goes liberal civilization east of the Rhine is dead.'

time, and in defiance of geography and strategy. British foreign policy cannot be a wholesale undertaking to engage in warlike action unconditionally, instantly and wherever offences against international order may invoke it; nor was it such in the mouth of the Prime Minister yesterday. But, subject to this sole limitation, it has again been put beyond all doubts where Britain stands among the nations. British arms and diplomacy cannot truly be devoted to the defence of British interests if they are not enlisted, year in and year out, on behalf of the common cause of civilization; nor can they command the united backing of British opinion upon any other terms.

Could any government go further? the leader asks. There follows a penetrating observation: Britain must not bluff.

A government answerable to public opinion is not free to bluff. It has neither the right nor the power to stake the sacrifice of life and possessions in the hope that a threat of force will not be seriously and sternly tested. It cannot rival the flamboyant language of dictatorship. To each system its own idiom. Democracy will employ a low rather than a high pitch, for its pledges will not lose by it.*

But should not Britain pledge immediate military assistance if the French-Czech arrangements come into force? No, insists B-W, doubtless recalling what had happened in 1914.

The decision whether or not this country should engage in war would no longer rest with the British Government. British diplomacy would no longer be free to exert its full influence in the way of mediation and prevention. It would abandon the control of events along with its ultimate freedom of choice.[17]

Opposition demands for a military line-up with other countries were premature. The Russian suggestion for a conference would lead not to a settlement but to concerting action against Germany, in circumstances not yet clearly predictable.

Suddenly and awkwardly, the argument moves over to non-intervention in the Spanish Civil War. Those who wanted to interfere there, it declared, in order to gain a decision to their liking would have provoked a general war 'upon an issue which

---

*Keynes, who occasionally talked recklessly outside his own specialities, wrote in a letter to Kingsley Martin a month before Munich: 'I agree with you that we should bluff to the hilt, and if the bluff is called, back out. I prefer meanwhile meiosis and bogus optimism in public.' (Kingsley Martin, op. cit.)

foreigners were incompetent to decide'. When the Opposition and other critics attacked the Prime Minister's personal effort to get Mussolini's agreement to respect the independence of Spain, what were they in fact doing?

Stripped naked it comes out as zeal for an anti-Fascist crusade, in Spain itself and in Europe generally, fortified with the doctrine of preventive war.

The country, the article concluded, would reject this overwhelmingly, although rearmament was now rightly to have first priority in the nation's effort, with concentration on air defences, active and passive.

Those who had been rebuked for their wish to take the country into an ideological war were again given a drubbing a few days later. A leader called 'The Primrose Path' is a good example of B-W's invective style, inspired by a disappointing discussion of foreign affairs (the House of Commons had staged for the dictators the spectacle of thirteen debates in nine weeks), and directed at Attlee and his front-bench colleagues.

The vagueness, wildness and contradictoriness of the alternative courses which they recommend encourage the belief that they refuse to be parted from bogeys of their own invention, partly no doubt because they passionately wish to blame someone for the world's woes — which is intelligible though unhelpful — and partly because it would be highly convenient if the electorate should be induced to agree with them in making the Government responsible. Unanimity in foreign affairs is not to be expected or demanded ... but it cannot help international causes, of which Labour and Liberal critics profess themselves ardent upholders, to work away with all the colours of exaggeration at a false picture of British policy as a prime *saboteur*.

For the record, it remains to add a fragment from the little evidence surviving in the files of the office to show the vigorous part played by the Paris team in informing the public and the office. Neither Dawson nor B-W put much faith in French morale and both distrusted French politicians; but they certainly did not foresee the collapse of 1940. Yet Thomas Cadett, and before him David Scott, had warned the office that France was deeply divided. A letter of 7 October 1938 from Cadett to Deakin says:

The truth is that this country is in an unholy mess, led, if such be the word, by a feeble and divided government with more than its fair share of characterless crooks. The worst is Bonnet, who from the very start has worked for the abandonment of the Czechs, but has sought to throw the entire blame onto us. It is not a question of quarrelling with his views on foreign policy but his methods, which include the suppression of the part of the Gamelin report on French military preparedness which was favourable secret attacks, followed by an inspired Press campaign, on the authenticity of the British guarantee; and a whole heap of other double-crossing activities. . .[18]

15

Liddell Hart Comes and Goes

For the most remarkable appointment made to *The Times* in the pre-war years B-W was personally responsible. The military writer, Basil Liddell Hart, who joined in 1935, had been known to him since just after the war, when the Captain was glad to supplement a meagre living by reporting lawn tennis and rugby football for the *Observer*. Now aged forty and writing under his own name for the *Daily Telegraph,* he had rapidly become a controversial and influential critic with a following among younger and forward-looking Army officers. His success for that paper had made conspicuous the absence of a comparable writer on *The Times,* which had a naval correspondent and an aeronautical correspondent but no one to look at defence as a whole.* In this respect the shortcomings of the newspaper were those of the Government. Just as successive prime ministers had seen no need for a single mind or Ministry of Defence to deal with the 'triple threat' (Liddell Hart's phrase for the dangers from Germany, Italy and Japan created by air power), so Dawson had thought a single defence writer unnecessary. Apart from the salary thereby saved, he may have had painful memories of the powerful and irresponsible position that Colonel Repington had created for himself before 1914 as Our Military Correspondent.

*E. Colston Shepherd was Aeronautical Correspondent and leader writer 1929–39, and was expected to cover, as well as the R.A.F., civil aviation and the aircraft industry. He agrees that to get accurate defence information, which could be published in the paper, was at that time extremely difficult, and that some of the figures that were used, notably by Churchill, in Parliamentary debate about German air strength were misleading. Rear-Admiral H. G. Thursfield, as well as being Naval Correspondent of the paper from 1932 to 1952, was editor of Brassey's *Naval Annual* and an authority on foreign warships and armament. Thursfield had access to almost any member of the Naval Staff and frequently secured for his paper advance news of important naval matters. But he seldom wrote on major defence topics.

After consulting 'thoughtful soldiers' about the wisdom of having this brilliant 'intellectual' to discuss their business in *The Times*, B-W made his first approach over lunch. Hitler had then been in power nearly two years. The diary comments:

The time has come for the paper to have a military correspondent once more. The years of experiment are over and the Army is beginning to take its post-War shape. Whether we like it or not, questions of defence are coming to the fore.... Liddell Hart is almost alone, by his own exertions, in that field. He has undoubtedly won many readers for the *D.T.* Six years ago he asked me to let him know when a vacancy should occur on *T.T.* To-day I told him it had. He is frankly ready to come. The methods of the *D.T.* have grown too catchpenny for his liking, though they have treated him well.... Would like to sign or initial. I told him we should want anonymity. Conversation committed neither of us.... I was glad to hear from him that his objective is peace.

I like him and he is undoubtedly able. My inquiries at the War Office, discreetly made, show that his appointment would be welcome to many there, including the C.I.G.S.[1]

What Liddell Hart expected from the change was not more money or a bigger audience (it would in fact be smaller) but escape from the attentions of a features editor and sub-editors who simplified and 'enlivened' his copy, and from the demand that he should cover 'spot news' of events, promotions, quarrels and changes in the Army. He wanted to be not a daily journalist but a pundit, a commentator. *The Times* should give him a platform for his ideas about mechanizing the British infantry, revolutionizing its tactics, and getting the cavalry away from their horses into fast and powerful armoured divisions. He hoped too to see the general policy of the paper based on sound strategic ideas which took account of air power and its effect on the Navy. When he and B-W settled the arrangements between them in December 1934, some points were left unclear, for neither man wanted to lose what the other offered. In this partnership, which was to last only four years, the seeds of misunderstanding were already sown.

Liddell Hart has given in his *Memoirs* a detailed account of his relations with *The Times* and of their differences over policy. If broadly convincing, it shows also a certain failure to understand the requirements of a newspaper office, which aims at forming and publishing a collective rather than a personal, attributable view. He felt he had a right to publish what he personally thought, because articles by the Military Correspondent would be read as his work. B-W felt equally strongly that defence policy was so vital a part of home and foreign policy that it could not be treated as a thing apart. That this disparity between the specialist and the journalist view must cause trouble became apparent during the Abyssinian episode and later during the Spanish Civil War. The paper supported non-intervention because it believed – correctly as it turned out – that the Spaniards would not hand themselves over either to Germany or to Russia. Its Military Correspondent believed, and went on saying for some time, that the Second World War had been already lost in Spain.

It is, indeed, difficult to acquit Liddell Hart of sometimes behaving in the *prima donna* style that Dawson, remembering Repington, may have feared. The audience of *The Times*'s readers was not big enough for him. By 1938 he was spending as much time advising the Secretary of State for War, Hore-Belisha* (whom he first met in June 1937), as in advising his paper. He had succumbed to the very weakness of which he accuses Dawson and B-W in his *Memoirs:* the wish to think and behave like ministers. His achievement in exposing nonsense at the War Office, clearing people's minds and pressing the claims of the armoured division and A.A. defence was magnificent but it was not journalism and could not be done mainly for his newspaper. In *The Times* of thirty years later the office would have used Liddell Hart as a columnist, giving him regular space to air his own views over his own signature, while maintaining in the leader columns an editorial view which might or might not be different. But both Dawson and B-W would have regarded an opinion column in *The Times* as striking at the root of the anonymous authority exercised in its leader columns.† Within restricted circles it might be known

---

*In his *Memoirs*, Volume II, p. 125, he makes the curious and revealing statement: 'The discontinuance of close relations with Hore-Belisha in July 1938 *set me free* to criticise publicly, with more pungency the slow pace and inadequate measures of the steps that were being taken to meet the growing danger of war with Nazi Germany.' The italics are the present writer's. No journalist, it may be remarked, should get himself into a position where he feels unable to criticise a minister whose confidence he has won.

†It was Colonel Repington whose behaviour provoked in 1913 the only comment on anonymity from Dawson that the present writer has seen recorded. 'I hold most strongly that *The Times* should stick to its old practice of anonymous

that Colin Coote wrote the brilliant 'sketches' of big Commons occasions, or that the sapient leaders on trade unions were by Radcliffe, or that Bernard Darwin wrote on golf and Colles on music. This could, Dawson, believed, do no harm; but once let names or initials appear, and vanity would intrude, and with it bees in bonnets and prejudices expressed in the first person. The Editor's right to maintain by alteration – that is to say by 'editing' – the necessary consistency of tone and policy would be under constant challenge.

Liddell Hart, like many brilliant writers before and after him, did not like being edited; and he seems to have found it hard to understand why editors dislike being asked to render an account of their reasons for omitting and altering.

All, at first, went well. The intellectual in B-W was stimulated by the historical approach to defence problems, and by the clear concepts brought to bear on inter-service rivalries in his new colleague's articles. Liddell Hart, for his part, was delighted to have as his chief someone with military staff experience, whom he remembered as one of the bright young men around General Sir Ivor Maxse in 1918, devising and writing about new infantry tactics. He found, too, that his new paper did carry more weight in the War Office than his old one. His first contribution was called 'Defence as a Whole', attacking the scramble for resources and money and men that went on between the Navy, Army and Air Force and the compromises between them that passed muster for strategic decisions.* Not only did the article demand one controlling personality, but it also insisted that this should be a civilian, advised by a staff of officers freed from dependence for a future career on the favour of their own services. This was the 'human crux of the whole problem': judgement of priorities in defence under the prevailing system was corrupt at the source.

To B-W, who loved campaigning, this was martial music. It foreshadowed his own advocacy, during the war to come, of an integrated general staff and even greater reforms of the

journalism, and that the members of its staff should be as far as possible unknown by name to the world at large. Personally I resist every attempt to discover the names of individual leader-writers, writers of special articles, etc. outside our own circle.'

*On 4 March 1935 a White Paper had announced a modest measure of rearmament. The sum allocated was a quarter of Hitler's known budget and the R.A.F. was revealed as sixth among the world's air forces.

military structure which were still not complete thirty years later. At this level Editor and Military Correspondent could agree without difficulty, even if Dawson in his more critical moods found the tall, gaunt, bespectacled newcomer rather sweeping in his comment. It was when he asked to be consulted about the policy of sanctions against Italy during her campaign in Abyssinia or about the strategic dangers of non-intervention in the Spanish Civil War that trouble began.

Both Dawson and B-W were used to making up their own minds on such matters and were not disposed to call in the strategist on what seemed to them primarily imperial, diplomatic and home political problems. If Liddell Hart and Thursfield would keep them informed of what the Navy could do in the Mediterranean and of what the Army thought of the threat to Egypt and Libya, that would be sufficient. He, understandably, felt that Britain's precarious position at the centre of a German–Italian–Japanese threat demanded that no step in her foreign or rearmament policy should be commented on without consulting a strategist. Looking back, it is clear that he was right; but his Editors' view made better sense then than it does at the moment of writing – the year of Liddell Hart's death. Comprehensive discussion of defence as a whole was rare, and was favoured by only a very few minds in each Service. The Admiralty was still dominant in Whitehall and its bitter rivalry with the Air Ministry was still bedevilling thought about what naval power could or could not do in the age of the bomber.

Liddell Hart made things no easier for himself or his colleagues by a manner which made those who disagreed with him feel rather foolish. He favoured that bugbear of all editors, the long written memorandum (copy for the files), which calls for an answer at the end of the working day. He was what Dawson called among his political friends 'a resigner'. When he found that he could not get into the paper views which he thought important, he suggested writing under his own name, publishing letters to the Editor instead of articles, or contributing articles to other newspapers not in direct competition with *The Times*. The indignation and impatience about what he found out through Whitehall contacts spilled over easily into writing. He wrote not only about the shortage of A/A guns to defend London and other cities and ports, and about the bad organization of the men to fight them, but also about the fact that some of them were unusable. B-W thought it unwise to state this last fact in *The Times,* on whose authority it would immediately become for enemies an item of first-class intelligence.* Liddell Hart wanted heads to roll and aimed attacks at those he believed to be guilty men; Dawson, remembering what happened when heads rolled in Whitehall, believed rearmament would move more smoothly if the spur was used instead of the axe. Liddell Hart by 1938 was cooperating with the militant group around Winston Churchill; Dawson, who had good reasons for distrusting Churchill's judgement and who said that national government would not survive his inclusion in the Cabinet, resented this – as he disliked his Military Correspondent's giving personal service to Hore-Belisha.

B-W, who decided what articles should appear in the leader-page turnover column, was more frequently in argument with his military colleague than was Dawson. Gradually the two men got on each other's nerves. Scathing references to Liddell Hart's sensitiveness are to be found in B-W's diaries and the *Memoirs* deal with B-W's suppressions and omissions. Typical of this deteriorating relationship was their argument after the Munich agreement. Liddell Hart wanted to argue that Britain must now prepare an expeditionary force to support France – an up-to-date mechanized and armoured force – because the loss of the Czech fortifications had deprived her of an important second front threat to German strength. B-W, who had earlier agreed that Britain must not repeat the error of 1914 and tie its strategy to that of the French, was prepared to support the new expeditionary force – but not by use of the Czech argument. For he had long urged that the French defence links in eastern Europe were unrealistic and that Czechoslovakia would never fight the Germans as a united country. He

---

*The deficiencies in the armed services, which were by then glaring, were examined by a sub-committee (Defence Requirements) of the Committee of Imperial Defence, which was not appointed until October 1933. Its findings would reach Printing House Square in bits and pieces of hints to Dawson and B-W from ministers, which they would not pass on to their service correspondents, and off-the-record disclosures to the latter which might reach the Editor in memoranda but not the readers of the paper. It is impossible to establish whether Dawson and B-W were fully aware of British military weakness.

therefore regarded his military expert's argument as wrong and opposed to what the paper had said.

It is hard to believe that some formula could not have been found to get around the difficulty, for the friendship between the two men was not yet seriously affected. Liddell Hart's persistence was encouraged by other members of the staff, like Coote and McDonald and Casey, who deplored the paper's treatment of Czechoslovakia. Many years later he wrote about B-W:

It had been a delightful experience to work with anyone so considerate as well as intelligent. . . . In argument he was most reasonable, and wonderfully patient with my persistence in pressing points that he was not disposed to accept. But I gradually became aware that, underlying his reasonableness in discussion, there was an inflexible will on which argument could make no impression. When he had made up his mind on an issue nothing would change it, except it was apt to be a complete right-about turn, and result in an equally positive move in the opposite direction, as happened over the Polish guarantee in the following year. His consistency, in whatever direction he took, was as marked as Geoffrey Dawson's variability.[2]

B-W had more than once charmed away his doubts and soothed his frustration. In August 1938, for example, he had offered his resignation to Dawson because he had 'no mind or heart to continue writing about military preparations that are likely to prove futile'. It seemed to him an 'inescapable responsibility to state facts that are necessary to a true judgement, within my own sphere'. A letter from B-W, then on holiday, coaxed him back. 'As usual he was so reasonable and persuasive and reassuring about future freedom to comment, that I agreed to defer my resignation and see how things worked out.' But by November they were at loggerheads again:

Each time that we have discussed national policy I have found an overwhelming sureness on your part as to the wisdom of the policy *The Times* was advocating. For my part, while pointing out various reasons for doubt, I have been ready, as you have remarked, to admit the possibility that it might prove the best policy—from a practical point of view at least. But each time the sequel has brought cause for increasing doubts—though not apparently to you.[3]

What is puzzling in the evidence available is the absence of any alternative to 'appeasement'. Liddell Hart was fully aware of the inability of the French Army to play more than a defensive role, and he warned the office as late as 1939 that to bomb Germany was to invite worse in return against British and French cities which had no A/A guns. He believed that Czech resistance to the Germans would be only temporary unless the Russians and the Poles joined in. And when Hitler's Polish campaign of 1939 was over, he dismayed – disgusted would hardly be too strong a word – his editors by saying that he now saw no prospect of defeating Germany and that Hitler should be encouraged to offer a negotiated peace. In his diary B-W noted:

LH seems to be playing for safety all round. For himself he wants to be wise after the event ... He is a monolith of egotism and vanity.[4]

Such cruel condemnation is rare in the diary, but it has to be realized how bitter was the irony of the situation between them now that war had begun. For years B-W had argued that a second German war could be averted, that the Germans themselves must in the end prefer negotiation to war, that the British could not fight them with a good conscience until certain German claims had been conceded. Now that their intentions had been revealed beyond any doubt, they must be fought wherever and whenever it was possible, regardless of risk, and with a good conscience. Yet his Military Correspondent, seeing the apparently hopeless strategic situation, chose this moment to be defeatist, as B-W saw it, and he would have none of his views in the paper. B-W had thought of himself as the realist, keeping Britain out of an unnecessary war. Now Liddell Hart thought of himself as the realist, trying to spare Britain an unnecessary defeat. And each was scornful of the views of the other. By 1940 they had parted company.

The turning point for both men had been, it is now clear, the Abyssinian war. They had begun by agreeing that collective security was the only defence policy for a weakened Britain; but they differed about its enforcement against Italy without the help of a reluctant France. The principle of collective security having been shattered – in fact it was little more than a formula – what was to take its place in the public mind and in the formulation of defence policy? Both were tempted, after their experiences of the previous war, towards isolationism; but British public opinion, indoctrinated with loyalty to the League, would not tolerate this. There must be allies. To Liddell Hart it was clear that the French security system in Eastern Europe, if it could be sure of Russian support, was the answer. To B-W it was clear that the set-up in Eastern Europe was unfair to Germany and that she was destined to economic mastery there, sooner or later, provided she did not use force to get it. The alternative was a direct Anglo-German confrontation on the lines of 1908–14.

What further light do the diaries throw on B-W's views of the Abyssinian crisis? Enough to show that he had become deeply committed, both with mind and heart, to the League resistance to Italy but not enough to show what part Liddell Hart's advice played in the movement of the paper away from collective security and towards bilateral dealings with the dictators. In September 1935 Sir Samuel Hoare, Baldwin's new Foreign Secretary, went to Geneva and offered the League of Nations British leadership in what was judged a remarkably sincere and bold speech. If other governments would follow such a lead, people said, then collective security might become a reality in spite of its failure against the Japanese in Manchuria. 'Thank God,' wrote B-W, 'Simon is no longer at the F.O.' The speech 'could not have been bettered. Firm, guarded, unprovocative, unequivocal'. The paper backed up Hoare and reported that the Empire was solid against Mussolini (as it was not to be for another four years against Hitler) with political leaders in both India and South Africa declaring support. B-W was elated; at last, perhaps, the secret of peace-keeping was being revealed. Yet, despite warnings from the Paris office, he underrated the reluctance of the French – with Germany rearming – to make enemies of the Italians, who commanded the lines of communication to their allies in Eastern Europe.

Nor could B-W ignore the views of men like his friend Admiral Gerald Dickens, lately Director of Naval Intelligence, who wrote in September 1935 denouncing the 'inconsistent and unpractical idealists' who demanded of the League action which could in fact be carried out only by a fully efficient British Navy.

I suppose none of them have any idea of how stretched and

worn is the fabric of the Navy. They only think in numbers of battleships and cruisers. They think nothing of reserves of stores and ammunition, of shortages of men, of deferred refits of ships, of delay in the provision of essential modern equipment.

Dickens conceded that it could in the end dominate the Italian fleet but insisted that *The Times* should remind itself and its readers of the general strategic prospect.

If we are landed with hostilities with Italy and lose a couple of battleships, I am prepared to bet my last shirt that Japan will deem it the moment to push that part of her expansionist plans which so far British sea-power has made too risky to undertake. Japan is the menace in any of these upheavals and Germany a close second. It is a fact—a humiliating one—that the British Navy cannot deal with situations of that sort and Japan knows it.[5]

B-W in reply defended the militant left as penitent prodigal sons, converted from pacifism by the Abyssinian episode, and pointed out that British rearmament henceforth 'will come with the united assent of almost the whole country and of all parties within it'.

I feel certain that it is a very simple feeling about right and wrong that has got the British shirt out. If the man in the street is hypocritical, at least he doesn't know it. What he does know is that feeble condonation, or still feebler disapproval and inaction, in face of the Mussolini method would infallibly have stored up trouble for himself. Then, indeed, we should have ceased to count in the Mediterranean or elsewhere and invited the Japanese and the Germans to take notice of it.[6]

The hero of collective security at this time for B-W was Anthony Eden.

Good talk at F.O. with Eden. It is largely thanks to his drive and determination that the League has been brought to life in this present crisis. Asked us particularly to insist that this is an affair of League principle, as it is, and not of Anglo–Italian rivalry. He returns tomorrow to push the reluctant and embarrassed Laval along. No side about Eden. Quite unspoilt by youthful fame.[7]

Both men, as survivors from the Western Front, represented a generation which had been encouraged to believe by its publicists and intellectuals that foreign policy guided only by national interest led to 'international anarchy'.

Dawson accepted the fact that the policy towards Italy of 'all sanctions short of war' then commanded virtually a national consensus. By satisfying the large League lobby, without alarming those who opposed war, Baldwin was able in the General Election of November 1935 to gain a majority of nearly 250 seats so ensuring the continuance of national government with an ineffective opposition. The Labour Party, by taxing the Government with lukewarm loyalty to collective security while at the same time accusing it of wrecking the Disarmament Conference, tried to win both the anti-war and the anti-Fascist vote – and failed. In less than a month came the tragi-comedy of the Hoare–Laval proposals that Abyssinia should buy peace from Italy by territorial concessions. At one time such an unprincipled bargain would have been defended as a way of bringing Italy back into the defensive front against Germany; for the course of the war was to show the immense value to Germany of Italy as a base for cutting Britain's Mediterranean communications and attacking the Middle East.

B-W, however, had no doubts then that the appeasement of Italy was wrong and unnecessary. No episode is more fully documented in the diaries than this. They reveal his moral indignation and shame; the feeling that this is a turning point in British policy; the conviction that Hoare must go; the fear that by discrediting the League he had destroyed the last chance of bringing Germany back into it as part of a European settlement. On the evening of 9 December, when the Paris Press leaked the agreement, Major Barrington-Ward, DSO, MC dined in London with his old comrades of the 14th Division.

One and all revolted by the Paris terms. . . . The League and the championship of the League served to win the election for the Government, and now the electorate is sold. So everyone will say. And how rebut it? On the facts it's irrefutable.

I went to bed utterly humiliated and dispirited and ashamed of my country. The first time that a public event ever so worked on me. We have sacrificed honour and interest together. Laval as tricky as a load of monkeys. Leakage of news in Paris obviously deliberate and intended to commit the British Govt.[8]

After three days of public indignation and embarrassment among ministers, which did not prevent the Cabinet approving the terms, *The Times* was still perplexed to find a way out without causing a crisis in the month-old government.

G.D. rang me at home in the morning and asked me if I had any ideas on 'this bloody position'. I told him I thought we should definitely urge the Government to admit the blunder and to get the proposals killed at Geneva. Later we talked at the office.[9]

The same afternoon the Editor let him know that Lord Wigram (the King's Private Secretary) had seen him and that 'the Monarch was more concerned with the possible collapse of the Government than with the collapse of League policy, apparently. He had impressed upon Wigram the necessity of seeing G.D. and had left a note on his pad before going out, "See Geoffrey Dawson".'

The outcome of much coming and going was a leading article which, if not the most important, was certainly the best remembered that Dawson wrote. The brilliant headline, 'A Corridor for Camels', echoed precisely the angry, derisive mood of opinion. The news, too, was a scoop for the paper, revealing – what had been suppressed in the published terms of the Hoare–Laval plan – that the Abyssinians would not be allowed to build a railway in the corridor they were to receive in return for losing half their territory.

It was apparently to remain no more than a patch of scrub, restricted to the sort of traffic which has entered Ethiopia from the days of King Solomon, a corridor for camels.... The suggestion seems so incredible, so completely at variance even with the most cynical interpretations of a 'civilizing mission' that its origins should be investigated before there is any fresh attempt at peace terms.[10]

During these days of excitement and uncertainty – with people asking would Hoare resign? was he the real culprit or was Baldwin? would the Cabinet split? who would succeed Hoare? – Dawson took charge, writing, interviewing, inquiring at the top of his form. He saw Hoare at his home and urged him to resign; the Prime Minister was coming round later, 'probably more culpable than Sam', notes Dawson. Meanwhile Colin Davidson, Baldwin's adviser, was calling on B-W and saying that Hoare must resign, the Government must 'frankly bow to the force of public opinion'; and B-W was urging that Baldwin must not try to frighten people with Mussolini's threats: 'it would unite patriots and Leaguers alike against the appearance of cowardice.'

Did Dawson take over most of the writing during these hectic ten days because he thought his Deputy too strong on sanctions in support of the League? B-W had been having a long and free run with his foreign policy articles, and had put much strain on himself. There is no written evidence of disagreement between them; had they differed, the diaries would surely show it. It is more likely that the Editor had pangs of conscience about the amount of work falling on his Deputy and decided to buckle to when mismanagement of foreign affairs looked like discrediting Baldwin's cabinet. Besides, he immensely enjoyed a political crisis in which *The Times* could take a hand.

To be in any newspaper office during a crisis is exciting; at *The Times* it was, in B-W's phrase, 'a great fortnight' with late changes in news and comment, a turmoil of gossip and speculation, with every office abroad and every editorial character contributing his voice, and everyone lunching and dining out on the story. On 2 December, two days after Hoare's resignation speech, he recorded a passage from the Londoner's Diary in Beaverbrook's *Evening Standard*.

The Times, recalling its ancient days, has never thundered to better purpose and the 'camel leader', which will certainly be historic, completed the disgust and bewilderment of thousands of the Government's supporters. . . . The Left, which denounced the betrayal of the League, was in momentary alliance with the Right, which denounced the betrayal of the Empire.

B-W added this characteristically loyal tribute:

The effect of our intervention was enormously increased by the reputation for detachment, self-control and common sense—good judgment in fact—which G.D. has won for the paper.[11]

Even the enemies of his German policy were reconciled – for a time.

This high point in leadership of a virtually unanimous public opinion is often forgotten when *The Times* of the thirties is comprehensively denounced. But it has to be remembered that Mussolini was being challenged from weakness. The Army, as Liddell Hart pointed out, was in no state to defend the Middle East and the Navy – without French support – could not be sure of dominating the Mediterranean and deterring the Japanese in the Pacific. The Hoare–Laval fiasco did reveal

British weakness to the British and B-W's caution about Germany was intensified.

Characteristic of the confusion of the time was a note in the diary of 22 December.

> G.D. told me that when the King sent for Eden the other day he gave him a great ticking-off. He was pushing the country to the edge of war by his conduct at Geneva, etc. Later the King was equally furious when he found that the 'peace terms' betrayed the national honour.[12]

King George V, in so many ways a representative Englishman, expected from his ministers a policy which would meet the needs of Britain and the Empire without the risk or threat of war. He, like his subjects, did not realize that the power to do this effortlessly had vanished for good. It was, perhaps, at this time that the truth was dawning on B-W. Otherwise the move away from collective security is inexplicable.

What Liddell Hart felt during this time and later controversial episodes has been felt by every thoughtful journalist at one time or another. Why cannot the Editor see this? Why cannot the Editor grasp that? Why does he disregard the warnings from Berlin, the advice from Rome? How can he believe that we are strong (or weak) enough to behave in such and such a way? Each specialist from his separate desk or capital sees a different opportunity for, or obligation on, British policy and is irate that the office sees it differently. Yet the Editor, if he is doing his job properly, is seeing the opportunity or obligation above all in terms of home politics: how will a foreign policy decision affect the stability of government, the relationships between ministers and between them and their parties? What is politically possible in a crisis when the electorate suddenly becomes aware of its power? On the answer to such questions depend business confidence, the financial and commercial judgements, on which the daily calculations of millions – and especially of readers of *The Times* – depended. These were matters on which the paper was expected to be particularly judicious and reliable. Here Dawson was in his element; and if he appeared much of the time to underrate the importance of foreign affairs it was probably for this reason.

16

Hitler's War

Appeasement ended with Hitler's march into Prague on
15 March – for Chamberlain, for *The Times,* for everyone.
Before describing how the paper reacted* and threw all its
weight behind the guarantee to Poland, let us consider for a
moment the main thesis of Stanley Morison's History: that
if there had been a foreign editor at Dawson's elbow the policy
of Printing House Square would have been different. The contention, quite simply, is that someone more expert on Europe,
with more direct knowledge of Germans, Frenchmen and
Russians, with the time to think on broad lines about foreign
policy and strategy, would have saved *The Times* from grave
error. It is a formidable list of qualifications, not easily met
from the newspaper ranks of the thirties.

The arguments with which Morison's thesis has been supported are not unimpressive but they overlook one probability:
it is that a foreign editor appointed, say, in 1930 would have
supported the inclusion of Germany in a general European
agreement, which was the office's main aim up to the very
eve of the war. Indeed, it is almost certain that a man like E. H.
Carr – who was Tom Jones's candidate for the post – would
have argued no less strenuously than B-W for agreement with
Germany. The real question is: for how long? A foreign
affairs specialist would have been even more conscious than
Dawson and B-W were of the Far Eastern threat from Japan, of
United States detachment and of the political difficulties
pinning down considerable British forces in the Middle East
and India. B-W noted in his diary at the end of 1938 after a

---

*The diary said: 'Hitler's first blunder – the forced incorporation of the
Czechs in the Reich. . . . The Germans have given a vast hostage to fortune.
And they have shown their hand. This is simple Prussian brutality again, unex-
cused, unredeemed.'[1]

lunch with Carr: 'He and I see eye to eye on foreign policy.'

In any case, British foreign policy – and the paper's ideas about what it should be – did not depend primarily on expertise about foreign countries. Political facts at home, the views of Government and Opposition leaders, the state of finances and armaments, the relative importance of European and imperial commitments – these were as weighty in the forming of a foreign policy as a Wickham Steed's experience of Central Europe or a Chirol's knowledge of India. Dawson had worked for years with such men and knew the limitations of expertise.

His decision to have a foreign editor or not – he certainly looked for one – was made no easier because he already had someone in charge of the ordering and receiving of foreign news, moving correspondents around, dealing with the news agencies, watching cable and telephone expenditure, and keeping abreast of the massive daily flow of foreign news. This was done between 1922 and 1952 by Ralph Deakin, an energetic and professional Foreign News Editor with an excellent news sense, trained under Northcliffe. A touchy and prickly man, holding down one of the most exacting administrative posts but uncertainly placed in the office hierarchy, Deakin was unconvinced of the need for a foreign editor and no one was more critical than he was of the appointment of Carr in 1941.* After the farewell lunch to Dawson B-W noted sadly in his diary that Deakin had stayed away because the new Assistant Editor, 'an amateur journalist', was to be placed above him at table. No one who has experienced the personal tensions of a newspaper office will judge Dawson very harshly for his hesitation over finding himself another Mackenzie Wallace or Valentine Chirol.†

---

*Deakin was a plump, florid, well-groomed little man, who swam twenty lengths of the St George's Baths each morning before coming into the offices. He showed glee in reminding gentlemen writers that a professional newsman like himself put THE NEWS first. There were foreigners who thought he *was* the Foreign Editor. '*The Times*,' he would say, 'stands or falls by its news service'; and his delivery of the name of the paper, which he served with devotion, sounded like the giant bell of St Paul's booming through the windows of his office. The long list of up-and-coming young men who were trained by him have reason to remember not only the aroma of his admirable cigars and his pleasure in being sometimes called 'Foreign Editor', but also his kindness and readiness to delegate responsibility to the rawest recruit.

†It was not until 1952 that *The Times* got its next Foreign Editor, twenty-four years after the death of Williams. The title went to Iverach McDonald, who was

There has been criticism of *The Times* – notably from Liddell Hart – for swinging so strongly in 1939 from the conviction that peace must be maintained at all costs and that Britain was not ready for war, to the view that Hitler must be faced with a fight to a finish over Poland. So far as B-W is concerned, the explanation is simple: his patience, like Hitler's, was exhausted. For six years he had tried to give the Germans the benefit of the doubt, argued for a general settlement that would give them justice, hoped against hope that some German resistance to Hitler would show itself.* Now the policy had failed utterly and the British were back where they had been in 1914, feeling morally bound to fight a European war at the side of France, but this time poorer, less prepared, more exposed than ever before. There was cause for more than exasperation; and all B-W's disappointment and moral revulsion against the Nazis flared through the leader he wrote for the morning of 4 September 1939. 'Hitler's War' it was called.

A peaceful and honourable settlement between Germany and Poland had been possible but Hitler would not have it.

Self-deluded and self-doomed, the Dictator of Germany has given the British and the French peoples no choice but to resist and overthrow him. Much as they loathe war, they love liberty more. The alternative that Hitlerism thrusts upon them is a surrender to organized brutality and treachery which would extinguish the last lights of freedom in Europe.

The British had sought peace with the German people, and the quarrel is with their rulers. 'Hitlerism must be extirpated from European relations now and for all time by the only means left. . . . There will be no peace without victory and no victory without peace.' That is what the guarantee to Poland meant.

---

principal foreign leader-writer, diplomatic correspondent and special correspondent at summit and near-summit conferences in the post-war years.

*That such a view of the German people was not as wishful as it is sometimes represented to be is suggested by the fact that those Germans who were plotting in August 1938 to seize and depose Hitler, the moment he began the attack on Czechoslovakia, also held it. John Wheeler-Bennett writes: 'Beck, and with him Oster and the *Abwehr* group, and also Goerdeler, held the view that the German people did not want war; and that, once the sinister motives of Hitler's foreign policy were unmasked, the glamour of his former successes in rearmament, in the Rhineland, and in Austria would disappear and that this same German people who had been willing victims of his hypnotic influences, would awake from the thraldom of the last five years.'[2]

'The most black-hearted episode in diplomatic history,' B-W called it.

In the eyes of the world the calculated invention of a German–Polish crisis, the atrocity, lies and finally the fraudulent 'peace' proposals are characteristic marks of a kind of stupid and suicidal cunning which has served only to aggravate the crime which it was intended to explain and excuse.... German youth is to die for the right to treat the Poles—and, after the Poles, other peoples—as Nazi Germany has already treated the Czechs.

And for good measure:

The 'spiritual rejuvenation' of the Third Reich culminates in the hoariest and most illusory aspirations of pagan nationalism. No one who casts up the balance of to-day can believe for a second that the future belongs to this truculent, degraded and bankrupt faith, and it is civilization itself which is mobilizing to crush it.

Following the tirade, the note of self-defence in the moment of admitted personal error:

For so long as it was possible to distinguish between the domestic and foreign policies of Nazism, it was rightly contended that the future of Nazism was in the hands of the German people alone. Even the peculiar and repellent vices of German authoritarianism could not shake the determination (of British policy) to leave German evolution in German hands.

Impressive though the invective is, let it be admitted that it is not difficult to write this kind of leader with a united audience, an overmastering theme, a rare anger and the feeling of danger in the air. B-W's last sentences are a peroration inviting a growl of assent from his assembled readers:

In his sober but splendid words to the Empire yesterday the King has spoken for us all. We fight to break the 'bondage of fear' daily encroaching upon the world. We shall do the right as we see the right, and we shall persevere as one man through all trials and all risks to the end.

There was silence about Germany in the leader columns for a fortnight; but then B-W felt impelled to comment on the Soviet invasion of eastern Poland. Angry and contemptuous in tone, the denunciation is in one sentence.

To the Soviet belongs the base and despicable share of accessory

171

before and after the crime, and the contempt which even the thief has for a receiver who shares none of his risks.

Had Hitler been more cunning than Stalin, or Stalin more cunning than Hitler? the leader asked. The question was not answered but B-W pointed out that Stalin had by moving into Poland re-established a common frontier with Germany – 'For the consequences to Russia of a common frontier with Germany *Mein Kampf* may be consulted.' When, at the end of the month, the Ribbentrop-Stalin agreement showed on what terms the Nazis proposed peace, the rejection by the paper was instant and complete. 'Whatever the "peace terms" might be, Nazism has left not the smallest ground or foothold for negotiation.' Again, six months after the outbreak of war, B-W took occasion to dismiss the idea of peace in the West while the Germans 'gain time for the reshaping, repopulation and consolidation of the East. . . . The certainties of six months are that there has been no *Blitzkrieg* in the West and that none in the strict sense is now possible; that there will be no shoddy and illusory peace; and that a new phase of the war is at hand.' So much for the peace-feelers then being put out from Germany, about which the paper knew but little.

This was the end of the road for B-W so far as Germany was concerned. No one, not even Kurt Hahn, could seriously interest him in the German resistance or anything but final victory over Nazis. One feels the orator here, savouring the words, the alliterations and the balanced periods. Yet the judgement would have been as true two or even three years before. Did silence about these things increase the chances of agreement? Some readers – and many of B-W's colleagues – felt that the condemnation came rather late; but he would have said that those who believed in the possibility of averting European war by a general agreement with Germany could not publicly say – even if they believed – that its people was too far gone in Nazism to make such an agreement possible. We need not doubt that B-W, although he never said so, had found appeasement and *Realpolitik* a gruelling experience, through which he was sustained only by his passionate resolve to do all that he could to prevent a second world war.

17

The Succession

> ...I refuse to sit and think about the 'immense responsibilities', 'unique position' and so on which figure in the letters of would-be kindly correspondents. The day's work is there and if I can do it there may be time to look back and reflect one day. *Ora labora*. What a glorious chance to get something done.[1]

The Establishment worked informally and discreetly in such matters as choosing an editor for *The Times*. One might expect the choice to have been made in much the same fashion as, until recently, the leader of the Conservative Party was selected. Four or five candidates would be listed; a few elder statesmen would be consulted; the list would be shortened; soundings would be taken at lower levels – and eventually the man would emerge. Of any such ritual in the case of Robin Barrington-Ward there is no sign or record. Doubtless there had been much discussion among a few *Round Table* friends before the young B-W joined Garvin in 1919, and again before he returned to Printing House Square in 1927. Astor and Dawson probably consulted before he was given the title of Deputy Editor in 1934. But that decision seems to have assured him the succession, though no one told him so.

As for the suggestion that he was selected and groomed for the job by the Astor family, it can be judged by the evidence of previous chapters. There was no consultation whatsoever between the two brothers, Waldorf of the *Observer* and John of *The Times*, about who should work for their newspapers or how they should be run; and B-W, after his marriage in 1926, saw very little of his patron, Nancy Astor. It is likely, therefore, that Dawson chose, if he did not actually appoint, his own successor. He certainly encouraged no rival in the office; that became clear when B-W was invited to be a candidate to succeed Reith at the BBC (see p. 4). But the most that Dawson had allowed himself to say to his deputy was that, if he himself died, he did not know who could edit the paper except B-W.

Few episodes in B-W's career display character and motive more clearly than the mood of his preparation for the Editor's chair after it was offered to him in the spring of 1939. For eleven years he had worked enthusiastically for this opportunity, giving loyal and laborious service such as few deputy editors can have matched. To succeed Dawson had become by then his sole ambition, and he had already worked out plans for changes in the staff and policy of his beloved paper. He enjoyed enormously the act of editing; and he was a glutton for responsibility. Yet, when the moment came on 18 May 1939 for Astor to send for him and make the offer, he had reservations, which he recorded that evening:

Reflecting on to-day's event. Do not feel as no doubt I ought to feel with life's ambition in sight. Better wait and tackle the job itself when it comes, without premature emotion.[2]

Unlike other heirs apparent, deputy editors regularly occupy the throne before succeeding, even though their powers are limited. So there is no spectacular change in occupying for four or five nights of the week a chair in which one has sat for one or two nights. Nor was the timing of the offer a surprise. In January Campbell Stuart, a director of *The Times* who much admired B-W, had warned him that Dawson had told Astor and Walter – but not the Board – that he would be leaving in six months unless war came. In April B-W, having learnt from the same source that Dawson's letter of resignation had 'gone in', discussed over lunch with the Manager the gap at the top of the staff that would be created by the Editor's departure – for it was the Manager who engaged and paid staff. The diary comments:

I do not wish to be tied up with anything like an intrigue. They can appoint whom they will. If I am asked to take it on, I shall do my utmost. If not, my philosophy will, I believe, be equal to it. All the same, I lay awake for some time considering what staff changes would become necessary if the responsibility fell on me. I should have far less assistance than G.D. has had and an even heavier burden perhaps.[3]

Dawson's letter of resignation of 4 April had the characteristic sardonic note. Considering that another two and a half years were to pass before he actually left the office on 1 October 1941 there is in it much unintended irony.

I have always had a horror of the sort of situation which I have seen in some other offices or businesses, where a man grows older and slower without realizing it himself and his friends are too kind to point it out to him. It seems incredible to me, but it is a sobering fact, that it is thirty-three years since I began to contribute to *The Times* as its South African correspondent and twenty-seven since I first was appointed Editor.

There must be, he said, a 'steady flow of promotion'. But ...

'the responsibility for editing *The Times* is so exacting, so continuous, and so delightful, that the temptation to cling to it too long is peculiarly insidious.... Nothing would distress me more than to feel that by yielding to it I was becoming a drag on the great institution with which I have been proud to be associated for so long.[4]

By this date, Chamberlain had given the British guarantee to Poland (31 March) and the probability of war with Hitler had sharpened. If it should come, at least a score of the younger editorial staff would be called up immediately for service of one kind or another, and whoever was Editor would have to fill the gap by improvisation, as well as by working harder himself. Little wonder then that B-W's pleasure at being assured of the succession before he was fifty had an undertone of worry about the circumstances in which he might take over.

There was by now not only real affection between the two men, but also a well-practised division of labour according to which Dawson acted as political prophet and news-gatherer among the elite, while B-W ran the office, supervised features and carried the main burden of writing on foreign policy. But who, hereafter, was to become the B-W to the next Editor?

The plan had been that Peter Fleming* should become day editor and do the news and feature planning which gets part of the paper ready for the night staff; but the first call on him was now from the Grenadier Guards. No one else had been

---

*Three years earlier B-W recorded his attempt to get an understudy:

'I have long wanted G.D. to get Peter Fleming to understudy some of my activities, chiefly the administrative, for my benefit and for F.'s – and for the paper's. It now appears that F. is willing to think of *T.T.* as a long-term occupaion, with occasional opportunities for travel. G.D. has talked to him. Accordingly I planned it with him this evening.'[5]

thought of for editorial responsibilities. Recruitment outside would now be difficult; and with a solid stratum of middle-aged special writers like Coote, Kennedy, Graves, Braham, and Morrah staying on, the Management would raise its eyebrows at new appointments.

The unexpected form taken by the 'phoney war' four months later did not relieve these anxieties. For nobody in late 1939 believed London would be spared much longer the devastating bombing promised by the pundits of air warfare. Lunching on 22 September with Harold Hartley,* a director whom he felt able to consult on personal matters, B-W asked whether it would not be wise to offer to stand down from the editorship, leaving Astor free to prolong Dawson's tenure if he was willing to stay beyond the end of the year. This was not a question he could ask Dawson to put to the Chairman. He must take the initiative himself; but he naturally did not want the purpose to be misunderstood 'as indicating any lack of confidence or fear of responsibility'. It would 'merely be to conserve the resources of the office in wartime'. Hartley agreed, and when he spoke on B-W's behalf a few days later Astor 'took it delightfully, as always, and agreed it would be best'. So Dawson, not at all reluctantly, stayed on to edit for his second world war.

For some reason, at which one can only guess, Astor was asking only two months later whether the original arrangement – that the Editor should leave at the end of the year 1939 – could not be revived. But B-W still insisted that 'there was no deputy in sight', though when the young men came back it would be different. As for Dawson, he said he had no wish to stay beyond the end of the war, which at that time people liked to think would be quickly over. The problem was frankly discussed between them more than once; and on their way down to a weekend with the Astors at Hever, they reviewed the position, assessed 'the young men' who might come back, and agreed that E. H. Carr should be got in as soon as possible.

So far reinforcement had been hampered by the frustration

*Sir Harold Hartley, G.C.V.O., F.R.S., M.C. born 1878. Hartley and B-W's much venerated eldest brother Fred, the barrister, were brothers-in-law, both having married daughters of the Master of Balliol, A. L. Smith. Hartley, a brilliant scientist, had known B-W as an undergraduate when Fellow of Balliol. One of the first academics to make a success of business and administration, Hartley was a Director of *The Times* from 1936 to 1960.

Edward Hallett Carr, B-W's mentor, aged 56. He joined *The Times* in 1941 after twenty years in the Foreign Office and ten years as a Professor of International Politics, Aberystwyth: 'a better pen never wrote leaders for *The Times*'.

W. F. Casey, Assistant Editor to Dawson and B-W, who took the chair as 16th Editor when B-W died.

1 WEDNESDAY [274—91]

[G.D. said in his "few words" at the conference "I have not stopped to think". Nor have I. ¶ This has been a very sad & disturbing and a striking — which no part of which I can say goodbye or tell him something of what I feel about his editorship and my regrets at him. But I have put it on record in his book. He will still be about the office and I hope to see him often, now and hereafter. As for me I refuse to sit and think about the "immense responsibilities", "unique position" and so on which figure in the letters of well-the kindly congratulations. The day's work is there and, if I can do it, there may be time & later to & reflect and ... one day. One, tomorrow. What a glorious ...

The new Editor records his feelings at the departure of Dawson and the achievement of his life's ambition.

attending negotiations with Carr. B-W had first met him at lunch in October 1938, when he was still Professor of International Relations at Aberystwyth. Tom Jones,* making it his business to help *The Times* find someone able to give his entire attention to foreign policy, had suggested that there in Wales was the future 'Director of the Foreign Department' (the phrase is used in the diaries) for whom the office had been looking since the death of Harold Williams in 1928. B-W liked him, but Dawson seemed unwilling to go beyond inviting the Professor to write occasional leaders. Already in July 1936 Dawson had written to Bob Brand, old friend and Director of *The Times*:

A really good Foreign Editor would be a great support. I *don't* think Carr would do for that. But I do think that his knowledge and experience and good writing would fit him for big foreign leaders, over and above the reviewing which he has been doing for some time.

For various reasons I doubt whether we have anyone on the staff at home or abroad who could take charge of the Foreign Dept as a whole. The fundamental difficulty with a staff of journalists is that the strain on them is very great and that their work suffers if they are disgruntled. You can't deal with them as you would with a regiment or a house of business.[6]

B-W was attracted by Carr's broad and ruthless approach to foreign and home affairs, by his readiness to formulate plans for the future, and by the facility with which he slipped into a readable if 'viewy' style of leader-writing. There are also several diary references to his 'excellent judgement'. But the relationship had been interrupted by Carr's appointment, when war broke out, to a senior post in the Ministry of Information. This he seemed unlikely to leave except for full-time employment with senior status; and to offer him such a prospect on *The Times,* with the young men just departed and the 'professional' journalists in the office suspicious of 'amateur' intrusion, might cause trouble with the staff – as eventually it did.

So, although in June 1940, the month of France's collapse,

*Dr Thomas Jones (1870–1955), an intimate of Lloyd George's at that time and an influential lobbyist behind the scenes of political life, had been Assistant and later Deputy Secretary to the War Cabinet between 1916 and 1930. As Secretary of the Pilgrim Trust he would be well known to Dawson.

G

there came a second offer by Dawson to leave, it met with another plea from B-W that he should stay until a number two had been found. Fortunately, Reith's decision to dismiss Carr from the Ministry solved all problems, and by November he agreed to come. Editor and Deputy Editor dined together alone – a rare happening in that long association – and B-W recorded that Dawson 'spoke as if I must soon take over'. Now, at last, he felt he could 'manage' with a combination of people. Carr would be a 'notable reinforcement', although he could not join the staff until January 1941. The Editor's reign might now, with his agreement, close at any time, for both felt confident that the smaller papers of wartime could be produced by a shrunken editorial team with auxiliaries from outside. Dawson was feeling the strain of the continuous air raids, which kept the paper's staff night after night virtually at battle stations. On 31 December 1940 in the brief epitaph with which he closed his diary each year, B-W wrote of 'the extraordinarily happy and confident partnership, if that is not too large a word, between us. No one else could have treated me with more consideration, and my affection for him and admiration for his great qualities is greater than ever.'

But the New Year of 1941 got into its stride, the war news grew worse and worse – and Dawson was still in the chair. Not until 5 May did Astor bring matters to a head by suddenly asking Dawson to fix a date for his departure which would give B-W time for a proper summer holiday. The suggestion that it was unfair to keep the duly appointed successor waiting indefinitely to step into his shoes took Dawson aback; but he quickly agreed that 'I ought to have thought of it sooner myself.'

On the same day the Chairman sent for B-W:

John Astor asked me to see him, unexpectedly, before the conference. 'It is this difficult question of the editorship,' he began. He asked whether I should now be ready to take it on, if required. I told him that we had been much strengthened by Carr's arrival since the question was last discussed and that, with Carr, Casey and McDonald behind me, I certainly should. I added that G.D. and I were extremely good and close friends and that I did not imply any readiness on my part to push him out. He quite understood that.

He then asked me whether Carr was happy—a leading question, to which I had to reply he was not wholly content. I told him of the plan which Carr had outlined to me in his recent letter. I said I had taken no action on it for two reasons—first, it was addressed to me personally and privately; secondly, it involved, really, a personal issue which no argument could assist, a mutual, temperamental antipathy [with Dawson]. I made it clear that for my part I regarded Carr as most valuable and saw eye to eye with him on policy and that his services ought not to be lost.*

I went on to say that I thought it the duty and opportunity of *The Times* to prepare for the great social changes inevitable after the war. Its function, I said, at all times is to apply common-sense, without prejudice, to issues as they arise and to gain general acceptance of novel but necessary moves by getting them rationally expounded. He most warmly agreed to all this and spoke particularly of the excellence of Carr's articles last year. All of which was good. We left it that he would see G.D. and see me again. Throughout the talk he was his generous and understanding self.

I imparted all this later to Stanley Morison, my sole confidant, as we walked through burnt-out Holborn and battered Gray's Inn to dinner at a little Italian restaurant, the 'Casa Prada' in (of all places) the Euston Road. It was a delicious meal and his company was particularly well-timed.[7]

The terms on which B-W accepted the editorship were the same as those laid down by Dawson for himself in November 1922. In policy matters he was to have complete independence of the Board and of the Chief Proprietors. Only the latter could dismiss him. 'The power of the Proprietors,' Dawson had written, 'is exercised properly by the appointment and dismissal of the Editor, not by interfering with his work or doing it themselves.'† It was his definition of the powers of the Editor that B-W was to evoke when one of the directors wished to challenge his policy at a specially arranged dinner in 1946. [See Chapter 13.]

By now, not surprisingly, rumours about impending change at P.H.S. were spreading and Dawson in July asked B-W to

---

*The reasons for Carr's disagreements with Dawson are discussed on p. 216.

†The memorandum in which Dawson, guided by Lord Milner, set out the conditions on which he would return as Editor in 1922 is given on pp. 79–80 of the *History of The Times*, Volume IV. It remains to this day an admirable analysis of the respective responsibilities of Editor and Manager in a newspaper office and of the need to distinguish between the selection of staff by the Editor and their appointment and payment by the Manager. Dawson saw it as his main task, after the Northcliffe – Steed period, to restore the reputation of the news columns for accuracy and impartiality and to restore editorial control over every part of the content of his paper.

draft an announcement about his retirement to appear in the paper. The very next afternoon, 17 July 1941, the *Star* scooped its rival evening papers with the announcement of the event and of B-W's succession, so obliging *The Times* to announce tardily and not at a time of its own choosing a most important piece of family news.* After all the havering it was perhaps fortunate that this leak occurred; there could now be no turning back. Letters from B-W's immense circle of friends poured in and the Press references to him were very friendly.

Dawson, too, had many letters to deal with. To John Reith, the Minister of Works and Planning, who had sent his good wishes for retirement, he replied:

I am sorry to go—particularly at such a moment—but it is a relief to know that it comes of having provided long ago for the succession and not from any friction or breakdown in health. I should in fact have retired last year, which was the limit I had always set in my own mind, if it had not been for the war; and it has been borne in upon me lately (not, I need hardly say, by him) that it is unfair to keep a duly chosen successor waiting indefinitely. This seems to me so reasonable that there is really no alternative; but I shall hope to find some other niche in the war effort when I finally depart from P.H.S.[9]

To a Canadian friend, Percival Witherby, he wrote that he had done all he could to make the transition 'smooth and unimportant'. B-W, he emphasized, had nothing to learn. 'For some years now I have had everything in common with him – people, papers and policy – and have made a point of taking his views at every stage.' Stanley Morison, while writing the History, was shown this letter and others, and noted on them: 'You would not imagine from the letters how loath to go G.D. really was. I don't in the least blame him. Few, if any, leave P.H.S. willingly.'

During the following week Dawson gave his successor dinner and listened to the plans for the future. 'I wanted to bring him

---

*The pother in the office was considerable. Two drafts of the announcement were shown to the Chairman, Dawson's and the one on which B-W and Stanley Morison had worked together. Astor preferred the former. B-W. who was due to dine outside London at G.H.Q. Home Forces that evening, risked losing his train and his dinner in order to get removed a reference to his distinguished record in the First World War. 'It would have been, to say the least of it,' he wrote, 'most inappropriate in my own paper.'[8]

along, as it were [B-W noted], in consultation and to expound
my plans to him, which I did. He was most helpful and receptive and indeed agreed with them all. I hope to preserve this
kind of relations, for all reasons, personal not least.'[10] Does one
detect here a lack of self-confidence now that the moment, so
long postponed, had come? For there was, in fact, little to be
done with the paper in its wartime size, and little to be done
with the staff save to edge out older colleagues.

Over the farewell lunch on 31 October at the Waldorf Hotel
the new Editor presided, with Astor there as a guest of the staff.
(Most chairmen of newspapers would have been less modest
and taken the chair themselves.) The task of saying goodbye,
B-W noted, proved not too easy. 'I described G.D.'s qualities
by imagining the attributes that should be ascribed to a great
editor . . .' Dawson replied at some length in his compelling
but matter-of-fact way, 'with some characteristically sardonic
touches'. He too reflected on some aspects of editorship and
said some very generous things about his host. Once or twice
he lost his thread; he was deeply moved (B-W thought) even
for 'a man who keeps his emotions far within'.[11]

Now, at last, Robin had joined his brothers, Fred, Lance
and Michael on the heights of professional success. It had taken
him twenty-two years, but he had climbed by the shortest route.
With influential friends to help him, B-W since 1938 had
been sufficiently confident of his future (as we have seen) to
refuse Reith's pressing suggestion that he should become the
next Director-General of the BBC. It may help us to understand
his reputation in those days if this chapter concludes with
Reith's description of the qualities he looked for in his successor. He should be 'just left of centre'; he should be 'a Christian
believer and should give the Christian religion a privileged place
in the BBC's output'; he should be 'firm in his dealings with
people'. All these qualifications, he thought, B-W possessed.
As for the comparative importance of the two jobs, the Editor
of *The Times,* Reith added, was 'one of the few people in
England to whom he would tip his hat' and was even more
important than the Director-General of the BBC.[12] Whatever
one thinks of his judgement, it is tempting to speculate what
would have happened if B-W had succeeded Reith and taken
the BBC, as he was to take *The Times,* well to the left of the
pre-war centre. He would have enjoyed greater power with a

much higher salary.* He would have become a public figure instead of an anonymous editor. He would have shed the burden of writing and re-writing, for that of administering a large staff. He would have ceased to be a journalist at the very moment that he was producing the most controversial articles of his life. It is hard to believe he would have found at Broadcasting House the pride and satisfaction he felt in Printing House Square.

The account given here of the succession will perhaps dispose of an anecdote which is sometimes heard when old *Times* men meet. John Astor, it is said, being a shy man of most delicate tact, planned to tell his Editor over dinner at the Athenaeum one night in 1941 that he must now, in fairness to B-W, set a date for leaving. His courage having failed him at the table, he conveyed the message later when they were together in the gentlemen's lavatory. Then, the story concludes, Dawson went out to his car and on the way back to the office told Horner, the Editor's driver, how and where he had been 'sacked'.

The story is so out of keeping with the characters concerned that it would not be worth recording if it had not been told with such confidence and relish. Lord Astor assured the author (in November 1969) that this account of an embarrassing episode is untrue, and we have Dawson's word for it – in his own memorandum of September 1941 – that the hint was gently if suddenly given in the Chairman's own room on 5 May 1941. More credible and creditable is the other office legend; that Dawson, when he left the office after editing for the last time, told Horner that he could think of nowhere he wanted to go to in blacked-out, bomb-torn London. Whereupon the devoted driver suggested that a cup of tea with Mrs Horner up in north London might be an acceptable send-off – and was taken at his word.

Dawson was to live only another three years, and bad health deprived him of that enjoyment of retirement, with activity in Yorkshire, and Oxford and London, which his friends hoped he would have. On the morning after he died, 6 November

*For work and responsibilities that were sometimes compared to those of the highest in the land the salary, though substantial, was not remarkable. B-W, on becoming Editor, received £6,000 a year and £1,000 expenses. The salary of the Prime Minister at the time was £10,000 and of the Chancellor of the Exchequer £5,000.

1944, a remarkable obituary was published in his paper, most of it written by Ned Grigg but partly revised by B-W himself. There was no doubt in B-W's mind that Dawson had been a great editor. The diary, not for the first time, recorded how deep the friendship between Editor and Deputy Editor had been:

He has bulked very largely in my life and I owe him much. Though he could seem self-centred at times, I was greatly devoted to him and had much admiration for him, acquired and sustained at the closest quarters.... And what he taught me—as a model and by example, for he was the least didactic of men—is not to be computed.[13]

To B-W's niece – the daughter of his eldest brother Fred – I owe this portrait of B-W just after he became Editor:

Robin was probably the best integrated personality of the nine brothers and sisters; but the dissimilar strains of an unusually diverse heredity were still apparent in him, making him to those who knew him well a person of contrasts, of light and shade both physical and mental. His spare frame, below average in height, his capacity for stillness and economy in words and movement, could give a superficial observer a misleading impression of insignificance. Then the dark eyes lit up, the lovely voice greeted you, the fine hands briefly emphasized the apt comment. A personality was suddenly irradiated, almost too ardently for its physical exterior.

Early balding emphasized the structure of forehead and temple. This, with the riding accident in youth which injured his nose, changed the almost excessive good looks of early manhood into a face that was determined and stern in repose. But the over-long upper lip, a dour legacy to so many sons of Ulster, was softened by a mouth of quizzical gentleness. Too active and practical to be dubbed elegant, his intellectual fastidiousness still had its physical —and sartorial—expression. This was all of a piece with his beautiful handwriting, and his great love of music and of natural beauty. One could join in the deprecating humour of the neat figure which, at a wartime lunch, suddenly showed his frayed shirt cuffs with a distasteful glance and exclaimed: 'My patriotism is becoming ostentatious.'[14]

Words in Churchill's Ear

The line between nagging and helpful counsel is
extremely difficult to draw.
First leader in The Times, *1 October 1941*

You can always turn the flank.
Churchill to the Editor of The Times, *March 1943*

War made editing easier for a man of B-W's turn of mind.
Policy was what interested him and in a state of national siege
it is the policy aspect of everything that is important. Although
newspaper sizes were heavily cut *The Times* leader page did
not suffer. There was much less room for news but little less
room for views. The biographer, therefore, faces a glut of
material spread over some 1,500 issues of the wartime paper
and over some 650 peacetime issues. It can be given shape only
by selecting a few leading themes which the diaries show to have
been uppermost in the Editor's mind. Those chosen are: (i)
the paper's counselling and chivvying of the Prime Minister,
with whom *The Times* in the past had had such acute
differences; (ii) his personal interest in post-war policies of
reconstruction for economic and social life; (iii) the part played
during the war years by his mentor and assistant editor E. H.
Carr, recruiting a new staff, shocking readers into thought about
the realities of Britain's future, and getting the paper argued
about by sympathetic radicals and outraged Tories.

To concentrate in this way on policy at the expense of the
vast news effort that *The Times* made during those five years
may seem unfair. But this was the bias of the man and it is
always this side of the paper's work that is best documented,
for of day-to-day decisions about correspondents, news
services, battles with the censors, the reporting of Parliament
and the home front there are almost no records outside the
pages of the paper itself.

Nor is there much of interest to record in the wartime life
of his family, of which he saw nothing save during weekends

and holidays. Mark and Simon were at boarding school and he devoted much of his leisure to his only daughter Caroline, still in the nursery, deeply attached to this gay but strict, entertaining and understanding father, who would read bravely on to the end of *Black Beauty,* defying the tears and the fears and then promise to begin a happier book the next night. His weekday life in London was simply work and meals and often interrupted nights. He and Stanley Morison, who had decided to share quarters and a housekeeper, had both been bombed out at home and shared the fiery ordeals of the blitzes on the City, all around Printing House Square. Out of those experiences grew a close friendship, an intimacy of opposites. Morison the technician and historian of typography; ex-Communist, Catholic, conscientious objector in the first war; tall, rumbustious, arrogant, argumentative, looking like a Jesuit in his black clothes and tie. B-W the ideas and writing man, scarred by war; unassuming in manner, neat and short, also argumentative in his calm and quick way; full of doubts where Morison pretended to be sure – in religion and politics – and full of confidence where Morison was obviously unsure – in social background and taste. A curious partnership, immensely stimulating to the Editor and a powerful aid to his friend's anomalous but powerful position in the office as a kind of Grand Vizier.

The new Editor's ideas of the relationship between his newspaper and Government, as represented by an all-powerful Prime Minister, were under test within a few weeks of his taking over. Proud though he might be of the tradition of stalwart independence which the word 'Thunderer' represented to him, he knew that the normal role expected of *The Times,* especially in wartime, was support of the government in power. In so far as the ministers' majority in the Commons truly represented the feeling of a majority of the voters, the paper was expressing public opinion by sustaining them. But if opinion changed, if the Prime Minister or the Government were visibly losing the confidence of the people, then the paper was not only free but also bound to draw attention to the failure, explain it and suggest the action to be taken. That, under Dawson, it had been doing already for two years. It is perhaps necessary to point out that there were then no polls of public opinion. Politicians and journalists and the House of Commons worked on hunches of surprising accuracy.

This does not mean that the paper, in B-W's understanding of its role, had to wait for a discontented majority opinion to form before voicing discontent. It must tell the public what those closest to the workings of government believed to be wrong with it, and give space to those who knew, or thought they knew, how the running of the country could be improved. In foreign policy, too, *The Times* would feel itself entitled to say even in wartime that this or that act of policy – for example the intervention of 1944 in Greece – was against the long-term interest of the country, knowing full well that its criticism would have unpredictable effects abroad and greatly embarrass the Foreign Office in its dealings with Britain's allies.

This being B-W's conception of editing it can be imagined what difficulties might be created by Churchill's uniquely personal methods of government. Between him and *The Times* office there were old grounds of suspicion and hostility. He had bitterly opposed its liberal policy towards India; in turn the paper had ignored – even deplored – his Jeremiads about German rearmament. Dawson, who remembered the fiascoes of the Dardanelles and the return to gold, distrusted Churchill's judgement. Two months before war began B-W had noted that there was 'much talk, newspaper and other, about getting Winston into Chamberlain's Government'. His comment is full of sense:

Winston is certainly a strong and capable figure who would no doubt impress the Germans. But this concentration on one saviour of the country is becoming a little ridiculous. Much better not to press too hard for his inclusion. If the P.M. did give way now it would look like abdication. And, if Winston did come in, the Cabinet would split. You can't have a War Government until there is a war. When the emergency is grave enough, any political combination will cohere—and Winston will be in.[1]

Churchill's appointment in September 1939 to the Admiralty and his dramatic leadership of the only service actually fighting the enemy pass without comment in the daily rush of adapting the office to war. But the diarist records what was told him by Ogilvie (Reith's successor at the BBC) about the First Lord's ways as a broadcaster:

Winston always determined to get for his broadcasts the best time for the largest public, including the U.S. Asked if he would not speak on Wednesday in the regular series of addresses delivered by Ministers, he replied: 'What! Stand in a row with that rabble?' His colleagues![2]

But, whatever B-W might think of Winston's choice of friends or his methods of doing business, his performance in the House of Commons was always appreciated. Alerted to a big occasion he went down to listen to the Battle of Britain speech of 20 August:

Heard Winston speak for an hour on the war. Very fine speech, sober though eloquent, full of reasoned resolution. One great phrase in tribute to the air pilots who have been winning the great battles of the last few days—'Never in the field of human conflict have so many owed so much to so few.' That deserves to live.[3]

B-W, like so many others, misquoted 'was so much owed by so many to so few' – but live it did.

These, be it remembered, were days of almost unbearable suspense, just before the Battle of Britain, with the shattered Dunkirk army regrouping, the Home Guard on watch through glorious summer nights, the whole people wondering what at last was coming to them: intensive bombing, invasion, a peace offensive, more phoney war? The mood was not all calm resolution: there was also irritability and impatience because preparations for resistance could not be fully seen and reported from the beaches, from the fighter airfields, and the radar sets. Discontent expressed itself (as in 1914) by demands for a Kitchener-type figure in charge of the home front, someone like the creator of the Royal Air Force, Trenchard:

I had a long and most interesting talk with Trenchard...Talked of the home command. He might have been—and ought to be—our generalissimo at home if he had been more patient and Winston more receptive. At their interview, however, he asked too much or too strongly in the way of conditions and they parted in heat.... Winston needs a big man near him, one who is not afraid to say 'No.'[4]

Here B-W was anticipating the verdict of most of those who worked with Churchill: the need for a big man at his side who would say 'No'. What he did not – and perhaps could not – understand was that this critical, resistant influence could not be exerted by an individual associated with only one of the fighting services. (It was in fact exercised by the Chiefs of

Staff in joint session.) For example, to the Admiralty Trenchard was a mortal enemy who had refused the Navy control of its own air force; to the War Office he was a rival who had attracted vast sums of money away from the Army. It is hard, moreover, to believe that the public accepted at that time the need for a superman even if Whitehall would have accepted Trenchard in that role.

The critical note is still sounded, though less often, in 1941. Clement Davies, the Liberal leader, talks to him of 'Winston's complete failure to face Beaverbrook – for that's what it amounts to – with a properly organized chain of command, one Minister settling priorities at the top'. And at a further meeting with P. J. Grigg, senior civil servant at the War Office, who as a young man had been private secretary to Churchill:

> We had a good dinner and a good gossip. Much talk of Winston whom he knows better than most people both in his strong and his weak points. Caustic about some others. I wish that P.J. were at No. 10, where he ought to be. He has a fine intelligence and courage. I have a great regard for him and respect for his common sense.[5]

The last month of this fearful and disappointing year, in which B-W had become Editor, was to give him the opportunity to meet the Prime Minister over lunch; but before that he went with his new assistant editor, Carr, to lunch in the private apartments of the Soviet Ambassador's 'Victorian Palace' in Kensington Palace Gardens.

> Treatment of Germany the main question, as being the essential problem of the peace. Agreed that peace must rest upon Anglo-Rusian-American tripod. Essential to get Anglo-Russian co-operation onto a fully cooperative basis. Maisky not very sound on how to tackle the Germans—too much 'retribution', 'dismemberment' etc.—but he may have been testing our views only. He gave us a superb lunch. After that proletarian feast a walk along the Embankment was much in order.[6]

The description which follows of Churchill's lunch at No. 10 on 1 December, with Brendan Bracken* the only other person

---

*Bracken (1901–58) was then Minister of Information and the principal channel of contact between the newspapers and the Prime Minister, whose intimate he was. He had a great reputation both inside and outside the House as a fluent and witty speaker. Despite his flamboyance Bracken was well liked and respected by B-W.

present, must be told from the beginning, for it was rarely that the Editor committed to his diary a report as long and detailed as this one:

Brendan came in first. Then Winston from a War Cabinet, looking (at 67) very fresh and young and spry. He is a different man altogether from the rather bloated individual whom I last saw (close to) before the war. His cheerful, challenging—not to say truculent—look is good to see just now; but it covers up a great deal of caution, even vacillation at times. Perhaps instinctively acquired. Anyway it is good to see, and the public thinks so too and it is the right 'face' to put on the vast responsibilities which he is discharging. A lack of the finer perceptions, no doubt! But no doubt either about vigour and purpose.

It is amusing to hear B-W, himself sometimes a cautious and hesitant person, perceiving that even the bulldog sometimes thinks twice, and to see the abstemious idealist from Printing House Square detecting in the patrician, self-indulgent Prime Minister 'a lack of the finer perceptions'. His host drank 'a glass of white wine, another of port and two small brandies. Not much by earlier standards.'

'I was invited,' the diary goes on, 'of course, as a critic – I won't say to silence criticism. But he was a little on the defensive. I was glad of the meeting, and all the more so because it was not brought about on my initiative.' The Prime Minister defended his Chiefs of Staff against the criticisms made in *The Times*'s leading articles and elsewhere.

Dill, he said,'has a fine, a refined mind' but implied lack of strength there. Alan Brooke more decisive. 'Pound,' he went on, 'is necessary to me. His slow, unimpressive look is deceptive!' Approves of Paget. Minister of Defence, constitutionally, must be either the Prime Minister or must hold all three defence portfolios. Described the elasticity of his system. Most often the Chiefs of Staff met without him. Sometimes he met with them, sometimes with them and their Ministers.

When the talk came to the Middle East Churchill gave his guest – what he knew he would relish above all – a piece of news, 'not yet given to the Cabinet', about Auchinleck's next move in Libya, 'for which he has reserves in hand'.

In their more casual exchanges Churchill asked about editors' hours of work, to which he doubtless received the reply, sixteen hours a day – eight till midnight – five days a week. B-W was advised that an afternoon sleep in bed was a good idea, and the Prime Minister wished that all those who worked with him would organize their day on the same lines. Otherwise they would wear out, like Dill. The parting was most friendly; B-W was asked to come and see him any time, and especially to keep in touch with Eden, 'a good mind with a real contribution to make'.[7]

Unconvinced by his conversation with the Prime Minister and Bracken, the Editor pegged away at his campaign to get more order into the running of the war and more attention to the home front. While Churchill was in the United States during January 1942, concerting future policies with Roosevelt, two leading articles in the Editor's own hand were being prepared. 'Likely to fall on deaf ears in 10 Downing Street,' he remarked, 'not perhaps elsewhere.' Visiting the House of Commons and talking to Members in the Lobby he had found a feeling that 'Winston was trying to ride the House on too tight a rein.' On 22 January he records a long private talk with Beaverbrook whom he respected more in the role of journalist than that of statesman. Churchill and Roosevelt, said the Lord, had 'clicked perfectly' and now changes at home must be considered. B-W said the Commons particularly wanted to get rid of Kingsley Wood and Arthur Greenwood, but he considered the vote of confidence to be asked for next week was a mistake because 'all but a handful wanted to see Winston on top of the Ministers'.*

Beaverbrook mentioned with a chuckle a General Election as another resource. We didn't discuss that seriously. Then he asked how long a man's 'indispensability' lasted. I said Winston's wasn't exhausted yet, though it would be one day. He recalled the precedent of Asquith in 1915. For two years everyone described him as indispensable to hold the nation together, and so on, but he was pushed out. I didn't think it a parallel. He favours a Minister of Production, to establish undivided authority over the factories. He went on to say that he himself had no wish for the job. He had

---

*There is an interesting parallel between B-W's efforts to get the direction of the war reorganized at this time and the campaign of Northcliffe and Dawson in The Times and the Daily Mail during 1915–16 in favour of a smaller body to run the war, and eventually in favour of Lloyd George against Asquith as Prime Minister.

been appointed first of all as Winston's deputy but every decision he took was reversed by Winston.[8]

A few days later, on 26 January, a short talk with Stafford Cripps, just back from Russia, elicited that he might enter a 'reformed and reorganized administration'. B-W thought it necessary to warn him that the Prime Minister would not 'part forthwith with all his stimulants, his necessities, to wit his Beaverbrooks'. But experience of administration, after Moscow, would make the Socialist lawyer a most valuable recruit to a Cabinet. 'If he returns to opposition,' the diary notes, 'he will, I think, decline.' The significance of this hint becomes clearer later when B-W finds himself interested, if not involved, in talks about a new deal at No. 10.

After conflicting rumours had kept Fleet Street guessing for most of January 1942, the Government changes were announced. Beaverbrook was to be Minister of War Production and Andrew Duncan Minister of Supply, with consequential changes below. 'They don't amount to much,' B-W grumbled to himself. 'No thorough reconstruction yet and even these moves require explanation.'

Exactly the same view was being expressed during the weekend of 7 February at Cliveden, which B-W had not visited for many a long day. It was one of the blackest passages of the war, with things going badly in Libya and unrelieved disaster in the Far East. On the 15th the news of the fall of Singapore, coming on top of the up-Channel escape of the battleships *Scharnhorst* and *Gneisenau*, had deeply shaken public confidence. Reconstructing the Government seemed the only positive thing that could be done. The Editor decided that he would devote a morning to writing on the subject himself.*

Went over to the quiet library at the Travellers at 10.15 and produced by 1 p.m. what is, I hope, a careful and considered appeal to Winston to reconstruct his government — men and machinery alike.[10]

*B-W's feelings about the 'high command' must have been influenced by his anger at the Singapore episode which had lost him his greatest war-time friend Major-General Merton Beckwith-Smith. Not until 19 November did it become known that he had died as a prisoner of war. 'It is a cruel, cruel loss. By the sheer stupidity of the high command he with his division was shipped to Singapore too late to effect anything, just in time to be captured. . . . He was the best friend that ever a man could have. A fine nature, unobtrusively rooted in sheer goodness, great sense of fun, admirable company, and ideal as husband, father and son. He will always be alive for me. . . .'[9]

When Churchill on the following Sunday broadcast at short notice, in an effort to steady morale, the effort was judged disappointing: 'a vague appeal for unity' – the diary calls it:

Who advises him? Doesn't Brendan Bracken bring him tidings of the outer world? He missed a great chance, on his return from Washington, of equipping himself with a new team of Ministers and a War Cabinet. Everyone could see what was coming, and it has come. The pressure of events will continue and, if Winston does nothing, it will push him out.[11]

On 19 February comes a moment of triumph. 'Most of what *The Times* has asked for has been conceded,' notes the diary:

The changes are good. Beaverbrook is out altogether. Cripps is in – as Leader of the House! Attlee deputy Prime Minister and Dominions Secretary. Cabinet of Ministers without, or virtually without, portfolio, except Bevin, Minister of Labour and National Service. Oliver Lyttelton recalled from Cairo. Arthur Greenwood out. This really is a large sweep, capable of re-invigorating the conduct of the war and public confidence.[12]

It is not surprising that B-W, contemplating his own first achievement as Editor, 'tinkered heavily' with the first leader after the first edition, finding the right balance between dignified approval and self-congratulation.* However, the event was not without disappointments: the reshuffle had cost Reith his job as Minister of Works and Buildings (with planning to come). Personal considerations apart – B-W much admired Reith's qualities – this was a blow to his hopes for the next campaign in favour of starting work on post-war reconstruction policy.

It says much for the relationship between B-W and his old editor that at such a busy time he should have written to him about the changes in a letter of the kind that used to go up from the office to Yorkshire in the old days – just to keep G.D. in touch. In February 1942, he wrote as follows:

When the pinch comes there is a blend of magnanimity and realism in Winston which commands respect. I think you will agree that

*Neither here nor elsewhere is it suggested that *The Times* was solely responsible for such events. Other newspapers and periodicals agitated too. But to the editor, however modest, the temptation to take credit himself is strong.

the changes have gone nearly as far as we hoped and a good deal further than we expected. As soon as I heard that the Beaver was out and Cripps in, I felt that the essentials were there. Not that the Beaver has not served an extremely good turn, but his bolt was well shot and he more than anyone or anything else was responsible for the *malaise* in the House and in the Government itself. It was Cripps in effect who put him out.[13]

Although the Cabinet reconstruction had much reduced *The Times*'s concern about the leadership, grumbles continued to reach the office. A trickle of evidence about inefficiency in Whitehall and in industry reached the Editor from many quarters. At a Lobby lunch* at the Savoy on 6 March he saw Winston, who was the principal guest, looking unwell. He made a defensive speech off the record to this select and critical gathering to which the political correspondents of the national and provincial press invite their proprietors, editors, assistant editors and political contacts. He appealed against unfair criticism in the Press and said 'in effect that we lost at Singapore the reputation for fighting quality gained in the Battle of Britain and under bombing, and must recapture it'.

The Times had not been alone in criticizing the Government and demanding explanations of the disasters of the year. In the popular and non-Conservative papers the tone had been much sharper, sometimes abusive, notably in the *Daily Mirror,* which on 6 March 1942 carried a cartoon with comment which ministers felt to be indefensible. The Home Secretary, Herbert Morrison, considering what action might be taken, asked B-W to come and see him, doubtless to find out how the Press would regard the use of powers not yet claimed – under Defence Regulations 2c and 2d. He had in mind a public warning in the House of Commons.

This was the kind of emergency with which B-W dealt admirably from his reserves of common sense. His advice to Morrison was:

*The collective body of political correspondents of national and some provincial newspapers was known as 'The Lobby' from the privilege they enjoyed of walking and talking with Members in and around one of the corridors of the House. They formed a powerful, self-governing group, with their own strict rules of behaviour. Their elected chairman would consult regularly with the Prime Minister's private secretaries or press officer about 'briefings' to be given to the Lobby, their timing and the extent to which they should be for use or for background information only.

I argued that the question is one of expediency, i.e. of politics not of law. I didn't believe that the *D.M.* cut two penn'orth of ice; a move towards control of opinion would react upon Winston and weaken the Government, which was not now strong enough (as it might have been in May 1940) to claim the authority to act as advocate, judge and executioner on its own behalf. Much better leave it alone. Rest of the Press perfectly sound.

Showed me draft Question and Answer. Latter long and turgid — 'a good leading article' he thought it! — and full of over-sensitive protest against criticism. I begged him, if he took that course, to keep the statement brief and pithy. Merely warn the *D.M.* that he had been advised he had discretionary power under the Regulations and would, if need be, use them; and add that the Government made no complaints of the Press generally.[14]

Then came the second of the lunches with the Prime Minister (30 March); a two-hour occasion, again with only Bracken present. The Editor on arrival presented a photographed copy of a letter, found for him in *The Times* archives by John Maywood, dated 1898 and signed 'Winston S. Churchill'. In it the writer regretted that he had been prevented by Kitchener from acting as correspondent of the paper in the Sudan. This memento of his journalistic youth seemed to give the host pleasure. After reviewing the good news of the recent St Nazaire raid and of American operations in the Pacific and agreeing that the collapse of Singapore was inexplicable, they passed on to the question of the *Daily Mirror*. B-W writes:

I said no Minister had yet named the conductors of that paper nor insisted on the impropriety of anonymous holdings (bank nominees) in newspapers — irresponsible control. If they closed down a paper with 1,800,000 circulation, there would be a widespread grousing and they would have a wolf by the ears.

Then Winston got on to the press generally (which he has rather on the brain). Thinks *Daily Mirror, Daily Mail* and *Daily Herald* campaigns were calculated to undermine the Army. Makes no complaint of *The Times* or *Manchester Guardian*: 'sober reasoned criticism'. Hopes we can give him a hand from time to time to keep things steady. I said people wanted some vision of the future, some hope. British would always fight best when fighting for more than their skins.

'What do you want me to say?' I said I wouldn't offer an off-hand reply but should be prepared to draft something. 'Get it on a few sheets of paper and send it to me.' I most gladly undertook to do so.

He went on to the importance of preserving free enterprise. Nationalization of the railways—no difficulty about that. But profit was not an ignoble motive. I said it was all a matter of determining where the profit motive could still usefully function and where it could not.

Winston said 'I am an old man (he didn't sound it), not like Lloyd George coming out of the last war at 56 or so. I may be 70 before this war ends.' (This was taking refuge in the view that reconstruction would be for someone else to take up in the future.) He cannot see what the assurance, and in some measure the accomplishment, of it means to public confidence and war energy *now*.* 'No man has had to bear such disasters as I have.' I said the nation had taken them very well.

Far from storming he bore my candour and listened most patiently. Not quite as fit and sparkling as at our last lunch. A very impressive person with strong limitations. His utter absence of pomposity is most engaging. He was wearing his one-piece 'siren suit'. Ate heartily.[15]

Not until 14 April did the memorandum on reconstruction plans go to Downing Street from Printing House Square. Carr wrote the first draft, but he and B-W and Casey took time to decide whether they should 'send all that we should like to hear him say or as much of it as we think he might accept'. They seem to have decided on the former, and the diary notes:

> The result will be precisely nothing. That doesn't matter in so far as I have not failed to take the chance offered. It will matter greatly, however, especially to him, if Winston goes on refusing to give any lead in reconstruction.[16]

By now, however, Downing Street and Printing House Square were grappling on another matter, far closer to Churchill's heart: the suggestion, at that time widely discussed, that there should be a Chief of the Great General Staff (CGGS), that is to say a serving officer performing the coordinating and chairing role with the three Chiefs of Staff which Churchill reserved to himself. After *The Times* had aired the idea, the Editor found on his desk a letter dated 17 April 1942 containing 'vehement

---

*Churchill, as Chapter 19 will show, took much convincing. Indeed, a year passed before his special broadcast on a four-year plan met *The Times*'s requirement.

but good-tempered argument' against it from the Prime Minister together with the offer of a talk with 'Pug' Ismay.

The Prime Minister treated with patient courtesy the Editor who was harrying him at this critical time.

Have you thought out the details of this campaign you are running for what is called the Great General Staff? There seems to be a number of questions which you and your correspondents are not facing. A professional chief without a department or Service is to be appointed C.G.G.S. Presumably he can give directions to the three Chiefs of Staff. What happens if they or any of them do not agree with him? As he would be inevitably the product of one of the three Services this is a very likely chance.

Next, what is to happen to the Service Ministers? They have a constitutional position which entitles them to access to the Cabinet and to circulate papers. In all probability they would make common cause with their own professional advisers and so would their whole office. It would then be my duty to advise the Cabinet and induce them to decide whether the C.G.G.S. was right or the Admiralty, War Office or Air Ministry. I fear I should be provided not only with solutions but with a whole series of disputes.

Again, have you anybody in your mind? Is he to be retired or serving? Old and sagacious or young and dynamic? Who is your man? Should he belong to the Army, Navy or Air Force? Have we any officer who has three-fold qualifications? It is very easy to suggest some unknown genius should be found on whom the Cabinet can dump their responsibilities to win the war, and whom the Services will obey; but I think you ought to name the animal.

These are only a few of the difficulties which would arise. It would be a very good thing if you first of all made yourself acquainted with the existing organization and of the very large degree of fusing which has already been achieved at the second and third levels of the Staffs. I shall be quite ready to let General Ismay give you the fullest particulars of this and I believe he would convince you of the difficulties of making the kind of change you have in mind.[17]

B-W's reply on 20 April was not one of his more convincing efforts, relying as he had to on the advice of others and lacking direct experience of the Chiefs of Staff functioning. He argued lamely that, if the project of a chief professional adviser to the Minister of Defence was right in conception, 'the office would be even more than the man, in the sense that it would itself elicit the cooperation on which he must rely and confer not a few of the qualifications to be sought.'

Two days later Churchill replied that he could not see how the scheme of a Chief Professional Adviser could work.

At present [he wrote] I am advised by the Chiefs of Staff Committee, of whom Sir Alan Brooke is Chairman. The advantage of dealing with the responsible executive heads of the Service Departments is that they have the great handling machinery in their control and can give immediate effect to what is decided. I do not quite understand what relationship the new 'Chief Professional Adviser' would have with the Chiefs of Staff. Would he be able to give them directions? If so, they and their Ministers would certainly appeal to the Cabinet, as they are fully entitled to do. Again, should I not run the risk of having conflicting advice given me by the 'Chief Professional Adviser' on the one hand and the Chiefs of Staff Committee on the other? What happens if I do not agree with the advice of the 'Chief Professional Adviser' and the Cabinet when appealed to agrees with me?[18]

The diary describes Ismay's visit to the Editor:

Ismay came, took a cup of tea and stayed an hour-and-a-quarter. I like Ismay. He is a cheerful fatalist or pessimist and gives himself no airs. But he is very much the P.M.'s A.D.C. A rambling talk. Discussed the combined general staff and C.G.G.S. It comes to this. He is not really against it in principle but says it will not be possible with this Prime Minister. 'Winston,' Ismay says, 'wages war all day.' Alas, he does. Ismay left me with a deepened impression of how personal the whole thing now is.[19]

The Editor's mind was in no way changed by the arguments of 'Bomber' Harris, at whose house near High Wycombe he spent a night in May while visiting the headquarters of his Command. Harris said Churchill was doing the job of keeping the three Chiefs of Staff together; but B-W noted how strong the vested air interest was.

A second front might make claims on bomber aid and interfere with the raiding of Germany: therefore no good. In some ways the Navy thinks the bombing of Germany waste of time. All the Services alike.... All competitive.

Whatever his feelings of frustration about war leadership, which he shared with most of the public, the Editor was strongly opposed to what he regarded as a dishonest Commons censure debate on 2 July, when Churchill replied in a speech of ninety minutes to critics, none of whom, in fact, wanted to turn him out.

I have never seen such a crowded House. He spoke till 5. A characteristic effort—sombre opening, some very good and disarming chaff later. A great victory in the House, but it won't dispose of the defeat in Libya. Debate as a whole poor.[20]

About this time, too, *The Times* expressed doubts about the Government's rejection of a 'second front' on the continent of Europe in 1942. At dinner with Maisky, the Editor, Carr and McDonald had heard British naval policy bitterly attacked, especially the scattering in early July of the large convoy P.Q.17 carrying tanks, aircraft and supplies to Russia. The Soviet Ambassador alleged that the British were now too frightened of air attack on their ships; as for the second front, he said (according to the diary):

They expect too great a margin of security, are too elaborate, and underrate the help to be expected from France. Must we wait for special landing-craft? We could contrive the necessary surplus of shipping by passing to the defensive in the Middle East and by cutting down our ample food supplies.[21]

This led the Editor to send for Thursfield, the Naval Correspondent, and Cyril Falls, the Military Correspondent, and instruct them to get at the true facts and make sure that the allies were still powerless to stage a diversion. 'Couldn't they go for North Africa?' he asked. 'I have always thought that our true offensive front,' and on the 28th Carr wrote a trenchant leader on the subject. Thursfield's visit to the Admiralty – where he had regular access to the Vice-Chief of Naval Staff, and to the Director of Naval Intelligence – had a curious result. Having passed on Maisky's criticism he returned to the office and revealed that the Admiralty wanted to publish a full account of the P.Q.17 disaster in reply to boastful German propaganda, but the Prime Minister would not hear of it. The next day B-W experienced the embarrassment that may attend a journalist's use of one high-level contact to influence or get news out of another source.

Vice-Admiral Moore [Deputy Chief of Naval Staff] rang me up. Admiralty sending another minute on Murmansk convoy to P.M. urging publicity. In view of the importance of the matter did I object to their mention of the source of the story brought to them by Thursfield? I felt bound to say 'no objection' but added that I did not want source or *The Times* compromised. I rang him up again later. He said there had been no mention of *The Times,* only of a 'responsible correspondent' in the minute to the P.M. I said I didn't want it to get back to Maisky. He said he couldn't answer for the P.M. I think the risk is justified. Useless for Maisky to talk to me if I take no action.[22]

It can be imagined what Churchill would have said if he had known that the Soviet Ambassador had accused the Royal Navy of cowardice in front of the Editor of *The Times,* and it is piquant to see the latter, properly anxious to protect the paper's sources and its carefully cultivated relations with 13 Kensington Palace Gardens, reassuring himself with the excuse a reporter makes to himself in similar circumstances: 'I would not have been told this if it was not for use.'

At the end of July the familiar figure of Ned Grigg (who had first introduced B-W to *The Round Table* and *The Times)* appeared in the office, advocating a revolt in the Cabinet to be led by Cripps. He had, he said, been talking to Waldorf Astor and others. He wanted to know whether *The Times* would support Cripps in a demand for a higher professional directorate advising the Cabinet on the conduct of the war; for a small War Cabinet without administrative responsibilities and in full charge; and for Churchill to hand over the Ministry of Defence to another man.

I couldn't have that [B-W writes]. It is not for Grigg or anyone else to pledge *The Times.* Moreover, as I told him, it is useless for Cripps to act alone. He would fail and be compromised and do more harm than good. Three or four members of the War Cabinet must act together. Nor is it sound to ask any Prime Minister to give up the Ministry of Defence or, even if the office is abolished, its functions. Asquith couldn't in 1916.[23]

The idea of a plot of this kind seems to have worried the Editor, who foresaw bad effects in Germany and the United States if there were a political sensation. On the other hand his old chief Garvin, now seventy-four and at last departed from the *Observer,* agreed with him when they lunched together in August that there must be a second front somewhere; for 'the world's future was now being gambled on the resistance of Russia, virtually unaided thanks to our unpreparedness.' 'Garve' was disillusioned with Winston, although not despairing:

Says he is already writing the history of this war. Large drafts already dictated. All his actions (as he has told the House of Commons) covered in writing, every contingency of criticism provided for. . . . No spiritual lead to nation from Winston, great as his qualities are.[24]

Some ten of the Prime Minister's colleagues shared the view of the malcontents. But Halifax maintained that colleagues did not submit tamely to the Prime Minister's view in Cabinet; 'when they are more or less in agreement with him and the hour is late they may suffer a monologue unresisting. Otherwise, they speak up'. However, Halifax agreed strongly that the country lacked the spiritual leadership which Churchill could not give it, and said he had been talking the problem over with the Archbishop of Canterbury.*

In September a visit to Cripps revealed a very unhappy man.

He is more and more left out. No talk with Winston lately. Even the business of the House, of which Cripps is the Leader, is settled between the P.M. and the Whips. Cripps has sent in a memorandum of his views on the conduct of the war and has had a negative reply. Feels he cannot go on.[25]

B-W urged that it would be futile and suicidal to resign except on a definite issue, but Cripps pointed out that he could not decently resign if catastrophe came. Churchill probably felt that a Minister who had now no party support, and therefore no political power, could be unshipped.

The Cripps affair soon came to a head and B-W went along to Gwyder House on 1 October to see him. The diary narrates the following:

At 2 a.m. this morning Cripps was asked to go round and see the P.M., was got out of his bed in fact. They had a firm and friendly talk. Cripps said he could not go on as member of a War Cabinet not fully consulted by the P.M. — they take the responsibility but not the decisions — or as Leader of the House without the full knowledge necessary for the job. Prime Minister said he could only run the war in his own way. So they parted. I told Cripps my bet was that he would get some kind of an offer from Winston.

So he did – and on the following day B-W again called.

---

*This touch of sanctimoniousness has provoked from a former colleague the remark: 'This gave me a good laugh. Imagine the people in the pubs, who used to hang on every work of Churchill's when he broadcast and waited for him to say 'Naazi', being spiritually wooed by Halifax and the Archbishop!'

He was again summoned to 10 Downing Street, 12.45 a.m. this morning. Fortunately he hadn't gone to bed. Was shown into an empty drawing room! Attlee and Anthony came in looking rather sheepish. Begged him to consider effect of his resignation abroad and on the army. Asked whether he would not consider a mission to the U.S. to organize British activities over there: alternatively whether he would dissociate himself from the War Cabinet and take on Ministry of Aircraft Production (said to be in a mess), as a technical non-political job.

12 noon to-day Cripps summoned to see Winston. Very friendly talk. Winston said he now saw it was a genuine personal difficulty and not the desire for a political coup which actuated Cripps. 'You are an honest man. If you had been Ll.G. you would have resigned on the issue of a second front.' Told him he thought the organization of the Government for war was, from Cripps's point of view, a bad issue for resignation.[26]

B-W then went off to lunch promising to reflect on what Cripps should do. Walking back from the Travellers along the Embankment, as was his habit, he ruminated. The results, as set out in the diary, are an interesting example of his methods of thinking, when asked occasionally to give advice to politicians:

If the true reason for his leaving the War Cabinet is to be disclosed (as it must be) even in a guarded form, the fat will be in the fire anyway. The blow to the Government will not be materially less because he takes M.A.P. [Ministry of Aircraft Production]. On the other hand he cannot now take office merely as a technical minister dissociated from Government policy. Suppose trouble at M.A.P., demands by Cripps which War Cabinet would not grant, and another resignation. Cripps would be fatally compromised. In fact, under these conditions he would be a prisoner at M.A.P., his stock would fall to zero, and the country's political reserves would be the poorer. Better a straightforward resignation.

The Editor sounds here and there as if he were thinking of Cripps as a potential leader, to be held in reserve, either in war or after. He continues:

He cannot withhold resignation: Winston's practice makes it impossible for him to continue; and his colleagues feel much the same even if they aren't ready to take the same action. If, however, resignation at this particular moment might have untoward military results, a bad effect on the troops, at a time when large military operations may be in prospect, then he can if he thinks proper, on the secret information which he possesses, hand it in post-dated by a month or so and carry on for the present. He alone can judge, with his knowledge of plans, of the importance of that.[27]

The end of the Cripps affair came on 20 November:

Winston has profited by his victories (El Alamein and the landings in North Africa) to revive the issue raised by Cripps in the October correspondence. Very friendly, of course, but it comes to this: that Cripps must either leave the War Cabinet and take the Ministry of Aircraft Production, or resign.[28]

In the event Cripps sent in his letter of resignation, in terms said to be stiff, and the diary records that the 'immediate result was several meetings of the War Cabinet and the circulation to its members of confidential military documents such as had not reached them before!'

Some consolation was found by the Editor at the time in discussing education policy with the young Tory R. A. Butler, who was planning big changes ahead, though doubtful of the backing he would require from his Party. 'This will be the great test of his character and career,' the diary notes on 21 October. 'He will be sunk if he procrastinates.' There should be interim legislation by next spring (on improved technical education and continuation schools and eventual raising of school-leaving age) and a big consolidating statute (which was to be the 1944 Act) could come later. B-W was also arranging with Beveridge over dinner to write three articles on his 'social security report', now nearly ready, and calling on Wilson Jameson, Chief Medical Officer at the Ministry, to talk about future public health policy.

At this nadir of our war fortunes and reputation there is something both heroic and unconvincing about his determination to plan the peace. Perhaps B-W did not realize how difficult it was for a man dealing with Roosevelt and Stalin, with commanders in the field, with the details of planning and fighting, to find time – let alone interest – for such matters. Very well, he would have said, that is the Prime Minister's job; and if he cannot do this as well as fighting the war then he should let someone else be war leader or someone else be Prime Minister. If the view looked doctrinaire in 1942, it proved right in 1945.

Even when a decisive victory came to relieve the general despondency, the diary (like Alanbrooke's notebooks, a private blowing off of steam) remained critical, even peevish, even though the paper shared in the nation's elation. Shortly after ten on 4 November came the news, 'Rommel's armies in full retreat.' The printers set the story at record speed. 'All things are now possible,' was the diary note of the day. But Churchill's order to ring church bells the next Sunday was not liked; the Editor's Puritan streak was affronted.

It is a stunt and this mistakes public feeling, and is a sign of the cheap, meretricious streak in the great man.[29]

Characteristically, with the North African landings achieved and the smell of victory in the air – although the tide did not really turn decisively until six months later – B-W produced a leader, meditated for some days, exhorting the Government to have a home front policy. It appeared on the day of publication of the Beveridge Report (1 December) and he noted that his colleagues were 'most congratulatory'. It is one of the rare occasions that a chink appears in the armour of his modesty.

In the brief epitaph recorded on the last page of each volume of the diary, he said of this first full year of editing:

What a year this is to have lived through. Only now are we beginning to take it all in.... Now we have to force this war to a victorious end. At the same time we must rouse ourselves and our imaginations to build a saner world at home and internationally.[30]

The New Year, 1943, produced not only another invitation to lunch with Churchill (29 March) but also, and before that, the statement of policy for which *The Times* had worked so hard. A friendly leading article of 16 March brought thanks from the Prime Minister delivered through the Chief Whip, James Stuart, whom B-W met at lunch with the Andersons. The Prime Minister, said Stuart, asked for more help from *The Times* and he was asked in reply whether any attention had been paid to its request for a lead on domestic policy. Yes, said Stuart, Churchill had the matter in mind – as was to be proved by a broadcast given the following weekend, forty-five minutes long and nearly all on domestic policy. As the advance text came in by driblets late on Sunday afternoon Carr began to write, leaving the Editor free to savour an occasion which had an element of triumph for the office.

His central idea is a four-year plan. There is much to be said for it. Contention will turn on the timing of its execution, which he seems to relegate until after the war. Still, the broadcast is a considerable step, advocated in a tone of real conviction. After hearing it I warmed up Carr's leader a degree or two.[31]

There followed a friendly gesture which Churchill must have appreciated. At the suggestion of Mason, the political correspondent, the broadcast was reprinted and copies were sent to the Prime Minister. 'Nevertheless, we must continue independent and critical,' B-W noted in his diary, 'but not hostile.'

The occasion on 29 March at No. 10 was more of a meeting of minds than the previous one. The Prime Minister looked back on great military successes: and that very day there had come news of the fall of the Mareth line. This time they were tête-à-tête for ninety minutes in the basement room looking on the garden. The host showed no sign of his recent illness: 'pinky, fresh in colour, hardly a wrinkle, voice firm, all his usual animation and emphasis'.

The main purpose, certainly, was to encourage aid and understanding from *The Times* and the invitation itself was a recognition of the truth, plain enough from recent leaders, that our campaign for a full, forward coalition policy bore no hostility to him personally. On the contrary he told me he had been 'much touched' by several references to him lately, including one which he had read while in Algiers. But, he said, 'you can always turn the flank' and he hoped I should not go in 'for anything viewy' — especially in finance, I gathered. . . . 'Remember,' he said, 'that there are a great many Tories in the country.' I replied that anything he said would 'go'.

One remark must have given special professional pleasure to the independent-minded Editor. Of the daily newspapers he read, said the Prime Minister, *The Times* came last but one. The last was always the *Daily Telegraph* 'because I know that will be all right'. The diary continues:

I said the business of *The Times* was to see things on their merits and that we had no axe to grind. 'I have no axe to grind either,' he said (to which I cordially agreed). 'I shall come out of this war an old man. I shall be 70. I have nothing more to ask for.' He would stand on his broadcast and the Tory party would fight on that.

When he turned to reconstruction he would give his whole mind to it and admirably he would do it. (This didn't sound like resignation.) I told him I was not and never had been a Socialist. I agreed with Oliver Lyttelton, in an early broadcast, that we needed 'all the private and all the public enterprise we could get'.

'I well remember that,' said the Prime Minister. 'I passed that broadcast beforehand. I remember inflicting a reading of it on the War Cabinet.'

B-W mentioned that the omission in his broadcast of China as one of the four great powers to organize peace had caused trouble in the United States.

Winston knew quite well he had been naughty (that is the word) about this. 'But China can have no part in the future of Europe! I cannot bring myself to talk rot.'

In general he was affectionately cynical and realistic about our Russian and American allies. Strongly in favour of full cooperation with Russia. 'I have wooed Joe Stalin as a man might woo a maid.' But he also favoured confederations of smaller states: 'I do not want to be left alone in Europe with the Bear.'[32]

Well pleased with his visit B-W noted the same evening:

A glass of sherry followed by two or three glasses of white wine and a couple of brandies do not conduce to my efficiency in the afternoon but make no difference to his.*

The way that the paper's reconstruction policy, in all its economic aspects, was arrived at is examined in the next chapters; but this is perhaps the place to refer to one criticism of it that was being made – accurately, as events were to prove. B-W mentions Keynes as inquiring at a lunch about the authorship of two economic articles which, he said, had shocked some people by their optimism; they were, B-W told him, by Nicholas Kaldor, who was to become twenty years later economic adviser to Mr Harold Wilson. Then he quotes an argument at dinner with Hubert Henderson, an eminent Oxford economist then

---

*How different were these feasts of talk from later meetings with Attlee; although the more B-W saw of the Labour Prime Minister the better he liked him:

'But not for nothing is he called "Clam" Attlee. I could get nothing out of him. He would not talk. If ever I failed to keep the conversation going, silence followed. . . . Yet there was one sparkle. I was saying that the Jews were the last people in the world who ought to resort to force; they were playing a card out of the wrong suit. 'Yes,' he said *instanter*, 'clubs instead of diamonds.'

working in the Treasury (and one of the few critics of Churchill's return to the gold standard twenty years earlier), who complained that the paper was encouraging in the public too great expectations. 'They say, in effect, that *The Times* is educating the public against a deflation after the war when inflation is more likely to be our trouble.'*

During June 1943 B-W had his first meeting with the new Tory Reform group, which invited him to dinner at the Connaught Hotel. Quintin Hogg and Hugh Molson are mentioned as the prime movers and others present were Hinchingbrooke, Peter Thorneycroft, and Alfred Beit. This group, he notes, came into existence to 'ginger up the Government over the Beveridge Report and supports the general line of *The Times*'. 'We ought to have a good deal in common,' comments the diary, 'it was refreshing to meet them.'

With that tireless appetite for ideas and causes which drove B-W on at this period, he was also interesting himself in detailed discussion of the future of the voluntary hospitals in a reformed health service. He invited Will Goodenough, Chairman of Barclays Bank, to dinner at his club for that purpose.

He seems to be fairly happy about them. Goodenough is very mature, solid and Conservative, much trusted, as he has been since early years. Trustee for all sorts of things. Suspicious of *The Times*, yet says himself that what we shall need after the war is a Left policy put through by the Right, from which I should not dissent.[33]

Other men of the City and industry were less sympathetic. Indeed, at the end of July he was told by the management of three industrialists who had ceased to give their company meetings to the paper on the ground that it was unsympathetic to private enterprise and had supported the Beveridge Plan. 'Some of these industrialists,' he commented, 'have little idea of what we are trying to do for a peaceful future in industry when the war ends, without which the fortunes of this island may be in grave jeopardy.' But the diary also reveals how argument with someone he respected – he had been talking of the future with Bob Brand – always had an effect. He mentions giving dinner

---

*B-W records without comment the remark made to him by the Duke of Devonshire as they parted at a dinner-party given by the Masseys. 'I have still to call your paper publicly the journal of the London School of Economics.' To which David Bowes-Lyon, himself director of the paper, added: 'The *New York Times* calls it the final edition of the *Daily Worker*.'

to his Deputy Editor, Casey, and giving him a 'general notion of the course we should steer at the moment – no sheering off from the general demand for reconstruction and reform, but no abstractions: stick to concrete and practical studies'. This remark is the essential B-W: enthusiastic for ideas but attentive to practical difficulties.

The summer then passes with no references of importance to the Editor's political or social objectives until late September, when he has a long talk at the Home Office with Herbert Morrison, the Labour Home Secretary and a member of the War Cabinet. For the first time the prospects of the coalition surviving under Churchill in peace – B-W wanted it to continue for six months after the end of hostilities – are surveyed. Morrison seemed to agree:

Wants continuance of coalition for one Parliament to get things done. Labour Party is apt to be a suicide club but if it takes the suicidal line he will go with it. Discussed the dilemma of holding an election without breaking up the coalition—a coupon election being barred. He thinks there might be a coalition programme with freedom to the parties concerned to contend that it should be reduced or exceeded according to the point of view. Pretty difficult. Morrison has much good sense and is an extremely able tactician.[34]

Brendan Bracken, shortly afterwards, touched on the same theme at lunch. Just returned from a visit to the United States, he was worried over the way in which 'as the war had improved the Right had begun to open its mouth again'. He wanted the coalition preserved and thought that B-W's suggestion of making Woolton a 'super-Minister of Reconstruction' might be adopted. Sure enough, on 11 November the news came that Woolton was to be in charge of reconstruction with a seat in the War Cabinet. Bracken rang up the Editor to tease him about Woolton's appointment: '*The Times* governing the country as usual.' 'I am delighted it has come off,' says B-W.

Soon afterwards he dined at Whitehall Court with Woolton who outlined a plan for meeting the recommendations of the Uthwatt Report: 'to freeze the use of land for five years, vary it only under licence, the State to take 80 per cent of betterment and to purchase development areas'. Then they discussed transport, employment, the future of industry and agriculture and the age and limited vision of some industrial and

207

financial leaders. 'Woolton's approach,' B-W noted with approval, 'is idealism tempered with business experience. He knows he is in a strong position with a great power of resignation.'[35]

There followed a long talk on 11 December with Beveridge, who said that the best instrument for carrying out his policies would be a Conservative Government with full responsibility and a fully established opposition. B-W wanted to ignore the parties 'and go for the programme as the test: for a coalition without action is dead'. Beveridge, however, thought that Churchill would show no interest in reconstruction. B-W argued that he must do so, once it was in the front place – and he did not see him resigning unless his health deteriorated.

The Times, though it grudged the Prime Minister no praise when the day of victory came, was critical – as might be expected – of his conduct of the general election of 1945. Barrington-Ward records a talk about him in July of that year with the Chairman of the Chiefs of Staff, Alan Brooke. They agreed that 'W. has let us all down by the cheap tone which he has given to this election and presented an unworthy picture of us to foreign countries'.[36] Three days later he worked all the morning on a leader about the choice facing the country.

How can I throw my hat up for Winston in his present temper or encourage people to vote for his Govt without the assurance that they are going to do as well as the late coalition or better, in fulfilment of its policy and pledges? How, again, encourage them to support ineffectual liberalism or to give Labour a victory which it would use for widespread nationalization? ... I wish some kind of resumed coalition Govt were still possible—best of all for the country for the next two or three years. ...[37]

When he met the defeated Churchill at lunch a month later their hostess, Ava Anderson, boldly put them next to one another. B-W wondered for a moment what their relations were to be. But he was greeted in friendly fashion.*

He is still astonished and mystified by the result of the election. He cannot make it compatible with the tremendous personal welcome given him at the election-time throughout the country. Even

*When Churchill boasted to the table that he had never allowed the social programme to distract attention from the war effort – indeed, that he disapproved of all social legislation in war time, B-W 'reminded him gently of his 1943 broadcast'.

The new Editor, aged fifty.

In the chair preparing to write a leader, freshly sharpened pencil to hand – and posed for *The Times* film.

now crowds hail him in the streets, people run up and kiss his hand and so on. ... He asked me was I surprised at the result. I confessed I was completely surprised. He offered no explanation himself except to say ironically that it might have been different 'If I had done my broadcasts differently and if we had had a little more of your support'.*[38]

No record of the relations between Churchill and Printing House Square over fifty years – and what a book that would make – should omit one mysterious, possibly significant incident. The Chairman told his Editor one day in 1946, guardedly and in confidence, that 'Winston had written him a letter of complaint' about the paper. He did not say when or in what terms: it might therefore have been from the wartime Prime Minister or from the peacetime Conservative leader. Whatever it was, the Editor gathered that Astor, with characteristic loyalty, had 'sent a sturdy reply'. If the letter's purpose was to encourage the Chairman, in his frequent informal talks with B-W, to ask a question or two about criticisms of Churchill, there could be no objection. But if it was a wartime Prime Minister trying to frighten a newspaper critic through his proprietor with warnings about the national interest, that would be objectionable and sinister.

The last recorded meeting of B-W and Churchill was in December 1946:

To 28 Hyde Park Gardens for lunch with Winston. He was looking well and young, nothing like 72. Countenance unwrinkled as ever, and free, too, of the studio portrait bulldog look. Began gloomily in matter though not in manner. Empire breaking up. India would go to Soviet Russia, Burma, Ceylon and Malaya would follow. He would not live to see it and did not wish to. We should be left under protection of the U.S.A. and he did not object to that. 'After all, I am half American.' I said our policy was implicit in all our undertakings from Queen Victoria's celebrated declaration at the supercession of the East India Co. onwards. The Government seemed to me to have given nothing improperly away and their statement last week was unexceptionable.

He said he did not quarrel with it; indeed, we differed with amenity throughout, aided by an excellent bottle of Pol Roget with port, brandy and cigar to follow. And we found a certain amount

---

*Lunching with Halifax in January 1947 B-W noted with pleasure that his host 'agrees that we were *not* all wrong before the war about W.'s judgement – no sense of politics. The war his supreme opportunity'.[39]

H

to agree about. The folly of the U.N. for example in perpetuating Franco by harrying him from outside. Also the defects of the rail and road nationalization Bill. When I rehearsed some of my criticism of it he said like a flash 'Will you say so?' I pointed out that we had said so. He said he was not necessarily against the nationalization of railways. Nor was *The Times,* I told him, though I was not a Socialist nor were those who worked with me.

He evidently took note of that. I went on to put to him my formula for the conduct of *The Times* which I put to Fred Woolton last week. He did not challenge it.* He then paid a great tribute to the news in *The Times,* admirable in its balance, proportion and accuracy. 'But I never read the leaders.' (Astonishing confession!) A little later I said to him, 'You won't have read the leader in *The Times* this morning on India.' 'Well, as a matter of fact I did read that one. You were kinder to me than I had expected.'

He was interesting on the atomic bomb. Ought it to have been dropped on a city? I asked. Ought it not to have had its powers demonstrated by being dropped first in some uninhabited or sparsely inhabited area? Evidently he now thought that would have been the better course. But it was wisdom after the event, he thought. We had to think of the lives of our men then at stake and of the tremendous importance of finishing it all off as soon as possible. . . .

Most cordial parting. Asked me to look in again. Told him we were opening up a little house between Dover and Deal.† 'You will be within the jurisdiction of the Warden of the Cinque Ports.' I assured him that that had already occurred to me.[41]

To anyone who remembers the veneration – a proper and professional veneration – with which the Editor spoke of *The Times* leaders, the exchange in which he traps the great man into admitting that he does, after all, sometimes read one of them – having said that he never did – is sheer delight.

Doubtless, if the question of serializing Churchill's memoirs had been raised at this lunch as B-W had intended, he would have been told that all was already settled with the proprietor and editor-in-chief of the *Daily Telegraph,* Lord Camrose, a close personal friend. He had been visiting the United States

---

*At dinner at Grillion's Woolton had said that the Conservatives in opposition were making no headway yet against the Government and gave the impression that he would be glad when 'Winston decides to pack up'. B-W explained to him that, 'while it is the duty of the Opposition to oppose, it is the duty of *The Times* to get the best it can out of the Government of the day. The King's Government has to be carried on.'[40]

†His cousin Jack Ward's house at St Margaret's Bay.

as Churchill's agent, and the price that B-W heard mentioned was £250,000, which was to go into a trust for the grand-children. It became clear that negotiations with Camrose had begun before Churchill had even started writing and that no chance for *The Times* was ever open. This was a portent to the Editor of the strong and persistent challenge to his paper's position that the *Daily Telegraph* was preparing to make in the post-war years, and which gathered momentum from the moment that improved newsprint supplies made possible bigger newspapers with more varied contents. Perhaps, too, he was being made to pay for 'turning my flank' – as Churchill called it – once or twice too often.

19

New Deal - New Men -
Carr Moves In

In the history of B-W's editorship the name E. H. Carr and the word 'reconstruction' are inseparable. The office might have conceived, but it would not have brought to birth and reared, a post-war policy for home and abroad without the thinking and writing of the Professor and of those he recruited for the paper. The interest aroused by his books on international relations and his contacts at the Ministry of Information made him a useful spotter of young talent, at a time when the war had taken so many away from London. Men like Dennis Routh, Donald Tyerman, David Owen, François Lafitte, Geoffrey Wilson, came to the Editor's notice, two of them to stay, the others to become eminent civil servants. *The Times* suddenly felt itself exposed to new influences from outside the office, from people with ambitions to achieve social change through the Press and who had a radical, sociological way of looking at events and issues.

Stanley Morison used to say, in his oracular manner, that every editor needed a mentor, because there was never time for him to do his own fundamental thinking; Dawson had had Milner, now B-W had Carr – as well, one suspects, as Morison himself. It is apparent, however, from surviving memoranda that the Editor believed he had succeeded in keeping Carr to the central political position he desired for the paper, urging on him a rather more persuasive style, a little less ruthlessness, a not-so-bold habit of generalization. Certainly the writing, both in books and articles, had a dogmatic, sweeping quality which achieved a deceptive simplicity and always provoked discussion, often indignant disagreement. To his critics of the right and centre Carr seemed always to be on the side of the big battalions, convinced that the tide of history was running with them, and that Britain, with its easygoing ways and inefficient

institutions, must learn not to row against it. Moreover, he felt
and showed impatience with those who, for lack of reading, or
imagination or courage, would not look at their time in his
fashion. As a former Foreign Office man of twenty years'
experience, with the time and opportunity to express long
views, he refused to be content with the hand to mouth, amateur
reflections of the daily newspaper. He was in Dawson's phrase,
'viewy'.*

Such articles – Garvin-like in their scope and Barnes-like in
their trenchancy – had not been seen in *The Times* for a long
while. Some readers felt that this kind of thinking and writing
would be better left to Whitehall or to the periodicals; but
when the British were fighting for their lives, it seemed more
acceptable than in normal times. The drowning man is said to
have long flash-backs. So the besieged ruling class addressed by
The Times was in a mood to listen – so long as the siege lasted
– to someone who would look backwards and forwards from
present disasters and offer prescriptions for the future. To put
the situation at its crudest: bombing would force the rebuild-
ing of slums; the U-boat war imposed efficiency in agriculture
and the working out of a minimum diet; evacuation of children
had shown the shortcomings of schools and parents; and, once
the German-Soviet truce had collapsed in the summer of 1941,
all those voices which had since 1939 stopped praising Soviet
methods of social and economic planning were heard again.

There was no party-political motivation in his writing, whatever Tory readers may have thought. Carr was no Communist.
His main purpose was to be 'anti-Utopian', to puncture the
kind of illusions (collective security was one) which had misled
the British in the thirties. Huge changes were going on outside
these islands; the scale of world politics was being transformed.
The facts about all this were being reported week by week in
the newspapers – but there was no strategy to cope with them,
no theory to give them coherence. At home, too, the newspapers
had not found room for the detailed and expert thinking on
the problems of industry and of social service which all kinds
of unofficial bodies had been producing for the last seven years.

*In a letter to Liddell Hart Dawson once wrote: 'My view of leaders is that
they should as far as possible be intelligent explanatory comment on the news in
the day's paper. Of course, it is necessary sometimes to launch them out of the
blue, and they may in themselves provide the news, but broadly speaking this is
true.'[1]

At the fringe of politics – regardless of past differences – civil servants, businessmen and academics had been conspiring during their leisure hours in groups like Political and Economic Planning to overhaul everything: national finance, local government, secondary education, foreign trade, population statistics, basic industries, depressed areas and so on. Carr was in touch with such bodies, much of what he wrote publicly was being written by many others privately.

Another main thread in the pattern of *The Times* and its new brains trust can be traced to the Ministry of Information, where Carr had been Director of Foreign Publicity. There, for the first two years of the war, a large number of gifted intellectual workers, eminent in home and foreign specialities, found themselves with too little to do, frustrated by the jealousy of the Foreign Office and the security-mania of the Services. They were employed to explain to the world why the British Commonwealth was fighting, what it planned to do with victory. But the Cabinet were too busy conducting the fighting to give thought to war aims, even though propaganda could not live for ever on Dunkirk, the Battle of Britain and the blitz. Sooner or later the nations which were to be liberated from Germans and Japanese would have to be told of Britain's plans for the future.

Also influential in the office, at first through the Editor himself and later through the *Times Educational Supplement*, was R. A. Butler, then thirty-eight years old and a Parliamentary Under-Secretary at the Foreign Office. In February 1940 B-W had a long lunch at the House with him, over which they discussed not only the war but also 'the new social revolution which is making its way and how to anticipate and meet it'. Butler said he had a committee working on future home policy, which was considered fairly urgent. For, incredible though it may seem, the Prime Minister believed – and so did Churchill at that time – that this would be a short war 'determined by ore and oil'.[2] Later B-W received drafts of ideas from Butler, of whom he thought highly: 'he should be of great use in politics hereafter if he also has enough fire in his belly'.[3]

Within a week of one another two diary entries, made six weeks after Dunkirk and six weeks before the Battle of Britain, show the forward-looking mood which we have already noticed in his dealings with Churchill.

I lunched with J. H. Oldham at the Athenaeum. He has responded with much conviction to the suggestions in *The Times* that we are fighting for a new Europe and not the old, and that the time has come broadly to define it. Question: who should be working it out? ... It is very necessary both as a shield for our own spirit in these days and as a spear against the enemy's—and also to get *our* fifth column going in the German-occupied territories.[4]

Then he talks with Carr (not yet on the staff) about a leader called 'Planning for Peace and War'.

The Times, almost alone in the Press and certainly first, is trying to get the right 'answer to Hitler' in a statement on our plans for war and peace to show that we are fighting for a new Europe not the old—a new Britain and not the old. I wholly agree with Carr: planned consumption, abolition of unemployment and poverty, drastic educational reform, family allowances, economic organiza-tion of the Continent, etc., but all this needs the right presentation.[5]

Then there was the state of home morale, which worried Whitehall more than was ever admitted then or later. Mass observation and other studies of public opinion seemed to show that enthusiasm and determination could be sustained only with clear-cut hopes for the future. Older hands in all parties remembered – B-W very clearly – how reconstruction pledges had been found necessary in Lloyd George's time, but had not been supported in wartime with proper planning. Often heard was the phrase 'it's no use winning the war if you lose the peace'. The Government's hesitations were compared by Carr and his circle with the ability of non-democratic regimes, whether of the left or the right, to decide quickly and act firmly. They seemed to be efficient in the way that American large-scale production was efficient; and the future lay with countries which, without losing their essential freedom, would limit it for the sake of efficiency and purposeful social policy. B-W himself was never a Socialist and never conceded any of the case for dictatorship; but it is hardly necessary to say that for some readers of *The Times* this was just 'Socialism'.

On New Year's Day 1941 Carr made his debut as a full member of the staff, although he had written a number of leaders from outside in previous months. B-W noted that this was 'the best possible beginning of the New Year'. At last he had, if not a future deputy editor, a number two who could write.

215

With W. F. Casey, an older hand than B-W himself (he joined in May 1913), to get the paper out and Carr to do the main thinking and writing, he felt he could face now the prospect without Dawson. At first all went well and it was noted that Carr was 'very willing to listen to counsel on how to put advanced views in such a way that they will seem to our constituency the most normal and inevitable truths'. But not unexpectedly the newcomer and the 'old guard' of the office did not always hit it off well.* He had come in very close to the top; he was not a journalist; he did not suffer fools gladly; and his wide-ranging leaders suggested to those who wrote on narrower themes an appetite for *Lebensraum*.

Only six weeks had passed before he was complaining of the Editor's attitude to his work; and B-W's entry on the matter makes a rare criticism of Dawson:

He [Carr] complains of G.D.'s 'insincerity', by which he means the rather transparent conventions that G.D. employs to stave off discussion of political or social issues. He thinks that there has been a 'change of climate' with respect to his reconstruction articles. G.D. fobs them off or doesn't use them when written. (Yet 10,000 copies have been sold of the reprint of Carr's leaders and the paper has reached its circulation 'ceiling'). He is not prepared to go on like this.... Though I know there is great truth in all this, I begged him to remember the extent of his achievement with us up to date, to recognize that reconstruction leaders (which have already put *The Times* on the map) must be spaced out, and above all to exercise patience.

I am much troubled and feel strongly the force of Carr's complaint. G.D. is not, I think, in real sympathy with the kind of article that Carr has been writing on home affairs, which has brought us so much credit. He does not seem to be aware that Carr is the ablest and best qualified man who has been near the paper for years. I have worked and worked to get him in, and now that he is there, I am ready to take on (with his help and Casey's) tomorrow. I cannot stand by tamely and see him depart. I can't have G.D. queering my pitch for lack of a little imagination and perception.[6]

Carr, looking back nearly thirty years, has compared Dawson

---

*Notable among them was Colin Coote, DSO a Balliol contemporary of Barrington-Ward's who had been with *The Times* since 1926 and was at this time senior leader-writer. From 1917–22 he had been a Coalition Liberal M.P. He was to be Managing Editor of the *Daily Telegraph* from 1950–64.

at this time to A. J. Balfour: 'If he was sceptical of change, he was equally sceptical of resistance to change. Much as he enjoyed being at the centre of things and exercising influence, there was no cause, positive or negative, which he wished to promote.' He was quite ready to pat the newcomer on the head 'as the bright new boy'. Carr tells an illuminating story of the origins of a leader by him which attracted much attention.

When Lothian was on leave from Washington early in 1941 he visited G.D. Either by chance, or summoned, I came into the room. Lothian, whom I knew fairly well, was explaining that the Americans now regarded unemployment, next to war, as the great social evil, and that we should hammer on that if we wanted to convince them of our sincerity. During the conversation G.D. turned to me, more or less as an aside, and said: 'You might like to write something about this.' That was the sole origin of 'Two Scourges', my first leader as a member of the staff of *The Times* that made a hit outside, being quoted with warm approval in the House of Commons.[7]

It is easy to imagine B-W's anxiety; if Carr looked like not staying long, then without some other reinforcement he could not take over the editorship. Dawson – in any case reluctant to go – would have a conclusive reason for staying. But B-W makes too little allowance for Dawson's view, which some journalists and some readers shared, that a newspaper is not the place for 'essays' and that to campaign on post-war prospects at a time when no honest man could say how the war was going to be won would be both irrelevant and boring.

Some people in Downing Street certainly thought this way. But there was some consolation in the evidence that readers liked the paper's new line. His brother Lance, the surgeon, brought to lunch at the Windham one day a colleague in charge of the buildings at the Great Ormond Street Hospital for Children. This man told him he had read Carr's articles aloud at night to his twenty-eight fire-watchers, all working-class people. All had felt in one form or another the injustices of the social order, but felt that if *The Times* agreed that many things were wrong then they would be put right. This would surely bring a sparkle to B-W's eyes: the picture of men and women watching the roofs above the sleeping children, facing all the risks of bombing, while listening to leaders read from his newspaper.

However the split in the office would not heal. He put into the paper one evening with 'timely modifications' a leader by Carr which Dawson had held up. The next day there was the following puzzled exchange:

G.D. returned after the afternoon conference. He said to me 'I see you got Carr's leader away' (as indeed I was determined to do)! *Self*: 'Yes, it was timely.' *G.D.* 'It was very good.' Odd man! As Bob Brand once said to me, it is impossible to discuss anything with Dawson because he always agrees with you! Later he asked Carr to write the leader on the reconstruction debate tomorrow. I observed that Carr was invaluable. He agreed. I added that Carr had no wish to 'plug' reconstruction in and out of season, only to maintain reasonably this interest which the paper had already shown in the subject.

The real trouble is that G.D.'s heart is not in it, and that, while he might admit its importance, he is not inclined by temperament to accept in advance or to prepare for (and so to control), still less to welcome, the upheaval which this war is now creating, and will create, or to see how a forward-looking social view will help the prosecution of the war by encouraging our own people, heartening the subjugated peoples of Europe and giving even the Germans some alternative to Nazism and a Nazi victory.[8]

He might have added that Dawson was visibly tired and in failing health.

Further interesting evidence of the impact of the radical policy of the paper came from George Pope, the assistant advertising manager, who said that some manufacturers were deeply interested in Carr's articles. Their author, however, still felt deeply unhappy and wrote to B-W that he saw no hope of doing what he wanted to do – 'improve the leaders, write constructive articles, based on a systematic policy' – under the present regime. However, in order not to force an issue which must deeply embarrass his sponsor, Carr said he would carry on until the end of June, and then resume the original arrangement under which he had come into the office two or three nights a week as a contributor without executive duties.

From this predicament both men were rescued by the Chairman, who had heard of it from the director Harold Hartley, whom B-W consulted, and probably also from Stanley Morison, who loved to take a hand in office politics and did not like Dawson.

Meanwhile, the campaign for reconstruction went on and

from Reith over lunch at the Athenaeum B-W heard the latest inside story from a strongly anti-Churchill witness:

The Uthwatt Committee has recommended and indeed assumed a central planning authority, vital to reconstruction, which cannot be left to take care of itself after the war. Resisted by Kingsley Wood, who thinks it will frighten the local authorities and is, in his turn, scared of them; by Ministry of Health and by Arthur Greenwood, both jealous for their powers and jurisdiction. Reith refuses compromise beyond a point, is backed by Anderson, and will resign if necessary. . . . The Machine really must be stripped and overhauled. Direction and drive from the top, that's what is wanted. Departments have lost sight of the war against the Nazis in their war with each other, and there are too many Ministers who have no national view at all.[9]

There was, of course, opposition to such views. The *Daily Telegraph* and the *Sunday Times* were both suspicious of thinking which seemed to be 'half way to Socialism', and there were plenty of critics in the Tory ranks. In July B-W dined with the 1922 Committee and was asked unexpectedly to 'say a few words'.

I took reconstruction, on which their party has set up committees under Rab Butler and on which chiefly the subsequent discussion centred. I had, incidentally, to make it clear that *The Times* was not a Conservative paper and that we regarded it as essential to be free to consider proposals on their merits.[10]

B-W was now moving steadily towards advocacy of permanent state intervention. If he did not believe the man in Whitehall to know best, yet he relished getting the expert to tell ignorant and selfish people what they ought to do, because the nation was in a state of siege in which people could not do just what they wanted to do. They were heady days and one suspects that Dawson, who had left the office for good on 1 October, may have felt some relief at parting with colleagues so full of ideas for improving the human condition by regulation and legislation. There had been a time in South Africa, thirty years before, under Alfred Milner when he might have been as eager as the next man to use the power of the Press for such ends. But he had experienced, with Northcliffe at his shoulder, the aspirations and disappointments of the First World War and by now was disillusioned. His successor, in contrast,

moved from idea to idea with elation. By the end of 1941 –
Japan having forced the Americans into the war – he was even
discussing with friends a joint Anglo-American (with China and
Russia) commission to investigate how to raise the world's
standard of living after the war.

Bob Brand, the Director of *The Times* who so often wrote to
Dawson and to B-W about policy matters, received in May of
that year a letter from an American banker friend, Thomas
Lamont, complaining that there was a barrage of suggestions
from London that the United Kingdom was going to be
socialized. He had noted two articles in *The Times* by Beveridge
which seemed to point to a 'regimented state'. 'I did not know
that Barrington-Ward had developed along that line,' wrote
Lamont, yet I never knew him well.' In contrast, Isidore Lubin,
Roosevelt's adviser, introduced on a visit to London by
Harold Hartley, said that the key to Anglo-American cooperation was a progressive policy in and for Britain. 'If we hang back
for fear of the isolationists,' B-W noted, 'we shall strengthen
isolationism.' Republicans and Democrats obviously saw the
future differently.

The new Editor, with his chief writer now firmly installed,
was finding time to drop in on ministers as Dawson used to do,
hearing their troubles and offering them advice, picking up in
the process excellent journalistic 'background' for commenting
on and anticipating political events. He now wrote seldom and
concentrated on the problems, difficult enough, of using to the
best advantage the few pages allowed to the wartime newspapers. If anyone in P.H.S. was in danger of forgetting that
'there was a war on', the state of newsprint supply was a
constant reminder. Since the spring of 1941 rationing of newsprint had been on a tonnage basis. Standard consumption for
each newspaper was fixed by reference to an agreed period in
1940 or the week ending 22 February 1941. This gave *The
Times* a hundred tons a week and allowed for a circulation of
182,000 copies of a ten-page paper against a peacetime average
of twenty. Later it suffered a twenty per cent cut which meant
a lower circulation and a reduction to eight pages twice a week,
an 'impossible' size for a paper of record, even with Parliament
meeting only twice or thrice a week.

There was also, in spite of the social round of lunch and
dinner that somehow maintained itself in the face of bombing

and rationing, time to think. At the weekend, up at Swines-head in Bedfordshire, he would ponder and comment on memoranda from Carr of a kind which had rarely passed between Dawson and him in the thirties. Some of these have survived with the annotations and show how the caution of the more cautious mind acted on the boldness of the quicker thinker. Much though he liked and respected B-W, and con-genial though they were in many ways, Carr found him slow to make up his mind, very obstinate about changing it, and inclined to 'preface any revelation of new thought with a platitude'.

Carr, great though his influence now was, often though he wrote, was not directing the Foreign Department in the way that had once been suggested. The staff attitudes that had made Dawson hesitate had the same effect on his successor, and Carr himself was interested only in finding a platform for ideas, not at all in securing a foothold for further advance as a pro-fessional journalist. He could not regard *The Times* with the reverence and sense of tradition that B-W and Morison brought to its service, 'as though it were a church'. Editing made no great appeal to him; but it is clear that the main strategic thinking on foreign policy was done by him, while colleagues like Iverach McDonald and Braham and Morrah concerned themselves with the day-to-day tactical treatment of the war and diplomatic and general news events.

A typical memorandum of January 1942 from Carr to B-W presented the following argument with some prescience:

Before the war British prestige suffered from protesting in advance against things which, when they happened, we tamely acquiesced in because we had neither the power nor the will to prevent them.

After the war Russian forces will probably march west at least as far as Berlin and dispose of Eastern Europe as they think fit. Is it conceivable that we shall have the power to interfere with them or that, even if we had the power, public opinion in this country (which, in large sections of it, shows signs of being almost frantically pro-Russian) would allow any Government to use it?

The end of the war will leave two great powers on the Continent, Rusia and Germany. We must not antagonize both simultaneously. They are natural antagonists so long as no third power tries to intervene in Eastern Europe. If we were to oppose Russian policy in Eastern Europe after the war, we should quickly reconstitute the German-Russian alliance.

221

We must give Russia a free hand in Eastern Europe if we wish to retain her as an ally against Germany.

'A free hand in Eastern Europe' for Russia: that was a portent of future trouble for *The Times* from exiled Poles, opponents of Tito, and friends of Masaryk. Remarkable, too, was the ignoring of the Americans. For Britain's dealings with Stalin Carr offered the following guidance: it should say to him:

We have all accepted the guiding principles of the Atlantic Charter, which provides for the maximum independence for all nations compatible with the overriding requirements of security and well-being. But the application of these must vary. Russia will interpret them in Eastern Europe and we will in other parts of the world. For our own part we shall not quarrel with her interpretation and application of them.*

This rejection of the moral and sentimental considerations which were to inflame British opinion over the Soviet investment of Eastern Europe made some people call the paper pro-Russian and cynically realist (one recalls Kurt Hahn's complaint ten years earlier that the Robin he had known had become a *Realpolitiker*). Yet basically all that Carr was doing was to puncture illusions – as he saw them – and reject an ideological foreign policy for Britain (just as B-W had rejected it before the war) on the grounds that she was not strong or rich enough to take the risk. She must not swim against the tide – or if she did it could only be in the company of the United States.

Another typical Carr memorandum, this time about home policy, ran as follows:

(i) Desire for monetary gain has ceased to work as the motive power of the economic system.
(ii) The profit system has ceased to provide full employment. Work is there to be done but it is not profitable to do it.

*Douglas Woodruff, formerly specialist in Empire affairs and writer of 'light leaders' on *The Times* (1926–38), who became Editor of the Catholic weekly journal *Tablet*, was one of the most vigorous critics of Carr's leaders. Writing about B-W to the author he said: 'What I particularly disliked was the way he let Carr write about "the new and vital forces in Central Europe", meaning in fact the small and detested Communist cliques who were installed in the wake of the Red Army, and have been kept under its shadow ever since.'[11]

(iii) The profit system is organized to benefit the producer and not the consumer. Restrictionist practices are the symptom.

(iv) Russia and Germany have not been inhibited from using new productive techniques by the wish to maintain the profit-earning capacity of capital already invested.

(v) Workers need some incentive other than money. Wage increases and bonuses have sometimes reduced output.

(vi) Coupons issued equally to all are a more important factor than money in regulating the distribution of the necessities of life.

(vii) The motto for post-war reconstruction is what F.D.R. said in his Inaugural Address of 1933: 'The measure of the restoration lies in the extent to which we apply social values more noble than monetary profit.'

Such ideas, familiar though they now are, would not have been considered in Dawson's day as possible leader themes for *The Times,* and were certainly not suitable for submission to Churchill.

The Social Round

To separate in the social life of B-W the cultivation of friends from the making of contacts is not easy. From the Editor's point of view, there are alway useful hints and sometimes valuable information to be picked up in the time devoted to the social round; and by others he is likely to be regarded as someone well-informed and therefore worth cultivating. One role leads naturally to the other; sources become friends and friends sources in certain situations. ... B-W was a gay and sociable person with a wide circle of friends outside the office, and he enjoyed good talk and the food and wine that went with it. The traffic of gossip and ideas in the West End clubs and what had been spared by war and taxation of London's social pageant are constantly referred to in the diary. Four days out of seven one might expect to run into him somewhere in that tiny and exclusive quarter of London which is bounded by St James's Street, Piccadilly, the Haymarket and Carlton House Terrace. His favourite clubs – the Windham in St James's Square, the Travellers and the Athenaeum in Pall Mall – were all within five minutes' walk of one another. Almost as much as Fleet Street, it was a professional *quartier* for those dealing with public affairs, who could walk to it from Westminster and Whitehall across the Horse Guards Parade or through St James's Park, up the Duke of York's steps and get from desk to table in fifteen minutes.

B-W was, like Geoffrey Dawson,* a keen hunter of news

*There is in B-W's files a good example of how devotedly and discreetly Dawson sought and communicated news for his paper. A hand-written note from Cliveden dated 7 August 1938 tells B-W for 'very confidential information and guidance', that Philip Lothian is going to succeed Lindsay as Ambassador in Washington. This, with war on the horizon, was an appointment of the greatest importance on which *The Times* would hope and try to get a scoop. Dawson's instructions are: 'The appointment will not be made until the end of the year, and

and views, in a London where, even after Hitler's war, information and press officers were fewer and less powerful in Whitehall than they were to become in the fifties. The Editor of
The Times (or his representative) could discuss with ministers
and civil servants without the reserve that might be shown to
reporters and special writers. Out of such official contacts friendships might grow; an example was James Grigg, the War Office
civil servant who became a minister. Likewise, as might be
expected, many of his friendships rooted in the past were
journalistically useful. Distinction at Westminster, Balliol and
the Union, his work with the General Staff in the last two years
of war, the connection with *The Round Table* and the *Observer*
made up formidable credentials for membership of the
'establishment' between the wars. He was to acquire by the
forties a prestige which opened all doors, even to tête-à-tête at
10 Downing Street. Both in his official and private circle were
influential, well-informed people in many walks of life – most
of them readers of his newspaper.

His interest extended far beyond politics: to literature,
music, painting and the theatre (in a middle-brow manner) and
sport of all kinds. Jelly d'Avanyi and Adela Fachiri were old
friends from musical parties. Adrian Boult's career as a conductor and his creation of the BBC Symphony Orchestra were
followed with keenest sympathy. The American impersonator
Ruth Draper and the actress Celia Johnson, who married Peter
Fleming, were good friends. Staying one weekend in Wiltshire
he spent an afternoon hearing the anecdotes of the jockey Cliff
Richards, and eighteen months before the Battle of Britain the
carefully guarded Hawker Hurricane fighter, which had been
flown from Edinburgh in forty-eight minutes ('actually forty-
three minutes,' says the diary, and at five hundred miles an
hour), was shown to him by its pilot, Squadron Leader Gillan.

Ambitious though he was within the sphere of *The Times,*
B-W was no social climber, and Mark, Simon and Caroline left
Adele little leisure. Snobbery is seldom a weakness of the
solidly rooted professional class. But they enoyed quality: a

it is very desirable (though I tell them pretty hopeless) that it should not leak
out till then, at any rate as definite. Lothian will be visiting Australia and New
Zealand for some weeks. I suggest therefore that if possible he should be mentioned
(if any revelation is necessary at all) as one of the people whose names are being
considered.'

house off Regent's Park, Eton for the boys (Westminster School, evacuated for wartime from London, could not then offer what B-W had known), the Ritz or Carlton Grill for special celebrations, a Hanover Square tailor, haircut by Mr Thomas in St James's,* but no expensive holidays abroad in winter and only the occasional shooting, at Hever, or in Scotland with Adrian Boult at Lagafater. With the children August spent at the seaside in lodgings in Pembrokeshire, still undiscovered by the motorist; or a week with Adele somewhere in Cornwall.

This time we had taken a chance on Aloe Cottage, Rock.... Turned out to be just what we had wanted: clean, good food and a sitting room to ourselves. Not dear—6½ guineas all in for both for a week.

Luxury was excluded on the salaries paid by *The Times,* despite the occasional bonus, and B-W was the kind of man whose savings go entirely into life insurance.†

Less and less, as the family of two boys and a girl left the nursery, did he and his wife go off on the kind of country-house weekend which was open to them. Nor until 1939 did they seriously consider a weekend cottage. The need to get the children out of London in the spring of 1940 (the fashionable idea of sending them to the United States or Canada was distasteful and barely considered) led B-W to rent for £60 p.a. a small house at Swineshead, in Bedfordshire. It was a converted inn, dating back to the sixteenth or seventeenth century, still called 'The Three Horseshoes'. Here he could spend weekends with the family, gardening, cycling, walking, reading and occasionally riding. From his friendly and regular contact with the farmers and villagers of this remote spot B-W had more

*B-W occasionally quotes the opinions of Mr Thomas, a veteran of the first war. During the abdication crisis he is reported as saying: 'Until a few days ago I would have died for King Edward VIII, now I'd die for Mr Baldwin.'

†When the Barrington-Wards moved into a larger house at the end of 1937 it was taken in the office to mean that he had the promise of the editorship, but this was not so. His own comment was: 'I have taken a considerable plunge with the new house. But we had to have a larger house to hold the children, we wanted Regent's Park and this house was cheap as they go... the place should be financially manageable until the time arrives to negotiate a new lease. When that time comes I shall either have a bigger post or I shall clear out, perhaps without loss.' The war obliged them to leave 19 Chester Terrace after less than two years residence.[1]

satisfaction than was to be found in the houses of the rich and the great.*

Swineshead reminded him of the happiest days of his youth in the Rectory and small farm at Duloe, of hunting with the North Cornwall on his horse Benjie and of the dog Saul, who had moved with him years ago into the Holywell digs. Arriving on a Friday night at Bedford Station with a stack of papers, he would try to clear his desk by Saturday lunchtime and then devote himself to the family. Long and strenuous walks; some pretty stiff tuition for the boys in plant-spotting and bird-watching; cycle rides to see village churches; hours of heavy gardening and log-sawing; reading in the evening to the children. His idea of rest was a change of work and plenty of exercise. He had given up golf, could not afford a hobby like collecting porcelain or prints, was bored by cards. The diary's account of helping a farmer neighbour with the war-time harvest is lyrical; his note of the local parson's sermon meticulous. Wartime weekends in Swineshead knit the growing family together, and it was sad that in the three years left between departing from there and his death they could find no house to call 'home'.

Escape though he could at weekends to the end of a telephone the need during the week to entertain and be entertained pressed hard. Until his house was bombed in 1940 he generally used the Windham Club, where the brothers were all members.†

This was 'the' club where many of the affairs of the paper were discussed and settled. Many young *Times* men were put through their paces at the Windham, accompanying B-W after lunch on his brisk walk back to Blackfriars through Whitehall

*A year after he married and in his earliest days back at Printing House Square, he had found time one weekend to go into retreat with Walter Monckton, at a house run by nuns in the Rochester Diocese under the aegis of the Society of the Divine Compassion. He was deeply impressed and refreshed and asked himself whether he should not live more spiritually. 'It cannot be without discipline, instruction and effort. Many of us have had a moral but not a spiritual training, and the former cannot rise to the true height of faith, certainty and consistency without the latter. The moral must live with the mystical and the mystical with the moral. But I am only in the beginnings.'[2]

†Henry Brooke, now Lord Brooke of Cumnor, who saw B-W regularly at the Windham, describes it as 'quiet rather than colourful, for people of wide interests, ranking with Brooks's and the Travellers. More quietly dressed than the Garrick, if you know what I mean. A good proportion of members living in the country . . . but no profession dominating. Probably a large percentage of the members had been at Oxford or Cambridge, but it was not a university club as such.'

and along the Embankment. Over lunch and dinner B-W would enjoy defining causes and plotting campaigns to 'get things done', looking over recruits, soothing down grievances, returning the hospitality which a junior colleague sometimes ventured to offer – little knowing how welcome it was. Sometimes there were surprises. The diary mentions with relish the day in 1934 when the Printer to Oxford University, the famous John Johnson, arrived to lunch wearing his hair with no parting, an old golf blouse under his coat and his trousers tucked into thick socks: 'An unusual man, properly contemptuous of this world, yet fully equal to its business.' They discussed the launching of the Oxford Society.

In a social club like the Windham, the transaction of business, the exchange and signing of documents is by tradition and for obvious reasons discouraged. If it were not, a club's rooms would be filled with low-voiced and secretive pairs trying to maintain the strictest privacy in what is intended first and foremost to be a place of casual but friendly meeting. However, neither rule nor convention forbids a minister bringing in his senior civil servant for a quick working lunch, and an editor is likewise free to entertain at dinner the man who is contributing some articles or going on a journey for his newspaper, or to scrutinize over a drink someone he is considering for a job. Hospitable and civilized interviewing of this kind, much though it saved office time, devoured B-W's leisure. One wonders, reading the record day after day, how often he ever ate his meal quietly alone and then relaxed for half an hour over the weeklies and monthlies. He may well have tried to do this, only to run into a fellow-member who would naturally welcome the chance of sharing a table or coffee with the man from *The Times*. During the war he would lunch or dine at the Travellers in Pall Mall, where he saw Portal, Chief of the Air Staff, taking his 'usual frugal and rapid meal – a single course and a glass of water'; or the Athenaeum, where he would meet Reith and other friends and discuss the Whitehall gossip.

For the company of men of affairs he also had the smaller and more intimate clubs, like the Beefsteak.* Dropping in

---

*The Beefsteak, in Irving Street, Leicester Square, was founded during the eighteenth century. After a period of decline, it revived towards 1900 as a supper club for leading actors. Gradually it widened its membership and has sometimes

there and sitting down to lunch in the first seat vacant at one long table, he would meet politicians, writers, men of the theatre, publishers. The great impresario C. B. Cochrane talked to him one day about the 'boy prodigy' Yehudi Menuhin and then about Noel Coward. Sitting next to Kenneth Clark led to the offer of an article on the forthcoming centenary of the National Gallery, a nice *coup* for the paper. Sometimes B-W would walk into a discussion – more often than not in the thirties a very heated one – about something written in *The Times* that morning, perhaps by himself. Occasionally he would be quizzed about authorship while lunchers watched for a tell-tale blush, but he stoutly defended the paper's anonymity. 'Why can't *The Times* be allowed a mind of its own?' he complained.

During the Munich crisis he had what he described as a 'slight passage of arms' with Harold Nicolson ('a vote-catching dilettante') and another member ('talking indignant tosh'). This face-to-face brush with critics of the paper's policy, he wrote, 'had warmed me up and I set about a leader'.*³

Just after he succeeded Dawson he was elected in February 1942 to that select and arcane body called Grillion's Club,† limited to eighty members. Public distinction in a candidate was taken by members for granted: the prime qualification was sociability and the capacity to argue without heat. This dining

been described as 'the sixth form of the Garrick Club'. Open for lunch and dinner, it offers none of the amenities of the bigger social clubs with their smoking rooms, libraries and bedrooms.

*In his *Diaries and Letters 1930–39* Harold Nicolson describes this incident with surprising self-satisfaction. B-W having entered the room, Nicolson said that *The Times* leader that morning was a 'masterpiece of unctuous ambiguity and I do not mind in the least repeating that in the presence of the author'. B-W, however, was not the author and Nicolson could not be certain that he was. B-W was fired to go back and write the leader of 21 September in which he referred to the 'light-minded, eagerly and irresponsibly misrepresenting this country'.

†Grillion's was named after the hotel in Albemarle Street, Piccadilly, where its first dinners were held. Occasions when only one member dined are recorded in its attendance book. When Sir Stratford de Redcliffe found himself alone he made a speech to the waiters at the end, and invited them to drink the uncorked bottles to the health of the Club and of Mr Grillion their employer. The privately printed history quotes one of the founding members as saying, 'At Berlin or Vienna such an association would have been dispersed by the Police as dangerous to the public peace, and at Paris its meetings would frequently have been adjourned to the Bois de Boulogne.'

club had been founded in 1812 because of the 'serious damage that London society was suffering from the violence of political controversy'. It was to provide a table where members of contending parties could meet and be sure of 'generous and courteous comprehension of diversities of political views'. Meeting twice a month during the Parliamentary session, members were not required to give notice of attendance, so that none would know whom he might expect to meet, or indeed whether he might not dine alone.

Only rarely does B-W describe an evening there. In February 1945 he found fourteen present, 'a large turnout', and they elected the new Archbishop and Rab Butler as members. 'Saw Camrose but did not fraternize! ... Late back after a very pleasant evening.' The rivalry of Lord Camrose's *Daily Telegraph* with *The Times* seems to have been much on the writer's mind at this time, and an entry in the following month refers to a warning from Brendan Bracken that its owner was threatening to give B-W severe competition after the war.

In general the club, when B-W joined it, was preponderantly conservative in outlook or non-political. The arrival of Labour, even with public-school men among the leaders, had passed it by. No wonder that he noted in October 1945: 'I was glad to hear Eddy Devonshire (the Duke) raise the question of getting some of the Labour people in – Jowitt, Shawcross, Pakenham, Cripps. Difficulty, however, will be to get them elected. Cripps has been on the list of candidates for a long time. Yet the club badly needs some such infusion.' Members at that time included Churchill, Portal, Wavell, Alanbrooke, Harold Macmillan, R. A. Butler and Alan Lascelles, latest of the Secretaries to the Sovereign who for a hundred years had belonged to the club, and a good friend of the paper.

Even though Dawson probably arranged it there was nothing automatic in the election of the Editor of *The Times*. Charm, says Sir Alan, was the quality which made B-W a welcome candidate, not only here but also in the equally old but less political Literary Society, to which he was elected in January 1944.

A very different person, the Robin of Balliol days, appeared at the annual dinners of the Circus, a dining club of old Oxford friends. On its tenth anniversary, in 1930, memorable to B-W because Walter Monckton was just taking silk, they dined at the Café Royal thirty-five strong. It was an uproarious evening, like that other occasion on which they had moved in a body to the floor where the Foxhunters were dining and sang the Red Flag to them from outside the door. B-W enjoyed himself hugely and wrote:

We sang the King's Regulations, as set by Alan Herbert to psalm tunes. Then Alan as Councillor Herbert made a witty speech. Then we sang Green Grow the Rushes O, with myself as conductor and other of our ditties. Walter [Monckton], K.C. and Laurence dancing the Apache dance after were good.[4]

But this was in the early days when the thirty-eight year old assistant editor still had a manageable day. The gay and youthful occasions become fewer and fewer, but suddenly in 1946 we come to an account of something more sedately hilarious: a dinner at Burlington House – not the great dinner of the Royal Academy given every June on the eve of its annual exhibition, to which most London editors expected to be invited, but a smaller occasion of sixteen guests at which B-W found himself under fire.

The composition puzzled me. I found various R.A.s including Gerald Kelly; Wilfrid Green and Cys Asquith; Watson (*D.T.*) and Ivor Brown (*Observer*). Good dinner in a charming room.... The speeches began. The Lord Mayor let off a harmless piece first. Then Munnings,* who had already introduced the Lord Mayor, made the first of several speeches. All were concerned with the infamies of modern art (Picasso, Klee, Braque) and, still more, of the critics who support or tolerate it. Cys was called on to speak as one who had written critically of Picasso in our recent correspondence, and did so gracefully and wittily. Gerald Kelly joined in, (more than once!) and, as the drink went round and the speeches went on, the abuse became still more violent.

This then was the purpose of the party—to educate the Press. It was all very ridiculous and extremely funny. We all laughed and laughed except the more earnest ones.... And it all became

---

*'Munnings' outbursts against virtually all art since Degas were the final salvo of a fusillade which the old academics had been keeping up ever since Manet added a female nude to the male picnic in the *Déjeuner sur l'Herbe* of 1863. His bravura displays, a little reddened by alcohol, gave the Royal Academy one of its few touches of colour in post-war years. Serious artists trying to earn a living in a cold climate found the P.R.A.'s fulminations rather less witty and pardonable. All the same, prices for his horsy tableaux have soared since his death, suggesting that he knew his market, if not his Matisse.' I owe this comment to my friend Edwin Mullins, formerly art critic of the *Sunday Telegraph*.

more and more concentrated on *T.T.* When old Munnings finally invoked me by name I felt compelled to say something. I defended the art critics as men who were being damned for their toleration — not a usual objection to critics — and said we should be grateful to those who were prepared to dedicate themselves to so thankless a calling. After this mild attempt at badinage, which they took quite well, I felt free to come away. Back to the office all too late after an amusing but still somewhat wasted evening.[5]

'A somewhat wasted evening!' That nagging conscience of B-W's at work again: time away from the Editor's chair was time wasted, especially time not spent on what was called in the office 'policy' – which meant in fact the paper's taking a hand in the running of the country. He should have been delighted to take time off for a confrontation with Munnings, who was then the butt of the more sophisticated art critics: as he was clearly delighted in that same year – when London was struggling to recapture its old rituals and splendours – to spend a gala night at Covent Garden, when the Sadlers' Wells Ballet reopened in the *Sleeping Beauty*.* The King and Queen were there, with the Princesses, and the poker-backed Queen Mary.

London has not seen such a gathering for a long time. Any kind of dress allowed (my first white tie since 1939) but the chic seemed to predominate. The ballet . . . was a new kind of achievement for this island, which could not have put on a native ballet of anything like this standard even ten years ago. Lovely settings by Oliver Messel, rather in the Rex Whistler manner. Dense crowd in the foyer between acts. Saw many people.[6]

Long before Hitler's war the Radical in B-W wondered how much longer the luxury and distinction of some of the social occasions he attended could survive; and the Edwardian in him was sad at the thought that they might not. Only a few weeks before the attack on Poland he and Adele were invited by the Astors to their son Gavin's coming-of-age ball at Hever.

---

*On a less public occasion he had to defend his music critic, H. C. Colles, against the conductor Thomas Beecham, who had asked Geoffrey Toye to pass on to the paper a letter of complaint. 'The old story. B. considers that we have not paid tribute to the artistic quality of his new Covent Garden season (which is certainly v. fine but in his opinion the finest ever given), that Colles is temperamentally incapable of appreciating his genius as a conductor, and that we pay undeserved tribute to other conductors such as Adrian Boult.'[7]

Hever, in spite of tropical downpour as we arrived, looked enchanting. Lights everywhere. Church flood-lit. Castle perfectly flood-lit—a block of golden, glowing stone. Great marquees. Fireworks over the lake, seen from the loggia at the end of the Italian garden. A sight to remember but always with the rumination, how long can these things last?[8]

Some of the survivals were remarkable. Ever since 1914, when they had entertained him as a young officer cadet, training near their house at Godalming, B-W had known Madeleine Midleton and her husband Lord Midleton. In 1937 he describes a dinner at 24 Portland Place.

The usual Victorian party. A card for the men on arrival telling them whom to take into dinner. All standing in a room almost empty of chairs before dinner. Then in to dinner arm-in-arm in procession. Host leading armed with the most important lady, that lady's husband coming last with the hostess. Table-cloths laid. Long dinner. Almost a survival in these days, but I wd not have it otherwise. Lord and Lady M. are admirable in hospitality and make the affair go well. I took in Mrs ——, a tiresome woman who seemed to have (anyhow for me) no topics of conversation and spent her time trying to identify the large company—24 or so.[9]

B-W particularly enjoyed meeting the characters and eccentrics of privileged societies. After a Gray's Inn guest night he recorded enviously meeting a 'ripe specimen' still practising at eighty-three: 'bright in eye and mind, snuff box in hand, full of good stories of the indiscreet past and full of candour about great men. He drinks nothing at dinner and they have a decanter of very special port for him after, most of which he floors. He keeps young, however, on six tumblers of water a day.' A memorable weekend was spent in May, 1938 at Eydon Hall near Rugby, the elegant eighteen-century house belonging to Bob Brand, Director of *The Times* and the Editor's most intimate and intelligent office critic. There he and Adele met the American airman Lindbergh, Tom Jones ('shrewd, wise and amusing as always'), Lionel Curtis and his wife, and young Moltke from Germany, great grandson of the great Chief of Staff.

Much talk with Brand and Lindbergh about Germany, defence etc. L.'s estimate of the gap between German and British air production, which is probably not far out, is very alarming.[10]

To this day the whole family remember with the keenest pleasure the wartime weekends at Dorneywood with Courtauld Thomson, from which B-W and Adele could run over to Eton and see Mark and Simon, sometimes bringing them back for a meal in that remarkable house, 'full of treasures and conceits'. 'Even-tempered, gracious, courteous, cultivated,' B-W wrote of his host in 1940.

His house and household faithfully express his qualities just as his philanthropy in peace and war expresses his public spirit. He has a secretary, a valet, a butler and a chauffeur. All have been with him for thirty years. All with their children form a patriarchically controlled family. They are more than servants. No tipping in his house.

Entertaining at home in Kent Terrace and later in Chester Terrace was necessarily restricted by the night work which fell to B-W's lot. But there was time for small dinner-parties, sometimes with a butler to help; for the occasional meeting of madrigal singers, which he loved to take part in: 'why don't we do it more often like Pepys?'; for serious gatherings like the Wives' Fellowship meeting which assembled at their home to hear Dick Crossman, then a Labour candidate and on the staff of the *New Statesman and Nation*.

To my surprise [B-W wrote] I found myself in almost complete agreement with his studiously non-partisan analysis of our present discontents. His stuff in the *New Statesman* is infected with the peculiar, petulant futility which blights all its pages.[11]

One catches in the diary glimpses of social life in wartime London, especially during the heaviest air raids. On 16 September 1940, the day on which *The Times* had been warned from Whitehall to expect the German invasion from across the Channel, B-W went to dine with the Canadian High Commissioner, Vincent Massey, and his wife at the Dorchester, into which many had moved permanently, for the safety of a steel and concrete building.

It was a lively night. The raids started soon after dinner began with a bomb in Park Lane and another in Berkeley Square. After coffee we moved from the Massey's first floor flat to the ground floor. Here was a strange, rather unlovely, sophisticated collection of cosmopolitans. Somerset Maugham was striding up and down with his jaw stuck out. It was exactly his milieu and he looked as if he was mentally recording the scene.[12]

What a contrast, B-W must have thought, to what he knew was going on two miles away in Fleet Street: the editorial staff packed together below stairs, elbow to elbow, producing the paper under conditions to which they were not yet hardened; the comps and machine-minders turning out their proofs and preparing the presses for a run that might never take place; the van-drivers wondering by what route through wrecked and burning streets they would be able to reach the railway stations. The next morning the population of the Dorchester would be sitting safely over their breakfasts, reading the latest news of the Battle of Britain gathered twelve hours earlier from every airfield of the Midlands and Southern England, and edited and printed under front-line conditions.

It should not be supposed that during the hungry thirties there was no thought or compassion for others in these two busy people, or that B-W was unaware of the poverty and unhappiness of some of his countrymen. On the contrary, he felt and thought deeply about the failure to cure their plight. To his personal contribution and Adele's the only reference in the diary is an entry of May 1936:

Some time ago, in answer to a broadcast appeal, A. 'adopted' an out-of-work family in Liverpool and has been in correspondence with them since. We send them food, clothes, etc. from time to time. Name *Schofield*. Husband a ship's steward, out of work four years. Mrs S. writes intelligent letters. We called upon them in her two-roomed Corporation tenement in Victoria Square where she and her husband live with 5 children. A very gallant woman. Saw some of the children. Pitiful lack of physical robustness, though cheerful. It is the kind of sight that cannot but make one passionate against our own times. The patience of the victims makes it worse. Mrs S. is a great reader. Has been reading Gorki. Interested in foreign politics. No bewailing her lot though she calls it, rightly, life under terrible conditions. Keeps all the family going. Tenement decent enough but—*two* rooms![13]

235

21

The Mentor Bows Out

I thought it the duty and opportunity of *The Times*
to prepare for the great social changes inevitable
after the war. Its function, I said, at all times is to
apply common-sense without prejudice, to issues
as they arise and to gain general acceptance of
novel but necessary moves by getting them rationally expounded.

B-W to J. J. Astor[1]

There survives from the summer of 1942 a memorandum from
Carr with pencilled notes by B-W. The gist of it is that the
military situation was probably now graver than at any time
since 1940 and the political situation graver than at any
previous time. The Government and the conduct of the war
inspired no confidence anywhere. Morale was 'slowly but pro-
gressively deteriorating'. The catchword 'We want the P.M. but
we want him to change his Government and methods' rang
hollower and hollower, for he clearly had no intention to oblige.
'Nothing but the lack of an alternative keeps the Government
in power.' Strong leadership must come from outside. There
was no *serious* candidate except perhaps Beaverbrook. (This
was underlined by B-W with 'NO' written in the margin.) Carr
goes on:

A leading M.P. must take his political life in his hands by resist-
ing and establishing himself as a constructive critic, building himself up as an alternative for the time when the popular demand for
a change at the top comes—as it will if there is a disaster.

Against the sentence about the 'leading member' B-W writes
in the margin, 'I contest this statement', and he notes too that
the disaster would probably 'not work that way'. This document sweeps onward: 'the paramount issue of the Second
Front must be tackled'; admittedly, military advice against its
feasibility could not be ignored, but in more than two years
the British had been unable to challenge the German strength

in the West, and that showed how bad the strategy and supply services had been. Carr wanted 'sweeping changes of methods and men'.

On the home front he was no less radical. Big firms were trying to maintain their positions for after the war. 'It may be necessary to comb labour out of non-essential small business, but what about redundant banks and big City institutions?' ('For what practical reasons?' B-W asks.) A post-war programme, Carr wrote, was needed now to put an 'adequate sense of purpose behind the war. Innumerable interests opposed to reform have enough of the ear of the P.M. to block any substantial commitment.' Again he demanded a leader from outside: someone 'who is prepared to make a direct popular appeal against these interests'. And against this B-W writes, 'back *whom* in politics?'

In considering the implications of such memoranda it has to be borne in mind that they were private to the Editor who, Carr knew, would pounce on practical or policy difficulties that they presented for the paper. But he may have overlooked – or may have deliberately ignored – the effect they would have on his standing in the office. No deputy deliberately encourages his chief to think him lacking in judgement of what can properly be said in his paper. But it should by now have been already clear to B-W, to use his own phrase, that Carr was not going 'to do for me what I did for G.D.'. Stanley Morison, who made it his business to study, and help to solve, the problems of the high command at Printing House Square, warned B-W in the following spring (May 1943) that he would be disappointed if he were to look to Carr to take a principal part in the organization of the post-war staff.

Carr does not seem to understand at all all that is involved in the position of *The Times* as an impersonal, national organ, closely related to the springs of political power, and, in particular, with public opinion. This illustration can be quoted: Carr said that he was aware that the Editor thought that it was not impossible that the P.M. would conduct a Coupon Election. Secondly, he said that the Editor believed that this would be a wrong thing to do. Carr then made the point that, although this was the Editor's view, it would not necessarily be championed in the paper. He expressed no criticism of the Editor beyond saying that *The Times* was not a 'fighting' journal. He was astonished when I said that, for my

237

part, I would not denounce a Coupon Election unless I felt sure that public opinion was either opposed to it, or so equally divided that the opposition of *The Times* would turn the scale. He agreed, however, that the one and only policy of *The Times* was to keep in close touch with the springs of real, not theoretical, power, i.e. of public opinion.*

I inferred from this illustration [Morison concludes] that it is too early to make him solely responsible for policy.[2]

Whatever we are to make of Morison's motives in this episode, it is improbable that he, having been in favour of Carr's appointment, was now undermining his position. But it illustrates how the typographer of the early thirties had become, by means of the editorship of the *History of The Times*, the adviser at the elbow of the Editor and, it should be added, of the Chairman.

When Dawson had retired in September 1941, it had been agreed between the new Editor, Casey and Carr that two out of the three should always be on duty together, so lightening the load on the man who took the chair and ensuring B-W's peace of mind at the weekend. For he never felt quite at ease when the newcomer was left in complete charge. He was liable to write – or to allow others to write – more candidly than the style of the paper required and to trail his coat before more conservative readers. Carr, on his side, found it impossible to identify himself with an institution in the way that the tradition of Printing House Square seemed to require.† Such reservations in the minds of both men made it likely that the partnership would not survive the national crisis which had made it possible, or find the paper a deputy editor.‡ In the event it lasted over five years, long enough to see the war out and a Labour Government in.

*In the Postscript of Volume IV of the History Morison seems to express precisely the opposite view.

†Buckle (Editor from 1884–1912), when making a stand against one of Northcliffe's first interventions, wrote: 'With me, as with Bell, the Paper is bone of my bone and flesh of my flesh. . . . The Paper is my life's work.' (*History of the Times*, Volume III, p. 756.)

‡W. F. Casey, who succeeded when B-W died in 1948, was in most respects already the obvious choice as Deputy. Relaxed, unambitious, slow of gait and speech, sceptical of journalistic pretension, he was the foil to B-W. He had longer professional experience than B-W, and he was liked and respected throughout the office as an expert dispenser of oil on troubled waters. His judgement was excellent but he was not a regular writer, was by preference a playwright, and had uncertain health. At that time he hoped to retire very soon.

A slow and reluctant disillusionment with the collaboration is traceable in the diaries. To follow it is fascinating for anyone interested in how a newspaper office works and for all who remember these days when *The Times* was the most discussed newspaper in the country. At first the leader-writing, which was indeed remarkable, gets unqualified praise: 'excellent', 'admirable', 'fine', 'brilliant'. But after Alamein and Stalingrad the Conservative critics of the paper recovered their nerve and made their voices heard in Printing House Square. After the furious controversy about the British intervention in Greece around Christmas 1944 and Churchill's public rebuke to the paper in January 1945 events brought about a distinct change of tone. A piece on the Yalta conference had to be rewritten; another in May 1945 on the Soviet arrest of the leaders of the London Poles is 'too apologetic' and is changed. Here are some typical entries:

Last Friday I passed the torso of a leader by Carr on Greece for possible use this morning. In view of yesterday's better news from Athens I expected him to modify it but deliberately abstained from ringing him up to tell him so. No good trying to drive the car from the back-seat. It was not much modified and seemed to me rather fiercer than it need have been.[3]

Already in earlier years B-W had criticized 'odd blind spots' in a leader on Lenin and he toned down another written on Stalin's denunciation of the Comintern in May 1943: 'The political effects of what Carr writes are not always plain to him.' The Editor's modifying touches – sometimes introducing qualifications in parentheses which brought sharp halts in the smooth velocity of Carr's prose – did not save either of them from excited charges of appeasing Stalin, betraying Mihailovitch in Yugoslavia, playing the Socialist game and producing a 'pink 'un'.* About a 'magnificent leader' on the future of Germany, which they had discussed together several times, B-W noted:

I never have any trouble with his contributions when we have talked them over beforehand. It is only when he goes off by himself and volunteers some unheralded piece that the rifts appear,

---

*Sir G. G. Williams, an old Westminster friend and contemporary, then a high official in the Ministry of Education, remembers meeting B-W at a party towards the end of the war and saying to him: 'My friends tell me you're gone all pink these days, Robin'; to which the Editor snapped back: 'That remark G. G. is a reflection on the intelligence of your friends.'

perhaps because he 'tries it on' me. But what a superb leader-writer he is when he stays in the team.[4]

A quite different complaint had to do with the evening of 6 August 1945 when the news came, entirely unexpected and uniquely sensational, about the atomic bomb attack on Hiroshima. Carr was in the chair and B-W was up at Swineshead hoping for a long summer weekend. When he heard of the attack from the BBC nine o'clock news he decided to return to the office next morning. His feeling that he would be needed proved right. The first leader was not about Hiroshima but about Europe's need for food and money.

Grabbed *The Times* eagerly from Bedford railway bookstall. Alas! no leader on the bomb. News fairly well set out but the general effect, without comment, is necessarily somewhat deadalive. From what I heard on arrival at the office a leader should have been manageable. I fear that Carr missed the significance of the event in the first messages. Too little journalistic imagination. At the same time Andrade [the science correspondent] refused to write a special article on the ground that he knew too much and was afraid of giving something away. Got him going to-day and, later, got Morrah on to a leader.[5]

How often was Dermot Morrah, by preference a special writer on home politics, the affairs of Royalty and big constitutional questions, called to the rescue in such situations. B-W was understandably exasperated at a failure to do justice to 'the news' and knew that there would be malicious chuckles in the office and in Fleet Street among the professional critics of the paper.*

By then B-W knew that the partnership was not going to last. Early in 1944 Morison had told him that Carr was seriously

---

*'What *was* there to say?' Carr now asks. Hiroshima was covered by 'an impenetrable cloud of dust' said the agency reports. It was not known how great was the damage done. It was more difficult to comment on that extraordinary Sunday evening than B-W perhaps realized.

The *Daily Telegraph* did carry a first leader the next morning, but it is obvious that only its first two paragraphs had been specially written and that they had been welded on to an existing leader about the prospects of allied landings in Japan! They praise the British Government's foresight in initiating nuclear research for war purposes and the efficient cooperation with the Americans. At the end comes the warning that 'unless we now so bear ourselves that the power of war-making is stamped out and peace among men of good will is securely established, the human race must go down to ghastly ruin.' B-W might have liked something like that written; Carr regarded it as cliché, pure and simple.

out of sorts, needed a rest, and was disappointed that no offer had come his way from a university. When they talked things over in March – on the eve of the 'buzz-bomb' attacks and the invasion of Normandy – Carr seemed to blame conditions in the office for his need of a break. It surprised B-W to be told that responsibilities in the office were 'blurred' and that the recruitment of new staff had been put off too long. He felt that he had 'nursed' his colleague and protected him from over-work – that was perhaps the trouble. But he agreed that when Carr returned from his leave he should be relieved of all administrative responsibilities.

He feels the need for reading, thinking and taking in after some years of putting out. I readily agreed and said I felt sure that the Chairman would be ready to treat this as leave on full-pay, though I couldn't commit him. Carr raised again the question of my recent refusal to let him write a Penguin on foreign policy.... (About which I am quite unrepentant: he cannot help to run policy in the paper and lay down policy independently elsewhere; pointless and prob-ably embarrassing.)[6]

A number of able and ambitious men have left *The Times* on account of its reluctance to share their services and ideas with a publisher, or a periodical, or the BBC. By the standards of that time B-W's ruling was perfectly fair and normal, and they parted good friends. But three weeks later there arrived a memorandum about reforms in the office which caused offence (see Appendix IV). Carr's twenty years in the civil service had accustomed him to clear lines of authority and delegation of duties. The situation at *The Times,* where no one except the Editor seemed entitled to give a decision, seemed to him con-fused and inefficient – as indeed it was – and Carr emphatically said so. The Editor, conscious of his own tendency to over-centralize decisions and trying hard to find in wartime London the nucleus of a younger staff, was annoyed and disturbed.

Proposes a delegation of control over leaders and letters which would be quite incompatible with an editor's duty and interest. Seems to think I work too much. But am I having the breakdown or is he? And so on. Truth is that (though I have to say it myself) I have not been able to put on Carr all that G.D. put on me and that his failure to get on with colleagues has not helped organiza-tion. However, I shall send him a tolerant reply.... Well, I must

241

I

reform myself where I can. But I wonder how Carr thought I was going to take his piece.[7]

During the next month B-W, with Carr's help, began to see a way out of his major difficulty with the appointment as assistant editor of a younger man, as great a glutton for work as himself. Donald Tyerman,* was to write leaders and look after feature articles. Here the hand of Tom Jones again showed itself, for it was his offer of permanent employment on the *Observer* to Tyerman that forced B-W, advised by Morison, to make up his mind quickly. Thus in mid-May of 1944 it became possible for Carr to come in only two or three days a week, writing leaders and making suggestions. This, the diary noted, 'is probably the beginning of the end of my cooperation with Carr, by no choice of mine'.

Tyerman was not the only new recruit. Peter Utley,† the young blind man from Cambridge, was writing brilliant political leaders; Rushbrook-Williams, a specialist on India, was to come in from the M. of I. to write on Middle East and Far Eastern questions; there were hopes of getting Maurice Green, the City Editor, out of his Anti-Aircraft command, now that the end of the war was in sight; Eric Wigham was to come in from the *Manchester Guardian* to be Labour Correspondent; and by 1945 B-W was negotiating with Con O'Neill to join as a leader-

---

*Donald Tyerman's rise in journalism was as spectacular as Dawson's had once been. As recently as 1936, having won a First in Modern History as a Scholar of B.N.C., he had been lecturing at Southampton University on Economic History and Politics. As secretary of the Appointments Committee there he received an inquiry from *The Economist* for a junior editorial assistant. Applying at the last minute he was accepted and quickly rose to Deputy Editor, taking Geoffrey Crowther's place whenever he was away on war service. During one of the seven years he held that position he also helped to edit the *Observer* (1943–4). It was there that he came to the notice of B-W.

With his north-country, grammar-school background and his economic knowledge, Tyerman at thirty-six brought to *The Times* the fresh contribution of a writer trained by the most brilliant editor of his day. He moved into the day-editor's job at the same age that B-W had taken it over twenty years earlier. By 1947 he had become just the kind of all-round writing deputy that the overworked Editor needed, although it was Casey who had that title and succeeded when B-W died. Tyerman was Editor of *The Economist* 1956–65.

†Utley was spotted by Carr while examining as independent examiner for the History Tripos at Cambridge, in which he got a 'starred' first. He was invited to contribute to *The Times* when he was only twenty-two. As a dyed-in-the-wool Tory he disliked most of Carr's opinions, except his 'obsession with Great Powers and his wish to organize Europe on the principles of the Congress of Vienna'.

242

writer on European affairs. With all this new blood coming in there would soon be a new problem of fitting in seven or eight fairly senior young men who were expected to return from the war. Colin Coote had left in 1941, treated surprisingly with less than B-W's normal fairness; Braham, the leader-writer on economic and American affairs, and Radcliffe, the Labour Correspondent, were retiring and Graves would be retiring shortly. Indeed, the Editor faced at this time difficulties of staff selection and management which were almost unprecedented – one of the duties he could not delegate to Carr or anyone else.

Their meetings and discussions continued in friendly fashion. One dinner-time conversation at the Travellers, against a background of long alerts and 'buzz-bomb' attacks, is worth recording.

Carr is contemplating a book on how much totalitarianism our economic needs will compel us to swallow and how it can be made compatible with personal freedom. . . . I am convinced that economic democracy is possible. He is troubled with doubts about the incentive being plainly insufficient. A moral purpose has to be rediscovered. To have any true vitality it must be rooted in religion, and our present-day religion lags behind the needs of the age, cluttered up with intellectual difficulties. Yet a restatement which cleared the difficulties would shatter the [Church] organizations.[8]

By the beginning of 1945 it was clear that Carr wished to be finished with journalism, in which he had never wished for a permanent career. He was now fifty-three and if he was to return to academic life regular office work must cease. He wanted to write books and Macmillans were ready to give him an office where he could work at a big book on Russia.* He had faced many difficulties caused by his outspoken views, some of which later turned out right. He had angered the left-inclined by attacks on Utopianism and by his attitude – or what was thought to be his attitude – to the Soviet treatment of Eastern Europe, and he had aroused bitter suspicions among the right-inclined by his advocacy of collectivist economic policies. He might be described as the *enfant terrible* of the liberal-minded Establishment, which was having to adapt itself simultaneously to the Soviet presence in Europe and the Middle

*This was the history of the Bolshevik Revolution on which Carr, since 1955 a Fellow of Trinity College, Cambridge, is still engaged. Eight volumes have been published.

East and to the Socialist presence in Downing Street. B-W realized that some people, even old friends like Archie James, thought of Carr as his 'evil genius'. In the spring of 1946 he was told by Christiansen, Editor of the *Daily Express*, that a syndicated article by Randolph Churchill had appeared in an Irish newspaper making this charge:

It says I have been under Carr's domination: that lately there has been a palace revolution, led by Casey and McDonald; that Carr is going, and that the paper's Russian policy will change. And the man is paid for writing this bosh!*[9]

'Bosh' though it might be, B-W was sensitive, as any editor would be, to the public suggestion that he was not in full charge. He even thought a leading article in the *Daily Sketch*, of all papers, worthy of a diary note:

Pompous leader, a column long, in the *Daily Sketch,* attacking *The Times* for yesterday's comment on Egypt. Refers offensively throughout to the 'leader-writer' (evidently meaning Carr who had nothing in the wide world to do with it). This line is meant to suggest that I am not in control, one of the allegations circulated by people trying to discredit the policy of *The Times*. No doubt ... with his morbid antipathy to Carr, was the disloyal source of a good deal of ill-natured gossip. Not that anything matters except what appears in the paper itself. If that is good enough *qu'on dise*.[10]

The next day, to rub it in, the *News Chronicle* had a leader defending *The Times* against the *Daily Sketch*, a rather comic piece of championship considering that most of the readers of both those papers never saw *The Times*. 'Friendly,' B-W wrote that evening, 'but could have done without it.'

The strain on his nerves at this time must have been great, although there is no indication of this in his diary apart from mentions of old-standing rheumatic and minor ailments. For a man entirely lacking in cynicism, sensitive in conscience and deeply mortified by his failure to avert – if anything written in the paper could have averted – the war now ending, the suggestion that the policy he was now following was not in the best interests of the country and was felt by some good friends to be

*As McDonald was travelling extensively at this time he was ill-placed to lead a palace revolution. Moreover, neither he nor Casey was the man to play such a role. Carr had in fact been on the way out, of his own volition, for over eighteen months.

a betrayal of principles and ideals must have been hurtful. Yet, as more than one of his old colleagues has pointed out, he enjoyed at moments of self-confidence being in a minority and became more stubborn under attack.

Some people were saying that those who had appeased Germany were now appeasing Russia. If by 'appeasement' is understood the search for a general agreement with a government which, on the face of it, was aggressive and expansionist, they were right. No one in the office disputed that it was necessary to live with the Russians: where there was disagreement was over the tactics to be employed towards them. As Diplomatic Correspondent in regular touch with all missions in London – in particular with the Poles and Yugoslavs – Iverach McDonald felt more directly than anybody from Foreign Office and foreign embassies in London the backwash of a Carr leader. We tend now to forget, he points out, how many people in the West, and not only exiled Poles, believed before 1945 that Russia would and should remain behind her pre-war frontiers.

I fully agreed with Carr that the Russians would have influence in and over Eastern Europe. My chief dispute with him was over diplomatic method. I would have preferred to let Britain and the other Western countries argue each case without *The Times* announcing that the conclusion was inevitable and that argument was useless. Where Carr would jump into the final position, I would have dragged my feet. Whether it would have made any difference in the end result I do not know.... Carr tended to write what he thought without regard to the country's diplomatic needs of the day.

Those close to the day-to-day dealings between the Big Three, seeing and hearing Molotov at his most disagreeable, were doubtful about the reasonable, conciliatory attitude that B-W favoured. He recommended what Churchill himself was to advocate seven years later as talking jaw to jaw and he regarded the great man's post-war speeches about European unity, the iron curtain and Anglo-American solidarity as provocative. Making every allowance for the fact that the Americans and the British were still formidable in power, though disarming and withdrawing fast from their wartime positions, the resemblance between the views expressed by the papers of 1946 and 1936 are so striking that sections of a leader by Carr of 9 March 1946 on relations with Russia are given here verbatim.

At the time the Americans were protesting strongly against Soviet activity in Manchuria and at the failure to withdraw Soviet troops from northern Persia. Having recounted the numerous actions of the Russians in Germany and elsewhere which had given offence, and the bitterness of their propaganda against their old allies, the article went on:

It may well be, however, that the situation seems very different to the men who shape the policy of the Soviet Government. It may be that in their eyes the actions which have inevitably perplexed and dismayed the western democracies stand as merely elementary measures of self-protection. Only the Russians can know by what hairbreadth they escaped not merely conquest but also slavery and extirpation at the hands of Nazi Germany, and they are acutely suspicious of any development in international affairs, or in the free flow of British and American opinion, which might indicate, however remotely, the possibility that forces hostile to the Communist culture and creed are finding a rallying point for a fresh onslaught.

Believing that western democracy is too easily captured by reactionary or Fascist influences, the Russians regard a close alliance between Britain and the United States, or between Britain and the countries of Western Europe, as a threat.

This attitude of suspicious aloofness and this conviction of sustaining a great cause in isolation against an indifferent or potentially hostile world spring no doubt in part from the difficulties experienced by the Russian Government since the Revolution and in part from sheer lack of knowledge. Friendly cooperation with other nations has never been a tradition in Russian policy; and two decades of ostracism have given little opportunity for the growth of a healthier practice in unfamiliar soil.

During the war understanding had improved but lately relations have deteriorated.

The guarded secrets of the atom bomb have impressed Russia as a menace. She has felt confirmed in her sense of isolation by the differences whch have emerged between her own views and the views of Britain and America upon the powers and procedure of the Security Council, upon the position of the Polish Government, upon the treatment of occupied Germany, and upon the regimes of certain Balkan countries. . . . The speech of Mr Churchill at Fulton,

246

with its emphasis on an Anglo-American military understanding, she now reads as a further confirmation of her fears.

The leader concludes with the suggestion that face-to-face meetings alone will resolve these differences.*

At a time when there was anxiety and resentment on both wings of British politics about Stalin's intransigence, even a feeling in some quarters that there was danger of war with the Soviet Union, this very fair – and in the light of present knowledge largely accurate – diagnosis of the Russian state of mind sounded to quite a number of people like 'appeasement' resurgent, with militant Russia instead of Germany as its beneficiary.

The Times's diagnosis was almost certainly right, as was its unexpressed feeling that neither the United States nor Britain would use force, or even threaten it, to undo what was being done east of Berlin. If intellectual arrogance consists in depicting a situation in plain black and white, ignoring all shades of grey, then the paper was guilty of such arrogance.

B-W recorded the views of some distinguished people who agreed with Carr's diagnosis of the Russian mood. At one of the regular V.I.P. lunches in the Board Room at Printing House Square – to none of which, incidentally, was Carr ever invited – he sat between the American emissary Averell Harriman and Sir Orme Sargent, then head of the Foreign Office.

Got Harriman going on Russia. Doesn't think them aggressive (as the Germans were) in any systematic way. Believes rather that they will try for soft spots and stop when they come up against something hard. Agrees that no one knows the play of forces in and behind the Kremlin. Evidently does not approve of Ralph Parker, our Moscow Correspondent.[12]

Before this he had called on Evatt, the Australian Foreign Minister, at the Savoy and found his views 'very sound'.

*Carr writes in 1969: 'I am perfectly clear where I stood at the end of the war. I hoped that we, in close association with the Western European countries, would be strong enough to make a third power comparable to the Americans and the Russians, or at any rate strong enough to be equally independent of both. Of course, I seriously underestimated our weakness and exhaustion. I did not guess that the Americans, far from favouring this arrangement, would discourage any close association between us and the Western Europeans, and prefer to deal with us separately, so that we were from the first in a hopelessly weak position. I did not foresee how quickly the cold war would break out between the Russians and the Americans, compelling us to join one camp or the other – necessarily the American. By the middle of 1946 all these trends were apparent and I was very much disillusioned.[11]

He believes that the Russians are still fundamentally on the defensive and have been given many causes or occasions for suspicion since the Anglo-U.S. atomic bomb agreement, and that our task is to avoid a premature line-up among the powers. He is particularly strong against accepting from the military a strategy or policy finally geared to war with Russia.[13]

Obviously a man after the Editor's own heart, although at that time some serious-minded people of the right were calling Evatt a fellow-traveller. B-W was likewise impressed by meeting at a Board lunch George Marshall, the US Secretary of State, and finding him moderate and cautious in his view of Russian intentions.

Parker* was later removed for six months from Moscow to the British Zone of Germany and his place was to have been taken by Michael Burn, who had rejoined after the war and had done a very good job reporting the trial of Cardinal Mindszenty. But he was refused a visa on this account and the staffing arrangements in Moscow were to give trouble for years to come, partly because of the great expense of keeping a permanent man there, partly because of the limited scope given for travelling, inquiring and freely reporting.

The time now came to recognize that Carr was no longer a staff man, though he would be looking in occasionally as a writer and B-W gave him a farewell dinner at the Carlton Grill at the end of July 1946 with Morison and Tyerman. It was the occasion for confiding to the diary the following *envoi:*

Carr has done the paper outstanding service. I owe more than I can say to his fresh, original, powerful mind. On the whole he has played up well as one of a team and has accepted the limitations of teamwork with good grace. No doubt he thinks me excessively cautious but I am certain that his work, and the paper, have gained because he has not always been allowed to offer all the provocation that he would like! A better pen never wrote leaders for *T.T.* It made its mark immediately. What has been done could not have been done without it. No one can take his place—and yet 'The same arts that did gain a power must it maintain.'[15]

*Parker's views were causing anxiety at the time. One of a group of M.P.s returning from a visit to Moscow in February 1945 had alleged that Parker was a Communist and that the Ogpu got at him by threatening the Russian woman with whom he lived. B-W remarked that the man who had said this was a 'Diehard' and that he would defend Parker if he were attacked, even though the correspondent had become 'too crudely propagandist in a lot of his stuff.'[14]

That the paper moved leftwards in these five years is clear beyond dispute – and without damage to its circulation.* The same movement was, indeed, also taking place in society itself, and in politics. Certainly B-W himself had wanted to see the centre of politics moved well to the left of where it had been before the war, but he would have called his personal attitude realistic Conservatism, not Socialism. He did not live to see in action the new Conservatism which he had discussed with Rab Butler, for he was to die in the third year of the Labour Government; but it is not difficult to guess what he would have thought of the Churchill of 1951 (the Churchill whom he had advised in 1945 to give up leadership of the Conservative Party, only to be told with a growl, 'I do not leave till the pubs close').

What, then, was Carr's role as mentor, to use Morison's phrase again? Because he wrote the main leaders in wartime he no more dominated B-W than B-W had dominated Dawson ten years earlier. He turned into patterns and words, clearer and more uncompromising than B-W would have created, ideas on which they both agreed. B-W had to a lesser degree done that for Dawson, too; but there was this great difference between the two relationships. Coming to Printing House Square as a mature and experienced Foreign Office official, Carr had a formidable equipment of knowledge and ideas to which in the office only McDonald, with his detailed knowledge of what was going on from day to day in foreign affairs, could offer effective resistance.† B-W had had no such advantage over Dawson.

Important, too, was the fact that the Professor had been spared the emasculation of style which Fleet Street inflicts on intellectuals, who on joining a newspaper are made to 'learn the ropes' by attending to the writing of others and wasting their powers of reasoning on 'straight reporting'. The ordeal was particularly arduous in *The Times* office, with its style book, meticulous attention to detail, and dislike of 'viewy' exuberance. Carr did not instinctively ask himself – as would the well-

*The financial year ending April 1944 had shown the largest profit in the history of the paper and its circulation was now bigger at 3d. than it had been a year or two before the war. B-W was naturally delighted, while well aware that war is good for newspapers and that small newspapers had meant reduced costs.

†Likewise, on economic matters only Maurice Green, City Editor, could stand up to Carr. Sometimes City page comment and the leader page were in contradiction.

trained P.H.S. man – what would be the paper's line; he stated his own opinion in terms which he hoped would just get past the Editor. Casey's cynical dictum, that the skill of a foreign correspondent was to be judged by his ability to get into the paper what was contrary to its policy, applied equally to leader-writers.*

It should help to recreate the atmosphere of the days immediately after the war, when B-W was working in his new staff, if the author recalls a typical evening's incident, throwing some light on the question of how much an editor should interfere with the presentation of news.

One day in March 1946, when I was acting as Diplomatic Correspondent in McDonald's absence, I came back from the Foreign Office with what seemed to me and to the night-editor (Russell) good Bill Page material. It was about the attitude of the Americans and ourselves to the refusal of the Russians to move, as agreed, out of northern Persia after we had left the south. I had been briefed in the News Department by Norman Nash – who had shown me telegrams – and also by the later notorious Burgess. There was the smell of belligerence in the air, because in those days Persian oil was a most precious asset to H.M.G. and Soviet behaviour in Persia a most serious anxiety.

I wrote three-quarters of a column of what I still regard as vivid, readable stuff about the serious view taken of Soviet behaviour. Indeed, Russell looked in during the evening to say just this, which pleased me, intent as I then was on re-establishing myself in the office. But sometime after dinner B-W came into the little Dip. Corr. room near his and said: 'McLachlan, this won't do at all,' waving my proof at me. 'What is wrong with it?' I asked. 'This is the kind of journalism that causes war,' he replied. 'But,' I protested, 'I have merely reported the briefing I was given at the F.O. I have expressed no views at all.' 'Maybe,' he replied, 'but we're not here to make propa-

*Casey had a quiverful of only half-serious epigrams with which he enjoyed shocking the eager young. The author, indignant at changes made in a piece he had written, asked Casey, one evening in 1946, who really decided the policy of the newspaper. 'The policy of The Times, my dear fellow, is decided by a committee which never meets,' was the reply.

ganda for the Foreign Office.' 'But,' I said, 'this is what the British and Americans have said to the Russians. These are facts, not views that I am giving.' He shook his head, put his spectacles back on his nose, and said: 'Anyhow, I have stopped the page. Come in and see me after the first edition and we'll see how we can alter it.'

Later Russell stormed into my room (his paper now running late) and demanded why I could not be more careful about what I offered for the Bill page. That, after his previous praise, was too much, and I let fly something in return. Lighting his pipe with furious gulps, and throwing the flaming match on to my floor, he explained with three or four oaths that stopping the page would cost a lot of money. That really did impress me and I went in to the Editor's office half an hour later as near trepidation as I had ever been in his presence.

The trouble was, he explained, that people all over the world persisted in thinking that *The Times* was the organ of the government. I said that I, just back from Europe, knew that only too well. It must therefore take care, he went on, not to reproduce provocatively or sensationally what it was told by the F.O., which gave the paper exceptional access to the facts. This was true enough. 'But,' I said, 'what I originally wrote has already gone over to Europe through the foreign correspondents in the office.'

Startled and irritated B-W looked up from his reading desk and said something – I cannot remember what – and then poised his pencil over one or two sentences which particularly troubled him. 'See if you can put that a bit differently,' he said; 'to be effective it is not necessary to be offensive.' The alterations turned out to be slight but he was satisfied. I was angry at the time, but I realize now that he was quite right: I had overwritten what I had been told – that was why the night-editor had liked it – and I was fortunate to be consulted about the changes made. The Editor would have been well within his rights if he himself had made, without telling me, more drastic alterations to my anonymous copy.

22

Then Was the Tug of War

The bitterest by far of all the storms that broke over B-W's head was caused late in 1944 by the paper's criticisms of the use made of British troops sent to Greece in the wake of the retreating Germans. For several weeks between December of that year and February 1945 the violent controversy between left and right, between Government and newspapers is mentioned almost daily in his diary, with here and there a note of misgiving lest the line taken may have been wrong. What especially worried him, with his deep respect and affection for the Army, was the charge that its officers and men were being stabbed in the back by critics at home, while they had to fight cruel and fanatical gangs expected to welcome them as liberators. Readers of *The Times,* in their passionate letters to the Editor, divided roughly two-fifths in its support and three-fifths against.

Indignation reached its peak on 18 January 1945, when Churchill made a long statement to the House of Commons on the course of the war, the first part of which defended his policy in Greece and attacked the Press.*

There is no case in my experience, certainly not in my war experience, when a British Government has been so maligned [loud and prolonged cheers] and its motives so traduced in our own country by important organs of the press among our own people. That this should be done amid the perils of this war now at its climax has filled me with surprise and sorrow.... How can we wonder, still more how can we complain, of the attitude of hostile and indifferent newspapers in the United States when we have in this country witnessed such a melancholy exhibition as that pro-

---

*The despatch which started the trouble was that of 4 December, beginning with this tendentious, or what Dawson would have called 'viewy', sentence: 'Seeds of civil war were well and truly sown by the Athens police this morning when they fired on a demonstration of children and youths. . . .' The message was referred to with approval by the *Daily Worker*.

vided by our most time-honoured and responsible journals [loud and prolonged cheers] and others to which such epithets would hardly apply [laughter].

Listening upstairs in the gallery and downstairs in his seat were respectively the Editor and his Chairman, the Conservative Member for Dover. Unconvinced by the Prime Minister's arguments, B-W was none the less shocked and impressed by the violence of the demonstration, as one colleague testifies who saw him on his return from the House. In his diary he wrote:

This—a direct and obvious reference to *T.T.*—immediately touched off the loudest, largest and most vicious—even savage! — cheer that I have heard in the House. It must have lasted a full minute or more. I went on with my notes and did not inspect the demonstration, but there could be no doubt it was almost wholly Tory.... It was a vent for the pent-up passions of three years, a protest against all that has, wrongly or rightly, enraged the Tories in the paper during that time.... This open onslaught by Winston must put a strain on the support which John [Astor] gives me.[1]

One Tory back-bencher described the left-wing Labour Member, Seymour Cocks, as 'bedfellow of the Editor of *The Times.*'

What then had the paper said? With Tyerman writing most, and Carr only a few, of the leaders, it had contended that the British role in Athens should be limited to creating and safeguarding, in the chaotic conditions left by the Germans, a state of affairs in which Greeks could freely choose their future government. If the British allowed themselves to protect right against left, or to give any sign of preparing the way for the return of the King, then they must expect the Communists, Socialists and Liberals of E.A.M. (the National Liberation Front) to treat this intervention as a challenge to civil war. Basil Davidson, who had worked in Yugoslavia and Middle East HQ and knew the realities of Balkan politics, says – although a man of left-wing sympathies himself – that *The Times* mistook members of E.A.M. and E.L.A.S. for a kind of English liberal. In fact, what had been planned before the British arrival was a ruthless seizure of power by the left which an equally ruthless right-wing faction, some of them trained and recruited under British auspices during the German occupation, resisted.

The Times suspected, as indeed did other British and American newspapers, that intervention was being personally directed by Churchill, who wanted a restoration of the monarchy.* It was known in the office that Stalin had recognized Greece as a British sphere of influence and that Churchill's plan to prevail there was partly inspired by disappointment at his own failure – and Roosevelt's – to prevent Moscow's recognition of the Communist Lublin Poles as a provisional government in Poland. However that may be, his critics protested that Britain and her allies had not fought this long war against Fascism in order to restore pre-war regimes of the right. Liberation must bring in its train true democracy and a new deal. Britain must not get involved in a civil conflict – what a later generation knew as a Vietnam war. His supporters insisted that the Communist resistance groups and their sympathizers were trying to impose their own dictatorship and should be resisted.

For newspapermen in Athens the working conditions were complicated and arduous. Penned for much of the time in the Hotel Grande Bretagne, living on army rations, without heat and often without light, dependent on communications controlled by the military, they tried to do a political job in what was a war situation.† As Deakin, the Foreign News Editor, explained to B-W:

> In each phase of the Allies' counter-invasion there has come a stage in which war correspondents have had to steer their work into political channels, and the machinery which might have ensured a better performance of their duties has so far been lacking.[2]

This had happened in North Africa, in Italy and in France; but Greece had produced the worst conditions so far. For the

*According to the diary, Eden told B-W on 9 January that eighteen months before he had almost succeeded in persuading the King of the Hellenes to agree to a declaration that he would not return to Greece without a plebiscite first being held; but Roosevelt had intervened and told the King to reject the idea. That declaration, wrote B-W, 'might, probably would, have averted civil war'. Sir Leslie Rowan, then Private Secretary to Churchill, wrote in *Action This Day* (Macmillan, 1968): 'I believe that during the whole Greek episode he felt more lonely than at any other time in the war; yet he never gave up and never doubted his own judgement'.

†*The Times* man wrote to the office in January 1945: 'December was the most uncomfortable and depressing month physically I can remember spending. It was impossible to get warm. Oranges cost 5/- each. We were living on half rations.'

reporters there was not one enemy but two or more rival factions at close quarters: 'When Greeks joined Greeks, then was the tug-of-war!'

Geoffrey Hoare, the special correspondent in Athens, was a staff member but knew more of Arab than of Balkan politics. He was handicapped by partial deafness, a point made much of by his critics; but B-W pointed out to a reader that J. D. Bourchier, the paper's great Balkan Correspondent of thirty years earlier, had been 'stone deaf'. Some who worked with Hoare thought he moved around less than he should have done and depended too much on the British mission. Others, however, praised his independent attitude and much of what he sent was confirmed by reputable American journalists on the spot. In April 1945, when excitement had died down but the post-mortem still went on, Deakin wrote to him: 'Your reports had the confidence of the office throughout the crisis and we were sorry to see that a certain amount of unjustified criticism was levelled against you personally.' Indeed, there is reason to believe that the paper's leader comment, the real cause of all the indignation, went further in criticism of the British than Hoare's messages justified. In February B-W's old friend Archie James, returning from a visit to Athens with a party of other MP's, told him that he thought Hoare 'an honest, decent man but below the quality of correspondent which the situation demanded'. Furthermore, Hoare had told James that 'he had sent nothing which could have justified the comment of *The Times*'. 'A strange statement to make,' commented B-W in his diary, 'and quite untrue.' But to read the leading articles now and compare them with the news reports is to get much the same impression. Moreover, B-W had shown his uneasiness about Hoare's judgement by sending a senior staff man, Lumby, to look at the situation for a few days in January.

However, the Editor staunchly defended his man on the spot. When a friend of the Chairman's complained of the paper's views and enclosed a letter from a son at the front, B-W felt it necessary to reply personally:

The letter comes from a man who has been in the battle and feels, like others with him, that he is concerned with thugs and blackguards. The longer the battle has raged and the more stubborn it has been, the more he feels that. Small blame to him. Any of us would think the same. If that were all, the affair would be simpler than it is, but it is by no means the whole of the picture. The enclosure, so far as it concerns *T.T.*, is inaccurate and unfair to Hoare. It illustrates the distortion that has been possible under the stress and strain of the worst kind of guerrilla warfare.

Anyone who looks back over his series of despatches will see that he has endeavoured to give a balanced picture of a heated and tangled business. Yet here he is accused, as *T.T.* itself is accused, of exaggerated statements, and sentences are quoted which are not to be found anywhere in our files.[8]

But the correspondence was not all hostile. From Margot Asquith B-W received a little personal note, with a cutting from a *Daily Telegraph* leader which said that '*The Times* and other papers have presented views on Greece which events have left without justification'; her comment was 'Enclosed would make a cat laugh'. To which B-W, feeling deeply the strain of constant altercation, replied:

I have just opened and read your little note and write on the instant to tell you how it has warmed my heart. Where so many people seem to have taken leave of their senses and of their power to follow an argument, it is indeed refreshing, though not in the least surprising, to have this token of understanding and friendship.

To other old friends and readers, many of whom had relatives in Greece, B-W had to explain that the paper's first duty was not to the Government or to the troops but to the truth; and in January he was able to claim that the Government was now following the course recommended by the paper: support for a Regency, preparations for free elections, disarming of rival factions, recruitment of a national army and economic revival. It seems to have struck neither him nor his leader-writers that proposals which were reasonable in mid-January might have been impracticable and premature in mid-December. Perhaps there was a failure or reluctance to understand, as in the case of the Nazis, how cunning and bloodthirsty the gangster politicians of Europe could be.*

*The simplest, expert comment on *The Times*'s handling of this episode comes from Hon. C. M. Woodhouse, who commanded the Allied Military Mission to Greek Guerrillas in German-occupied Greece from August 1943:

'It was a failure to see that E.A.M., though it included a fair sprinkling of well-advertised liberals, was in fact purely and simply an instrument of the Communists; and the only object of the Communists was to secure complete power. It follows that *The Times*'s policy (plebiscite on the monarchy, elections, parliamentary democracy etc.) was irreconcilable with their sympathy for E.A.M.,

Churchill's displeasure with the paper was expressed in more than one way. The leading article of 7 December, he believed, represented 'the opinion of Professor Carr', and he wondered 'whether this might not be the occasion for some straight talking to Mr Barrington-Ward'. His secretary was told to consult Brendan Bracken, the Minister of Information. That the rebuke was passed on is suggested by B-W's diary note, 'This morning's leader is said to have enraged Winston. But it is he who had made it possible for the Greek troubles to be laid at our door.' A fortnight later, shortly before midnight, just as B-W was trying to get away from the office for a few days of Christmas holiday, Churchill rang up to explain the new call-up for the forces.

Then with no encouragement from me he got on to Greece.... I said (wishing to end the conversation and let Horner catch his train) that what all wanted was an early conclusion to the affair. 'So do I, but not at the price of a humiliating skedaddle by British troops.' Then he said I must come and see him. I said I had been waiting for a signal. 'No need to wait for a signal.'... I said I was pulling out for a few days if I could. 'You're going off to eat turkey I suppose, and all that. Ah well, I shall have to stay on here.'... I said I would approach him later and we could talk then. On that, at last, he rang off.[4]

What Churchill did not tell B-W was that two days later he would be in Athens with Eden, personally intervening in the dangerous situation and doing some of the things *The Times* had recommended. On 1 February Tyerman told B-W that Bracken had told Waldorf Astor (owner of the *Observer*) that *The Times* would not be forgiven over Greece until it had climbed down. 'Very well,' B-W comments in his diary, 'it will not be forgiven.' Then five days later he and Bracken lunched alone:

I then told him that I made no complaint of Winston's attack on *T.T.* Ministers were entitled to defend themselves. Equally *T.T.* would defend itself. (He assented and said that the attacks on *T.T.* had been overdone.) I went on, however, to say that I found Win-

because if E.A.M. had come out on top, none of the rest of the policy would have been allowed to take place. The Foreign Office's error, on the other hand, was that by excessive loyalty to the King, they forced the liberals in E.A.M. to make common cause with the Communists instead of breaking away from them in 1944. (Letter to the author, January 1970.)

ston's onslaught surprising. He had talked to me just before Christmas, had asked for some help (which I have given him), and spoken of Greece (and I had gladly offered to come and see him after Christmas). *T.T.* had printed a most laudatory leader about his Christmas visit to Athens (Brendan nodded), had congratulated the Government most warmly on the conclusion of a truce, and was preparing to give Winston unqualified credit for developments from it. . . .'

Then he told me that he and Max had restrained Winston from sending me a scolding letter, with references to 'Munich' too. Brendan had told him, 'You can't berate an editor like that. He may be wrong and I think he is but he has his point of view as you have yours. Beside you can't tackle him on "Munich", that was Geoffrey Dawson's responsibility.' 'Ah well,' said Winston (according to B.B.) 'he has made a better thing of *T.T.* since Geoffrey Dawson went.' (I received this with no special satisfaction and exhibited none, having no desire to profit at G.D.'s supposed expense.) Further, according to Brendan, Winston was intending to say much more about *T.T.* in his speech. Here Max restrained him. 'No, no,' said Max, 'look at the whole record of *T.T.* and its fine work in this war. And which paper gave you the best leader on your birthday?' . . . I have a v. warm spot for Brendan. He is v. easy to talk to in the most candid way and, though he may take some colour from his company, that helps the process.[5]

There could not be a more revealing picture of Bracken at work on behalf of his master; conciliating, flattering, explaining and informing. One can imagine B-W's quick, sparkling smile of pleasure when the Minister of Information, at a party where they met during this stormy time, said that the Government's daily prayer was 'Give Us Peace In Our Times, Oh Lord'. For, although it was very disturbing to a conscientious and patriotic man to feel that his judgement of a dangerous complicated situation might be wrong, it was also very exciting to the journalist to know that his paper was being eagerly read on both sides of politics, was being argued about and was influencing Government policy. Among the directors of the paper, however, there was one who thought criticism was going too far.

23

Skirmish at Carlton House Terrace

Only once during his time in the chair did B-W feel that his independence was being challenged by his employers, the Joint Proprietors and Directors. It was in the summer after the end of the war, when public opinion was coming to terms with what promised to be a permanent Russian presence in central Europe and a long, if only temporary, Labour presence in Downing Street. The challenge was quite unorganized and developed into nothing more than the politest of skirmishes over the dinner-table. It worried the Editor none the less, for there was in 1946 enough querulous gossip and open criticism of the paper's policies outside the office without the added embarrassment of snipers within the gates. In fact his position was virtually unassailable. The paper was prospering and had made record profits in 1945; Astor liked and respected him; he was protected by the clear agreement about the respective roles of Editor and Board which Dawson had drawn up before returning to the chair in 1922.

He was to be free in the fullest sense of the word to use his own judgement. He would – and should – consult the proprietors, but there would be no interference from the Board, or the Manager, or the Managing Director – who was then (1922) Campbell Stuart.* The Board would be chosen part by Astor and part by Walter – not from members of the staff – and would attend to the financial side of the paper. The Editor would be present at Board meetings but he would answer

*As Managing Director during Steed's brief editorship (1919–22) Stuart's powers had been considerable, and he was the main channel of communication between Northcliffe and the editorial staff. His position in the office had been strengthened by the frequent absences abroad of an editor who felt that no important international conference was complete without him. How the agreement was arrived at, with Milner acting as Dawson's chief adviser, is described in the *History of The Times*, Volume IV, Part 2, pp. 774 ff.

for his work only to the Chief Proprietors, who alone had the right to appoint him.

It is reasonable to assume that B-W had read, though he nowhere mentions it, the clear and vigorous memorandum of 18 November 1922, in which Dawson stated his view of the Editor's rights. The document is as fresh and relevant today as it was fifty years ago.

The conduct of a newspaper [Dawson wrote] differs from every other business in the world inasmuch as it has two quite distinct objects which are ultimately both dependent on one another, yet are in constant opposition. They can only be achieved by the closest cooperation and by daily compromises.... These two objects, of course, are (1) to reflect and guide public opinion by producing a good newspaper and (2) to make money by producing a profitable newspaper.

Inevitably, Editor and Manager would often clash: for example, over the relative space to be given to advertisements or over the cost of foreign correspondence. But so long as each consulted the other, differences could be overcome. The right of the proprietors of a newspaper 'to do what they choose with their own property' was not in question. But their intentions should be known in advance by those conducting the property. Then comes the key passage:

Every Editor worth his salt must have a 'free hand' to conduct his side of the paper as he thinks best so long as he is in charge of it. The power of the Proprietors is exercised properly by the appointment and dismissal of the Editor, not by interfering with his work or doing it themselves.

This sentence is obviously aimed not at the Walters, but at the late Lord Northcliffe.

This was the relationship built up by Dawson in his second period of editing and inherited by his successor. There were occasional grumbles from John Walter V, a few doubts expressed by the tactful and modest John Astor and emphatic, protesting letters about 'appeasement' and defence policy from Bob Brand – but written as from an old friend and not as a director. If the proprietors and directors felt worried about the paper's policy they had no right of formal protest or control. But there was nothing to prevent either Walter or Astor asking the Editor questions in private and informal conversation. It was something of this order that David Bowes-Lyon had in mind when he and other directors met the Editor at dinner in June 1946, at their Chairman's invitation. How was this meeting brought about?

One evening in May 1946, B-W was dining alone with Astor at 18 Carlton House Terrace to discuss office problems.* His host, quite casually, asked if he would mind meeting the directors one night at an informal dinner party. Made in the Chairman's low-voiced, diffident manner, this was not an alarming suggestion; but some Editors might have refused.† B-W said he saw no objection, provided that it was not regarded as a meeting to discuss the paper's policy. Dinner was fixed for 5 June. He thought no more about it until he met by chance Campbell Stuart at a Lancaster House reception.

He pulled a long face on seeing me and we had a very brief talk. 'I don't like this dinner at all, this discussion of policy. It's dangerous.' I said I would not budge an inch. 'No, I know,' he said, 'and I'm your backer.'[1]

He was now wondering whether his ready acceptance had not been rather unguarded. Although the Chairman had remarked that David Bowes-Lyon was 'a bit of a diehard', he had not made it clear what was the purpose of the dinner.‡ Why should he, the Editor, be called on to defend his policy just because it was disapproved of by some Conservatives with friends on the Board. 'The flourishing condition of the paper' should protect him, as he put it, 'under our own roof and in our family.'

Lunching with Stuart a few days later, he learned what had happened at a dinner on Astor's birthday which he had missed

---

*The Editor's confidence in his Chairman was complete and the diary has many references to their friendship. He realized how important was Astor's support, as a respected and wealthy Conservative, for the radical policies the paper was advocating. 'Apart from my deep personal feeling for him, including admiration for the most truly modest man I have known, he is essential to *The Times* on its present line.'[2]

†Lord Astor to the author, October 1969.

‡David Bowes-Lyon (1902–61) was an uncle of Queen Elizabeth II and became a director in February 1939. He had entered merchant banking from Oxford and his outstanding contribution to the war effort was made when he moved to Washington in 1942 as head of the Political Warfare Mission. He did much to foster good Anglo-American relationships and Franklin Roosevelt became one of his admirers. He was an outspoken Tory and, according to one colleague, 'a good hater'.

owing to illness. Bowes-Lyon, with some slight support from Walter (who was worried about the paper's attitude towards the Russians), had argued that the Board must have some right to judgement on editorial policy, only to be quickly disabused by other directors. Indeed, Stuart said, Astor had been 'absolutely stout and loyal throughout' and was supported by Laurence Irving and Harold Hartley. He added that dinner on 5 June would involve the Editor in no more than a review of events at home and abroad 'in the light of the special knowledge coming in to the office'. He thereupon decided to stand without protest by his acceptance of the invitation. The momentous evening came and proved something of an anti-climax. Four directors, apart from Astor and Walter, came to dinner and the Editor's dignity was not affronted.

Campbell . . . put me a leading question and we had a general talk on politics, keeping it all clear of the paper and its responsibilities, though I was glad to be able to point out once or twice what independence in journalism means and what kind of criticism it is likely to attract. In the end it all seemed quite useful. I judged that we ended up a united party. Back very late into the office.[3]

Some people had come to think of *The Times* as a Conservative newspaper because for fifteen years it was supporting Conservative politicians, albeit in national or wartime coalition governments. Now they saw it giving friendly but critical support to Socialist policies at home and showing abroad a measure of understanding of Moscow attitudes greater than the Foreign Secretary, Ernest Bevin, thought right. Not surprisingly, anyone who knew a director of *The Times* and disapproved of its policy – members of the Board had connections in the City, in the Royal Society, at Court, in the world of the theatre and press – would ask why the paper was 'going pink'. It may well have been embarrassing for a director to explain that his power of intervention was non-existent.

On the point of principle B-W was right, and he had no more trouble. If his attitude seems over-sensitive, it has to be remembered what were the social pressures that could be brought on a man in his position. A passage from his diary illustrates this:

To Westminster for a sherry party given by the Head Master and Mrs Christie at 17 Dean's Yard. B. of B. [Balfour of Burleigh] says he is always defending me against attacks from his Conservative colleagues. Apparently I am accused of knocking the paper to bits. I told him how the circulation stood. He said he was very glad to hear it. B. of B. has real integrity and independence.[4]

He was, in fact, thrilled to be writing and editing against opposition: 'I should not budge an inch' is characteristic. 'He was not at all put off, but was rather reassured,' wrote Iverach McDonald, 'if he was writing against his own natural instincts. If he took a line that some might call unpatriotic, he was the more sure he was right because it was against his own strongly patriotic instincts. All this set up great tensions inside him.'[*] We can see now – what he perhaps did not perceive at the time – the irony of the situation: a man who before the war had been treated by Socialists and Communists – and some Tories – as almost a traitor to his country, for advocating peaceful co-existence with Fascists and Germans, was now being regarded by the right and some Socialists as a traitor to his class and its newspaper for advocating peaceful co-existence with Communists and Russians.

What did the Editor mean by the 'independent journalism' which he had defended over dinner? It was for him the expression of views and the support of policies which the privileged, powerful and wealthy might regard as threatening their interests. To see *The Times* advocating, however persuasively, new economic thinking, drastic social reforms and good relations with Stalin was irritating and disturbing. As leader of the Conservative Party in war, Churchill had not encouraged such thinking, despite the efforts behind the scenes of Butler and others; the paper had attacked what it regarded as his short-sighted and mischievous leadership.

People of these views understood, some of them, that *The Times*, as a national institution, was expected to maintain an objective, restrained tone and to give Socialists a fair crack of the whip; but they also felt, most of them, that Socialism at home and the appeasement of Russia could not possibly be in the national interest. Twenty-five years later the argument still goes on; and some believe that the movement leftwards of *The Times* assisted the spectacular post-war increase in the circulation of the *Daily Telegraph*, with its more predictable

*Iverach McDonald, in a letter to the author, 1969.

and intransigent views. B-W himself believed that men and women of the moderate left must play an ever greater part in the running of the country and must now be treated with the respect due to His Majesty's Opposition – and as probable readers of the paper.

It is tempting to speculate that he may have been influenced by what he had learnt while editing the History during the early thirties. Stanley Morison's researches had revealed for the first time in detail the radical strata in the paper's tradition and the greatness of Barnes (1817–41). Living memory was then still of the editorship of Buckle (1884–1912) who thought of his staff as a fellowship and of his paper as an institution. The reminder – for some it was the first inkling – that Barnes had backed Reform, and the new men of commerce and industry against inherited wealth and the power of land caused some surprise in the office. B-W, who edited much of Morison's and other authors' drafts, was probably more impressed than anyone and perhaps felt his 'radicalism' rekindled. 'Independence' then, in this sense, has much to do with the tradition that has made *The Times* an institution.

A. P. Wadsworth, while he was Editor of the *Manchester Guardian,* praised B-W for restoring the 'political independence' of his paper. The judgement is only half true. It would be fairer to say that he corrected its class image. Dawson had no more kow-towed to Conservative Ministers than B-W did to Labour Ministers. Indeed, on a number of occasions he asserted the paper's independence in sensational style. He talked policy with Halifax and Chamberlain as an equal and as a friend, as B-W did later with Bevin and Cripps. His real offence, in the eyes of progressive circles, was his indifference to fresh thinking about the way the economic and social life of Britain – and other countries – might be directed. For this, B-W, as we have seen, tried to make amends from the very first month that Carr was on the staff. And it was this trend, expressed in Carr's trenchant style, which understandably roused the hostility of Bowes-Lyon of Eton, Magdalen and Lazard's.

24

Last Years

Geoffrey Dawson is 58 to-day and has shown no
sign of retirement; Barnes died at 58; Delane
went mad at 58; I resigned at 58; and no man
can edit *The Times* after 58 and live.
            George Earle Buckle to Dermot Morrah, 1932

I may or may not live a few months, but my real
life ends here; all that was worth having of it
has been devoted to the paper.
            Delane on retiring from the editorship.

During his last three years of life (1946–8) B-W strove hard,
probably too hard, to maintain his fitness. None of the doctors
whom he consulted about persistent minor ailments could find
anything seriously wrong with him. Early in March 1947 a
very bad bout of influenza kept him away from the office for
nearly three weeks, during part of which he was treated 'very
much as an invalid' at Dorneywood. But in April he was
congratulating himself on a nine mile walk and just after that
on doing fifteen miles with his younger son Simon. 'I am
much out of condition,' he noted – his standards being high.
In May a specialist gave him a thorough overhaul with the
usual result: 'Gave me an absolutely clean bill of health but
evidently thinks I am overworked and overtired as indeed I am
– look at my tell-tale handwriting.'[1] The hand's failure was a
symptom of the palsy which was to show itself clearly later
in the year. Colleagues noticed a falling off in his performance
but he himself grew impatient with doctors who could find
nothing wrong with a man who claimed 'to feel extremely well'.
In July they insisted on three weeks in bed and it was arranged
that he should take his rest at a house on the cliffs of St
Margaret's Bay in Kent which was rented for the summer from a
cousin, Jack Ward. Here he lazed and read in a garden chair
through wonderful sunny weather; he was allowed no bathing
and only the mildest walking. The office kept in touch and

265

Casey and Morison visited him. Some improvement showed and he thought in September of returning to the office, though they implored him not to.

I still feel no real recuperation ... slow and tired, handwriting difficult. These are symptoms attributed to overwork. But I think there must be some more specific cause.[2]

And a week later: 'I am slow, weak and a little unsteady in my balance. . . . What can the cause be?' One day he wrote that he would like to try his own specific: 'plenty of rest *and* plenty of exercise', the familiar, demanding weekend ritual.

This slow, sad collapse of the fifteenth Editor of *The Times* was discussed and measured as anxiously as the mortal illness of a king. Stanley Morison, full of concern for his friend, was at the heart of it all, and discussed the symptoms with Adele. She warned him that Robin 'always looks very disturbed at the slightest reference of his being unwell'. 'The difference, and it is striking,' wrote Morison to Astor, 'lies in the slowness, compared with the old rapidity of mind and body.'

His voice was flat: he had that difficulty in speaking which marks the overtired man. His silences were longer and more numerous and his walking even slower than when I saw him a month before. His shaving exhibited a very uncharacteristic lack of precision. The whole of his processes had decelerated.[3]

This was on 2 September and Morison warned the Chairman that no amount of rest would bring back the B-W of ten years ago. He must never be allowed to re-establish the old four-teen-hour day. Indeed, a reorganization of the editorial department should make such a thing impossible for B-W or any other editor.

When B-W returned to the office in mid-September he seemed a little better, and by early October a good deal better. Astor, the Chairman, so tactful and reserved, congratulated him and said he had nearly spoken about his apparent weariness, where-upon B-W assured him that he would shorten his day by sharing work after dinner with Casey. But soon the symptoms returned and one day in November, after a Board meeting, Astor came to B-W's room and urged him to get away for at least three months. The Editor protested that he could not do this with the nation's affairs as they were (it was the day that Chancellor Dalton on his way into the House leaked his Budget proposals to the political correspondent of the *Star*) but Astor firmly pointed out that there would always be crises of one kind or another and that if one waited for a lull in political excitement it would never come.

The doctors agreed with the idea of a holiday abroad. A neurologist was consulted – surprisingly, for the first time – and it was admitted (to Adele but not to the victim) that there were signs of serious illness. Campbell Stuart, the director of the paper who took most personal interest in the Editor, kindly cleared the way by offering passages in the *Durban Castle* bound for South Africa. This meant leaving on 1 January. So B-W reluctantly gave final instructions to Casey and Tyerman, said a round of *au revoirs* to his staff and cleared his desk for the last time. The last letter he wrote was to the Master of Balliol recommending two names for the Montague Burton Chair of International Relations: first his old college friend Namier, and after him his old colleague Carr. Neither of these formidable personalities was chosen.

For seventeen days he relaxed, even neglecting his diary, reading with delight *Tono Bungay* and the *History of Mr Polly*, as well as some Marlowe presented to him for Christmas by Mark. When they reached South Africa the physical symptoms had not improved but he was able to pay a round of more or less official visits combined with sight-seeing. Was this really the kind of holiday he needed? They met Cecilia, Geoffrey Dawson's widow, who was shocked by B-W's appearance and strongly advised against continuing their journey in another ship through the heat of the east coast. But B-W was not to be deterred and on they went to Zanzibar, Lourenço Marques and Tanga. . . .

A few days after his fifty-seventh birthday, on board ship in the steaming heat of Dar-es-Salaam harbour, B-W died quickly and mercifully of cerebral malaria. This was no sudden collapse of slowly returning health or unexpected crisis in the Parkinson's Disease which had driven him to take a long holiday. It was caused by one of the most deadly infections of the East African coast, which he was in no state to resist for long. In a letter home to Robin's sisters Adele described how, after two days in bed, having no idea that he was dangerously ill, 'his temperature suddenly soared on the Saturday evening and he knew nothing'. She found some comfort for herself and the family in the thought that Robin had been spared a crippling and humiliating advance of his palsy, the symptoms of which had already caused him embarrassment in public and anxiety in private. To lift a proof from the desk or to handle steadily a knife and fork had become an ordeal, for him and for those watching him. The handwriting of the diaries had slowly deteriorated. On his previous birthday there was a premonitory note in the diary:

56 today. Barnes and Delane did not last beyond 58. So far I have had great luck. Should like to do more writing myself. Must keep fit.[4]

On Monday, 2 March, the unexpected news sent by Alan Neville, the paper's local correspondent with the *Tanganyika Standard*, was given top position on the middle column of the Bill page. Modest headlines for the late Editor had to compete on one side with 'Cairo Haifa Train Mined: 20 British Soldiers Killed and Wounded – the Stern Gang at work again' – and on the other side with 'Communists Consolidating in Prague', a juxtaposition – having regard to the past role of *The Times* in that country's affairs – of sad and malevolent irony.* The leading article that morning was entitled 'March Winds' and opened with a sinister sentence:

While Czechoslovakia is hammered into shape without open pressure from the Soviet Union, the Russian sickle flashes warningly at Finland.

Under the bare announcement of death there was placed a personal tribute, composed at the shortest notice, probably by Casey himself, who had been left in charge during B-W's absence, with help from Morison and Tyerman.

Barrington-Ward's standards, personal and professional, were high. By nature he was just, scrupulous, exact. The strict rule he applied to his subordinates he imposed upon himself. No servant of Printing House Square in the present generation has exacted more from himself in the endeavour to maintain the tradition of *The Times*. He saw his task as a mission to be fulfilled and he fulfilled it always with courage and devotion. It cannot be said that his contribution was made without effort. Rather it was made by conscious direction of the will, strengthened by a native sense of duty.

*Only ten days later Jan Masaryk was found dead in Prague in circumstances which suggested murder by political enemies.

Barrington-Ward was a man of genuine religion. He brought to
The Times a rare combination of talent, conscientiousness and
modesty. No Editor in a long line had given to his work greater
integrity and honesty of purpose.

He was completely unselfish in his dealings with his colleagues,
ever giving reward where it was due and taking to himself none of
the credit for the work of others.

He was austere yet humane, ready to forgive conduct in others
that he would not tolerate in himself. He took great pains over the
contributions of his colleagues, so that little of the comment on
the news that went into the paper did not bear, though invisibly,
the mark of his hand.

His keen sense of the errors of Versailles and the logical nature
of his mind led him, even after 1939, to work hard for peace. As a
soldier he knew what war was and was prepared to go far to prevent
a repetition of its destructiveness and wastefulness.

If there are reservations and omissions in this judgement, which
the reader who has come thus far in B-W's biography will at
once detect, it has to be remembered that this death was a
shocking surprise to the office generally and to the Deputy
Editor in particular. Casey, who only a year earlier had been
considering retirement, found himself in sole charge. No
plans had been made for the succession, and he was suddenly
expected to compose an epitaph to the man whose place he
did not wish or expect to take. Was he to comment on the policy
of the thirties in which he himself had cooperated – or
unsuccessfully opposed? But that, in the eyes of the world, had
been Dawson's policy, not B-W's. Was he, too, to ignore the view
– widely talked about in the office – that the late editor had
worked himself to death? There was, in any case, the balancing factor of a long and stylish obituary notice on another
page.*

Other newspapers were noticeably friendly, as they had been
when B-W became Editor. The *News Chronicle* called him a

---

*John Walter V, descendant of the paper's founder and still a part proprietor,
who had been more than once alarmed at the trend of policy under B-W, sent
the following tribute to his widow:

'Of all his qualities the one perhaps that appealed to me most was that fine
sense of honour that impelled him to discharge the obligations of his position
without regard to his own comfort and convenience. Such rare integrity of
character is not often joined, as it was in him, with a disarming naturalness of
manner and a genuine desire to understand and make full allowance for the views
of those who disagreed with him.'[5]

'liberal reformer' who 'disliked privilege and was suspicious of doctrinaires'. The outlook of his paper, it said, had been revolutionized during his editorship: 'That the revolution was so quietly accomplished by so unassuming a personality should not blind anyone to its importance.' He had seen that the debate of the future would be 'to define the frontiers of freedom and social security'. The *Manchester Guardian*, too, went close to claiming B-W as one of its own. Under him *The Times* had become 'much more open to liberal influences and took a courageous part in commending bold policies of social reconstruction (sometimes bold to the point of heresy)'. It is remarkable that neither of these papers took the dead man to task for those leaders on Germany which ten years earlier had them foaming at the mouth. Had they forgiven or forgotten? Or were they just being generous to the dead, more generous than they had been to Dawson?

On 2 March the funeral – which took place at once as there was no possibility of cremation and bringing the ashes back to Britain – was briefly reported by the local correspondent:

> In the hot, sandy square of the new cemetery at Dar-es-Salaam a little group of people yesterday paid their last respects.

It was the bleak burial of an exile. To keep the widow company there was only a handful of local officials and personalities who had helped to make the Barrington-Wards welcome during their visit. The next day Mr James, a linotype operator from P.H.S. who was emigrating to South Africa on the same ship, had the gracious thought to pay his respects on behalf of the Compositors' Chapel. He wrote back to *The Times House Journal* that he found the cemetery surrounded by a four foot wall and shaded by mimosa, flamboyant, and coconut palms, with the open side overlooking the sea.

> When I reached the newly-made mound, the wreaths of flowers on which had already wilted in the hot sun, my thoughts turned immediately to P.H.S. I remembered Mr Barrington-Ward's cheerful 'good evening' to all who worked in the basement during the blitz and how we used to chat while 'on the slate' and agree among ourselves that he was 'a decent sort and a good editor'.[6]

The *New York Times*, following the courteous tradition that each of the great newspapers of that name should take a friendly interest in the affairs of the other, wrote in a leading article:

He drove himself hard and it may accurately be said that he was a casualty of the war and of his own deep sense of responsibility in trying to set a wise course in the trying days that followed the war. . . . He was gentle in manner, eager for ideas, tolerant of the opinions of others.

In fact, there is no evidence that the war shortened the life of this strenuous man. The strain on him was greatest when he was trying both to edit and write, that is to say, in the thirties. That the wartime years, with their smaller papers and concentration of attention, were less arduous is evident from the diaries. The final collapse was due not to overwork but to an illness for which, in those days, there was no cure and the early diagnosis of which was difficult. There is no medical reason for believing that if he had rested more and driven himself less fiercely his editorship might have been much prolonged.

The Memorial Service was held on 31 March in St Paul's Cathedral where B-W had often sat a while in prayer, or hearing part of a service, when the state of the news brought him to London on a Sunday or during an Easter or Whitsun weekend. The family were amazed at the size and distinction of the congregation. The Prime Minister and the Lord Mayor were represented. Wavell, Trenchard and Ismay were there; Samuel, Dawson of Penn, the Governor of the Bank, Beaverbrook, Haley from the BBC and Reith. From Oxford came the Master of Balliol and other University representatives.

Many of those who came to St Paul's that forenoon would have been sources and contacts of the journalist become friends of the man. Tributes which appeared that morning in his own paper praised his 'gift for friendship'; one called him 'a gentle soul who won the DSO and the MC'. The notice in the Court Page mentioned the bowl of primroses on the chancel steps – a yellow speck of spring in the vast building – which came from the Vicar of St Bride's in Pembrokeshire, where Robin, Adele, Mark, Simon and Caroline had made many friends during those memorable seaside holidays. None at the time, except perhaps Stanley Morison (still working at his History of the paper), seems to have noticed that here was yet another Editor dying before sixty, sharing the fate of Delane and Barnes. But the coincidence was noted later, and to recall it here is to raise the question how far the comparison can be in other respects sustained.

25

Fifteenth Editor

Any comparison of stature between Barrington-Ward and previous editors of *The Times* is bound to be in part speculative. To show what he could do on his own he had only seven years, four of them war years and the rest a time of small papers and scarce newsprint. Had he lived he would have taken his newspaper into the fifties, a period of Tory supremacy under Churchill, Eden and Macmillan, and of retreat from imperial responsibilities. It is reasonable to guess that its attitude during the years between Attlee and Wilson would have been critical and crusading; for as B-W gained self-confidence he became more radical. It is unlikely, however, that he would have found a substitute after 1947 for the powerful influence of Carr. *The Times* would have stayed slightly left of centre but its role would have been less conspicuous than it was, say, in 1944.

The name that immediately suggests itself for comparison is that of Thomas Barnes, the eighth editor under whom (1817–41) *The Times* became known as The Thunderer, and who was 'the first man to become a responsible editor in the sense familiar to later generations'. The quotation is from Geoffrey Dawson's introduction to the first volume of *The History of The Times,* published in 1935, on which B-W laboured long and lovingly at polishing Stanley Morison's prose. Barnes's greatness was, indeed, Morison's discovery, and its impact on B-W was strong. It revealed a radical tradition in Printing House Square of which the vast majority of readers knew nothing. Barnes, unlike the great newshound Delane who followed him, was a writing editor. Under bitter attack from the right, he supported political reform, attacked social abuses and encouraged the new middle class and the workers against privilege and reaction.

When B-W succeeded in 1941 the middle-class had been in power for over half a century – that was why they regarded *The Times* as the organ of the Establishment – and it was their turn to concede and share power. That this was the basic political problem of the twenties was overlooked by Dawson and barely appreciated by B-W at the *Observer*; but it had become apparent ten years later and to deal with it was part of B-W's plan when he took over at *The Times*. In this respect then – that he made the paper move with the times and saw the opportunity to win the interest of readers with backgrounds, education and interests quite different from those of the traditional reader – B-W can stand comparison with unquestionably the greatest personality to sit in the chair at Printing House Square. Like Barnes he showed courage, independence and dedication.

In other respects the comparison is not to B-W's advantage. He was a less formidable, immediately impressive figure. Clear and eloquent though he was in his writing, he suffered from the inhibitions bequeathed by Victorian predecessors who believed – or feigned to believe – that *The Times* must be always oracular and never conversational, always judicious and never partisan, always ready to keep the King's government going on. B-W could not have written about the Tolpuddle martyrs as Barnes did:

We have been called enemies of the working class; but by whom? By miscreants who cheat and prey upon them. We are too upright to be flatterers of the wealthy, and what honest man will dare charge us with having *ever* abandoned or betrayed the poor? ... Who would now open the poor man's eyes to the snares and treacheries which his mock friends are practising against him, who but this *Times* journal? – the object of every villain's vengeance and of every slanderer's abuse. On such creatures we disdain to waste words – we despise and defy them.

However, like Barnes B-W wrote leaders to get things done; and it was Stanley Morison who praised as 'Barnes-like' two of B-W's early leaders about appeasement. Likewise, the judgements of contemporaries do not accord to the fifteenth Editor the personal brilliance of Barnes, who was a Bohemian figure, unconventional and full of gusto, reckless with his health, convivial and hearty. As an editor he made himself a figure of

273

mystery and was seldom seen around town; B-W was accessible and much seen around town, though unknown to the general public. The vital difference between them in experience and mood was that Barnes, at the age when B-W was fighting in the trenches, was idling in London running through the few thousands he had inherited after leaving Cambridge.* High seriousness, sometimes with deep pessimism underlying it, was not uncommon among those who survived the First World War.

As original and brave an editor as Barnes, but a less impressive and colourful personality – that seems a fair verdict. But for B-W's critics it does not answer their questions about his judgement: judgement first on the Nazis and later on post-war Russia. Did he not err so greatly as to forfeit the right to such comparisons? However, *The Times* under Barnes also made serious errors of judgement, as controversial newspapers always will, and Barnes was probably as much influenced by Brougham as B-W was by Carr. The previous chapters should have shown that B-W was not deceived by the Nazis, or by the Communists, but underrated their readiness to use violence, fraud, blackmail and conspiracy in a manner virtually unknown to British politics outside Ireland. So deep was his horror of war and his fear of what another conflict would do to Europe, that he gave both enemies of Britain the benefit of every jot and tittle of doubt that he could sustain. About the Nazis he said later that appeasement had ensured that the Commonwealth went into war in 1939 united and convinced of its cause. What he would have said later about the Russians is not easily guessed, even though his scepticism about Stalin was growing just before he died.

Such errors of judgement in international affairs are not unusual in the generous and liberal-minded. As Stanley Morison wrote in the History:

> With him justice was a principle of individual, national and international obligation; not an item of his policy but an article of his creed, loyalty to which in national and international affairs served him in place of ideology.

*Barnes was educated at Christ's Hospital and was a fine Classical scholar. Anyone interested in comparing his youth with B-W's will find it described in Derek Hudson's biography *Thomas Barnes of The Times*, Cambridge University Press 1944.

What Morison, his intimate friend, failed to see was that there was no contradiction between the pre-war champion of 'appeasement' and the post-war champion of social reconstruction. His work was consistently dedicated, as he said in 1919 it would be, to 'the creation and organization of peace, above all things, and for the liberating truths at home, at whatever cost to conventional opinion'.

The judgement of a younger colleague, Basil Davidson, who left *The Times* for the *New Statesman* after B-W died, is illuminating. He succeeded Con O'Neill as a leader-writer in 1947, aged thirty-three and with a reputation for 'leftish' views. Davidson wrote to the author:

B-W wanted to open his columns to a large number of things that were new and strange; he encouraged one to secure interviews with unlikely people such as Tito and Thorez; he knew that many landmarks and secure points in his early landscape had gone for good, and he was ready to discover whatever new ones, good or bad, that there might be now.

Had B-W survived, he suggests, the benefit to *The Times* would have been great:

Never since then has the paper achieved that same mixture of tough and determined pride in itself combined with an eager curiosity and readiness for whatever might be new and difficult. B-W edited out of his own character and convictions, not evading issues, not baulking at personal responsibility, always taking the burden himself.

Donald Tyerman, another younger colleague, who was thirty-six when he joined B-W as assistant editor, shares Davidson's admiration but is critical on two counts. He found it remarkable in the Editor that he seemed to have no rules of thumb for new situations, but pondered deeply in each case how *The Times* should react to each of them. In his own words:

B-W was altogether a principled man but not a man of principles, wanting all the time to do the right thing but searching round to find what the right thing was, looking always for the right principles to apply, and supported always by reserves of common sense.

Tyerman thinks that B-W lacked any real programme; but in the diary for 5 April 1942 there is a clear statement of aim: 'to create through *The Times* a central bloc of opinion agreed on a national minimum and prepared to see it through – peaceful revolution'. B-W certainly had a political faith. It is stated in his diary for 27 April 1934:

Democracy, self-government, political neighbourliness—call it what we will—is an essential to human progress, and the only form of social structure which is true to Christ's own idea of the Kingdom of Heaven *on earth* (not in a next world), nor yet to be brought about by Messianic and miraculous intervention . . . I feel a sense of liberation in worshipping Christ without miracles. His message is for us on earth and in our own day, to build or to build towards his earthly commonwealth. . . . Time will expose the emptiness of the Fascist and Nazi 'philosophies'. What are they but registrations, like the Greek tyrannies, of democratic breakdowns? Inevitable, for their time, they probably are; and may serve a turn in holding society together. But systems with the power and right to survive, No. They must deny true growth to the human organism.

He had, it is true, just been reading Lionel Curtis's *Civitas Dei*; but this is not the only evidence that he was a man of long views.

Perhaps the intellectual difficulty in which he sometimes found himself is best described thus: a natural fluency was hampered by the feeling that he must say what *The Times* would say – a point of view which Carr found it hard to accept and which would have meant nothing to Barnes. There went on in B-W's mind a three-cornered debate between what conscience prompted to believe was right, what instinct made him spontaneously feel, and what his understanding of the paper's tradition told him should be written. His instinct in 1945 may have been to vote Tory; but reason told him that led by Churchill the Tories would not carry out the social programme that B-W's conscience demanded. His instinct was to boil with rage when he heard what the Nazis were doing to the Jews and their political opponents. But his reason made him ask whether *The Times* would increase or diminish its influence in Germany by compiling a 'Bradshaw of political atrocities' such as his conscience made him feel was due to friends like Kurt Hahn.* Yet B-W had plenty of that cheerful, cynical, down-to-earth

*The phrase is used in a letter from B-W to Kurt Hahn dated 7 March 1939 in reply to complaints that the paper was giving insufficient attention to the persecutions going on in Germany: 'We should be able to help and, in a crisis we certainly can help. But I think we shall weaken our power if our Press *merely* becomes a sort of Bradshaw of atrocities, minor and major, from day to day.'

common-sense which among the British gains a man the reputation for being 'sound'.

In his earnestness and success in producing a serious newspaper B-W may be compared among his contemporaries with Hubert Beuve-Méry of *Le Monde*. In his determination to be independent and to make independence pay, he can be compared with C. P. Scott – who, however, had the great advantage of being his own Manager. If he did not fully grasp the significance of what Lord Camrose was doing to make the *Daily Telegraph* the great rival of his paper (its circulation by 1939 was over three times that of *The Times*), he did a lot to make *The Times* look as lively and elegant as possible. His eye for controversial topics and love of argument would have been approved by Northcliffe, who used to tell Dawson that the first object of a newspaper must be to get talked about.

Not unnaturally B-W's critics on the staff saw some of these achievements in reverse. For them Carr was not a mentor but a master, in exclusive conspiracy with the Editor. 'Appeasement' they condemned as a mixture of bad judgement and moral cowardice, even in a man with such a war record. His enthusiasm was to them cranky, his radicalism out of place on *The Times,* his meticulous scrutiny of leaders finicking and time-wasting.

His introduction of new men between 1944 and 1947 was seen as unfair to established writers of reputation, and it was confidently predicted that the specialists would be unreadable – which at first was in some cases true. It is not to be expected that such critics will admit that *The Times* in 1948 – when B-W died – was a better paper than it was in 1938, when he was expecting the succession and refusing Reith's invitation to the BBC.

Whether *The Times* itself will ever revise the judgement of B-W by Stanley Morison in his final volume remains to be seen; but on its verdict will depend largely whether posterity calls him a great editor or not. Had he lived he would not have approved publication of a premature verdict on Dawson and the years of 'appeasement'. He knew, it is true, on what lines those final chapters were being planned, but no more. In the event they were written without consultation with any members of the staff of those days that this author has been able to trace. When completed, the volume was passed without editing by any second person, seen – it appears – only by the Chairman and by the Editor, then W. F. Casey. Shortly before his death, Morison told the author that he regarded his own treatment of B-W as 'perfunctory' and hoped that greater justice would be done to him. Here, it is obvious, the task of the biographer ends.

Appendix I

EDITORS OF THE TIMES

1785–9	John Walter
1789–95	William Finey
1795–1802	William Walter
1803–8	J. W. Walter II
1808–9	H. Crabb Robinson
1809–13	John Walter II
1813–16	John Stoddart
1817–41	Thomas Barnes
1841–77	John Delane
1877–84	T. Chenery
1884–1912	George Earle Buckle (at 29)
1911–19	Geoffrey Dawson (Robinson till 1917)
1919–22	Henry Wickham Steed
1922–41	Geoffrey Dawson
1941–8	R. M. Barrington-Ward
1948–52	W. F. Casey
1952–66	William Haley

Appendix II

Less than two years before his death B-W had occasion to visit the Foreign Secretary, Ernest Bevin, to discuss the release of Con O'Neill, who had been engaged as a leader-writer on foreign affairs. In two or three cases the Editor had been successful in getting quickly out of the Services or civil service key men for his reconstructed staff. In this case he not only met resistance but had also to face a counter-attack, which is described in the diary as follows:

'Then he turned to an extraordinary attack on *T.T.* He said it had no policy. It was "spineless". It was "a jelly-fish". It was neither for him nor against him. (Why should it be?) He wouldn't mind if it was either. But it was always "balancing" – (he made the gesture of twisting his hand with outstretched fingers). (All this was of course about Russia.) The *Manchester Guardian* and even the *News Chronicle* stood up to Russia.

The Times did great harm. It was taken abroad for a national newspaper. He was going to tell the H. of C. that it was not, and that it was pro-Russian and not pro-British. I had a lot of pink intelligentsia down there and he didn't believe I was in control. (Not intended as a compliment, I fear.) He had a policy. He put it to the H. of C. on 21 Feb. and *T.T.* took no notice of it. (Actually we had a leader on it.) He had a plan, though he wouldn't say what it was. Give him three years and he would build a new Commonwealth without regard for Russia or America. "I will build it up just as I built up the union" [Transport and General Workers']. He would fight etc.

This tirade was eked out with a great deal of repetition, many of the things being said two or three times. Naturally, it all took me by surprise. I had come quite unprepared for a slanging or shouting match with the Foreign Secretary. The onslaught was so crude that it was almost embarrassing for that reason alone, while the vanity and egotism of it were repellent. I kept calm – too calm, I was annoyed to think afterwards – and told him that *T.T.* had a perfectly definite line, was as ready to defend British interests as anyone else, and did its best to apply reason to foreign affairs, and so on. What I might well have told him was that his bulldozing outburst amounted to an attack on the freedom of the Press, that *T.T.* meant to show itself possessed of a mind of its own, and that people like him were usually in favour of a free and independent Press and against a free and independent newspaper. He also deserved to be told that he is self-centred, touchy, and intolerant, and more also.

I should add that I asked him if he had the U.S. with him. He said he had. I asked him what the U.S. would do. He could not say. In truth, I suppose, some allowance should be made for a harassed Minister in an admittedly awkward situation. But my opinion of Bevin is not what it was. Vain men are always limited. He was a fool to try and tackle *T.T.* in this way. It could do me no good nor him either. Having got all this off his chest, he shook hands with me twice at parting!

We also clashed over Greece. I told him that I had only supported the postponement of the elections when I found that reputable and responsible Greeks considered it essential. He said "Have you ever known a reputable Greek?" Very silly. Rendis, the foreign minister, and Aghnides, the excellent ambassador in London, are as reputable as anyone I know. But Bevin thinks that Russia has stoked up the E.A.M. in Greece and is turning the heat on him there too.'[1]

Appendix III

TREATMENT OF CORRESPONDENCE FROM BERLIN

It has been frequently alleged that the Editor of *The Times* regularly suppressed and altered, for reasons of policy, despatches from Berlin and other offices abroad which might weaken the paper's advocacy of 'appeasement'. The charge has been encouraged by quotation of Dawson's letter to Daniels of 23 May 1937 in which he said he had done his utmost 'night after night, to keep out of the paper anything that might hurt their susceptibilities'. (See p. 131 where the context of this statement is examined.)

Inquiry among former correspondents and sub-editors who dealt at one time or another with correspondence from Berlin leads to the conclusion that such a sweeping charge is either without foundation or arises from misunderstanding of what was expected of correspondents and sub-editors respectively.

Three points are clear. First, that no sub-editor (not even the chief foreign sub-editor) had authority to change the views expressed or implied in a despatch from abroad. In fact, the expression of views by correspondents – except in feature articles or memoranda to the office – was discouraged by the Editor; and his policy in this respect was enforced by an Assistant Editor, Casey, who saw all foreign despatches and advised the chief foreign sub-editor, G. L. Pearson, on their handling.

They would either themselves delete or alter messages which infringed this rule – dealing at the same time with the verbosity, obscurity and inconsistency which are inseparable from reporting done under pressure – or they would instruct a sub-editor to do so. So far as possible sub-editors would specialise in a subject or country. Thus the present writer subbed most of the Berlin messages between 1934 and 1936, unless he was in the Berlin office as a relief. In his absence they would generally be done by J. D. L. Hood.

There were, it is true, complaints from Ebbutt, Douglas

Reed and others who worked in Berlin – and in other offices – about the treatment of their messages in London. This is normal in any newspaper office. More often than not cuts would be made because other news left too little space available for all that the correspondent wanted to write. Sometimes they were made because there was too much detail or complication for the ordinary reader (e.g. over the German Church dispute); sometimes because the message was badly constructed. Correspondents did not generally realize how much the readability and accuracy of what appeared in the paper owed to the work of the sub-editors. Norman Ebbutt in Berlin, himself a former sub-editor, did realize this and was always careful to distinguish between good and bad subbing of his despatches.

The picture of Dawson sitting night after night – as one of his critics has written – suppressing and distorting the *news* from Germany is therefore false. That the paper's known views on policy towards Germany affected the writing and behaviour of the Berlin office is, of course, true; but Ebbutt, who had fought hard for the German case against Versailles in pre-Nazi days, was as well qualified as anyone to understand the reasons for the Editor's insistence that a settlement with the Germans should be attempted before war was accepted as inevitable. He, on the other hand, became more and more doubtful that Hitler and the gangster element would be displaced by moderate men.

This statement has been seen and approved by the following former sub-editors in P.H.S. and correspondents in the Berlin office:

Iverach McDonald, now Associate Editor of *The Times*
James Holburn, Editor of the *Glasgow Herald* 1955–65
G. L. Pearson, chief foreign sub-editor of *The Times* (under Dawson and B-W)
J. D. L. Hood, foreign sub-editor of *The Times* (1932–6), later Ambassador of Australia to the United Nations.
Euan Butler, foreign sub-editor of *The Times* and correspondent in Berlin (1934-39)

Appendix IV

MEMORANDUM FROM CARR TO B-W. APRIL 1944
(This is referred to on p. 241)

Fifty years ago the editorial side of P.H.S. – at any rate above the sub-editor level – probably required little organization. Its numbers were small; the issues of policy confronting it were relatively few, straightforward and non-technical; and the bill of fare offered to the reader was less varied. Questions could probably be settled as they arose by informal and unorganized personal contacts. This was the period when, at the Foreign Office, the Secretary of State was expected to read all incoming, and to write all outgoing, political despatches, and when nobody beneath the rank of an under-secretary ever wrote a minute. This happy-go-lucky age was already passing away when Northcliffe descended on P.H.S. But the Northcliffe whirlwind, while it uprooted much, planted little or nothing; and when it was over, P.H.S. sank back with an exaggerated sigh of relief into pre-Northcliffe traditions. The introduction of a crossword puzzle and the change of type and lay out modernized the external aspect of the paper. But the editorial system – or lack of system – remained substantially what it had been fifty years before.

In these circumstances it is not surprising that the organization at P.H.S. today still violates or ignores many elementary principles of sound administration. The lines of delegated authority running from centre to circumference are blurred and indistinct – a fact which explains why inquests on mistakes seldom lead to any useful result. In some cases, there is overlapping of authority: for eighteen months I strove to establish the simple rule that one person only should be responsible for sending leader-page articles to the printer, then gave it up as a bad job. In other cases, there is a complete hiatus of authority: for more than two years I have enquired in vain who is responsible for seeing that letters and documents do not accumulate on the desks of absent leader-writers; and more than once I have been compelled to discuss with the management accommodation for new or occasional leader-writers simply because this was, on the editorial side, nobody's concern at all. Far too much of the daily routine is concentrated on the editor, with the result that other important questions are postponed because he has no time, and others no authority, to deal with them. All this lack of system is inimical to smooth and efficient working, and adds quite unfairly to the burden on the editor and his principal collaborators.

The first pre-requisite of any sound administration is that the head of it should be above, but not in, the machine. He should be familiar with the working of all the principal wheels, but it should be no part of his daily duty to turn any of them. The results of failure to observe this rule are conspicuous in the present Government. The Prime Minister's personal preoccupation with the day-to-day conduct of military operations unbalances the whole administrative machine and makes confusion, procrastination and indecision endemic in other parts of it. The contrast with the last war, when Mr Lloyd George kept himself free from day-to-day routine and was thus ready to intervene decisively at any point where delay or deadlock threatened, is glaring. Translated into P.H.S. terms, this means that the Editor should on occasion write a leader, handle the 'letters to the Editor', vet an article or a despatch, and decide on the arrangement of the news, but that he should not habitually, as a matter of routine, do any of these things. Every part of the editorial function should, under the Editor, be the primary responsibility of an assistant editor. The Editor should act personally only on issues of importance, or where failure is apparent or differences of opinion arise, or where the assistant editor refers a matter to him.

Under the Editor, therefore, the linch-pins of the organization should be three active assistant editors (X, Y and Z), each responsible to the Editor for a specific sector of the editorial function. The division between them is obviously arbitrary and would depend in part on the personalities and capacities of those concerned.

Scarcely less essential than the three assistant editors is a responsible Editorial Private Secretary. In any large organization the private secretary of the chief is a key-man in the machine; and his absence is an important cause of present inefficiency at P.H.S. The post is not hard to fill; a modicum of intelligence, a lot of tact, a ready but non-committal pen, a not too shabby old school tie and a bedside telephone manner are the chief requisites. The duties of the EPS are plain and straightforward:

(a) The Editor of *The Times*, like the head of any large organization, is burdened with a host of well-meaning people who, on the strength of a slight personal acquaintance or an official position (MP's, headmasters, bankers, bishops, etc.), inflict on him letters of comment, enquiry, congratulation or expostulation. The credit of the institution requires that they shall be civilly answered. This is the job of the EPS. He will consult an assistant editor, leader-writer or lobby or other correspondent if necessary before replying; but only on the rarest occasions will he find it necessary to bother the Editor himself. It is neither necessary nor desirable that the Editor should reply personally to any of these effusions. A letter signed by the Editor of *The Times* to an outside person ought to be an extreme rarity – almost an event.

(b) The EPS will regulate access to the Editor both in person and on the telephone. No large organization can work efficiently if the head keeps open door. It is quite wrong that a senior member of the staff, wishing to consult the Editor, should have no way of ascertaining whether the Editor is free to see him except by going to the Editor's room to find out – a time-wasting process which may be repeated two or three times before he is successful; it is even less right that, having obtained access, he should not be able to count on ten minutes' consecutive conversation unbroken by the intrusion of some other member of the staff or by a telephone conversation on some routine detail. All this should be managed by the EPS. He will know whom the Editor wants to see, and who is entitled within reasonable limits to see the Editor on request; he will make arrangements accordingly, notify those concerned and while the Editor is engaged prevent interruptions. Except for a few close personal friends, only the assistant editors (who will not abuse the privilege) and perhaps Cabinet Ministers are entitled on their own initiative to be put through on the telephone to the Editor. Other callers should be told that the Editor is not available on the telephone and dealt with by the EPS or referred to an assistant editor or other member of the staff.

One other appointment of major importance and urgency is of what I will call an Editorial Staff Secretary, whose job will be the recruitment of editorial staff. It would probably be desirable that he should work under the direct supervision of a small committee consisting of Editor, Manager and one or more of the assistant editors. For the present and immediate future, the recruitment of staff is a matter of such vital and pressing concern to P.H.S., there is so much lee-way to make up, and conditions are likely to be so difficult and complex, that this is beyond doubt a full-time job for the next few years; after that the merging of this duty with some other job might be reconsidered.

It should also be the duty of the ESS to survey the whole field of journalism in its broadest connotation, to know who are the promising writers, and who is writing what, particularly in fields in which P.H.S. itself is weak. It should not be thought undignified for *The Times* to recruit writers from other papers, daily or weekly; on the contrary, every effort should be made to establish the tradition that to come to *The Times* is a natural promotion for any outstanding writer. What is undignified is to employ inferior writers when better could be found. The same applies to news as to articles. For instance, home news is on the whole at present better handled in the *Daily Telegraph* than in *The Times*. The ESS would know who is doing it and whether he is the sort of person who would be useful at P.H.S.

Other journals and other businesses are already earmarking recruits for after the war. If *The Times* is content merely to wait for something to turn up, what will turn up will be another generation of third- and fourth-rate writers. The first- and second-rate writers will be discovered and secured only by long, arduous and systematic enquiry; and this is not a task that can possibly be performed by busy men in their spare moments. It is a job in itself.

One further question, though not directly one of organization, has some effect on recruitment of staff and may be mentioned here. Professional part-time correspondents who are to some extent necessarily and rightly spokesmen for their professions, may write technical leaders, but should not be allowed to write policy leaders. For example the agricultural or

287

medical correspondent may write a leader on the virtues of carrots or penicillin, but not on agricultural policy or on the relation of the medical profession to the state. Whatever the views expressed, experience shows that it is impossible to eliminate from such leaders a no doubt unconscious note of apologia for the profession, which is perfectly natural but none the less inappropriate in *The Times*. Such leaders should be written by economic and social leader-writers respectively. It is true that Falls [the Military Correspondent] has written some useful leaders in the past on military organization. But this was rendered possible by the fact that the most controversial issues were those arising between the Admiralty and the RAF; and anyhow this is a precedent to be eschewed rather than followed in future. The Diplomatic Correspondent rightly does not contribute to the leader-page. But he also should not be allowed to write disguised letters elsewhere. If he can say that this or that is the view of the Government, or of the Foreign Office, or even of 'official circles', that is news; and the opinion can, if necessary, be criticized in leaders. But to write 'it is widely felt here', or 'it is hoped that', or to discuss the merits and drawbacks of a course of action taken or proposed, is to usurp the function of the leader-writer; such things should be said, if required, in leaders.

Sources

INTRODUCTION

1 P.D., June 1938
2 P.D., 23.vi.38
3 P.D., 26.vi.38
4 P.D., 28.vi.38
5 P.D., 23.11

CHAPTER 1

1 P.D., 8.iv.38

CHAPTER 2

1 B.W.L.
2 *Georgian Adventure*, 1937 by Douglas Jerrold
3 P.D., 11.v.41

CHAPTER 3

1 B.W.L., 1909
2 B.W.L., 1909
3 B.W.L., 12.vi.10
4 B.W.L., 18.iv.11
5 B.W.L., 5.xi.11
6 B.W.L., 23.ii.12
7 B.W.L., October 1912
8 B.W.L., 20.xi.12
9 B.W.L., 19.iii.13
10 B.W.L., 31.vii.13
11 P.D., 28.iv.47
12 B.W.L., August 1913
13 Balliol College Library

CHAPTER 4

1 B.W.L., 5.viii.13
2 *The Times*, 6.viii.13
3 B.W.L., February 1914

CHAPTER 5

1 B.W.L., 11.viii.14
2 B.W.L., 2.vi.15
3 B.W.L., 7.vii.15
4 B.W.L., 3.viii.15
5 B.W.L., April 1916
6 B.W.L., August 1916
7 B.W.L., 13.v.17
8 B.W.L., September 1917
9 B.W.L., 3.iv.18
10 B.W.L., 7.ii.19
11 P.D., October 1918
12 P.D., 29.xi.18
13 P.D., 27.xii.30
14 P.D., 30.x.44

CHAPTER 6

1 B.W.L., 13.i.19
2 B.W.L., March 1919
3 B.W.L., 21.xi.19
4 B.W.P., 7.iv.20
5 P.D., 28.vi.20
6 P.D., 12.vii.20
7 B.W.L., 8.iii.22
8 Lord Riddell: *Intimate Diary of the Peace Conference*, 1933 pp. 339–40
9 P.D., June 1919
10 P.D., August 1920
11 B.W.W., 30.viii.21
12 B.W.W., 2.x.21
13 P.D., 23.ii.22
14 B.W.L., 1924
15 P.D., 19.iii.24
16 P.D., 17.v.24
17 B.W.L., May 1926

CHAPTER 7

1 P.D., 23.vii.26
2 P.D., 14.iii.24
3 B.W.L., 20.ii.26
4 B.W.L., 23.x.24
5 B.W.L., 6.ix.26
6 B.W.L., September 1926
7 P.D., 23.i.47

CHAPTER 9

1 P.D., 11.i.29
2 P.D., 19.iii.29
3 P.D., 22.iii.29
4 P.D., 18.ix.34
5 P.D., 25.x.34
6 Memo. from Nicholas Barker
7 P.D., 15.x.34
8 T.T.A., Letter of 27.x.34

CHAPTER 10

1 P.D., 1.x.35
2 T.T.A., September 1946
3 P.D., 7.iv.39
4 T.T.A., 2.ix.47

CHAPTER 11

1 P.D., 25.x.38
2 P.D., 6.ix.38
3 P.D., 25.ix.38
4 B.W.L., 27.iv.39
5 B.W.L., April 1938
6 T.T.A., 22.ix.36
7 T.T.A., 4.xi.36
8 T.T.A., February 1937
9 T.T.A., 6.iii.37
10 P.D., 6.vii.38
11 T.T.A. 8.ix.51

CHAPTER 12

1 House of Commons Debates, Vol. 5, Ser. 310, Col. 1458
2 *Le Deuxième Bureau au Travail* by Général Gauché, 1953
3 G.D.P., September 1938
4 P.D., 8.iii. 36
5 Memo. from Arthur Barker, 1969

6 P.D., 10.iii.36
7 *The Times*, 9.iii.36
8 *The Times*, 10.iii.36
9 T.T.A., 24.iii.36
10 P.D., 10.iii.36
11 P.D., 11.iii.36
12 P.D., 20.iii.36
13 P.D., 7.iv.36
14 P.D., 2.v.36
15 *The Times*, 4.v.36
16 T.T.A., October 1935
17 P.D., 5.vi.63
18 P.D., 5.vi.36
19 P.D., 3.vi.36
20 P.D., 4.vi.36
21 P.D., 6.vi.36
22 P.D., 19.vi.36
23 T.T.A., 29.v.35
24 T.T.A., 20.v.35
25 P.D., 27.vii.36
26 G.D.P., 4.ix.36
27 P.D., 25.ix.36
28 P.D., 17.ix.36
29 P.D., 23.ix.36
30 P.D., 18.xii.36
31 P.D., 14.i.36
32 Memo. from Arthur Barker, 1969

CHAPTER 13

1 T.T.A., 23.v.37
2 T.T.A., 16.v.37
3 T.T.A., 5.v.46
4 T.T.A., October 1912
5 P.D., 28.v.37
6 P.D., August 1937

CHAPTER 14

1 P.D., 21.ii.38
2 P.D., 1.iv.38
3 P.D., 25.v.38
4 P.D., 28.ix.38
5 P.D., 19.xi.38
6 T.T.A., 2.x.38
7 P.D., 24.xi.38
8 *The Times*, 23.ix.38
9 *The Times*, 29.ix.38
10 P.D., 6.viii.38

11 P.D., 7.ix.38
12 B.W.L., 7.ix.38
13 P.D., 9.ix.38
14 P.D., 17.iii.38
15 P.D., 11.iii.38
16 P.D., 14.iii.38
17 T.T., 25.iii.38
18 T.T.A., 7.x.38

CHAPTER 15

1 P.D., 26.xi.34
2 Liddell Hart, *Memoirs,* Vol. II,
   pp. 148–9
3 B.W.L., 8.xi.38
4 P.D., 2.x.39
5 B.W.L., 18.ix.35
6 B.W.L., 19.xi.35
7 P.D., 2.x.35
8 P.D., 9.xii.35
9 P.D., 12.xii.35
10 *The Times*, 16.xii.35
11 P.D., 21.xii.35
12 P.D., 22.xii.35

CHAPTER 16

1 P.D., 15.iii.39
2 *The Nemesis of Power*, by
   John Wheeler Bennett, 1953,
   p. 406

CHAPTER 17

1 P.D., 1.x.41
2 P.D., 18.v.39
3 P.D., 26.iv.39
4 *History of The Times,* Vol. IV,
   p. 964
5 P.D., 8.vii.36
6 Brand Papers, 18.vii.36
7 P.D., 5.v.41
8 P.D., 17.vii.41
9 Reith Papers, 1941
10 P.D., 24.vii.41
11 P.D., 31.x.41
12 Lord Reith to author, 1968
13 P.D., 7.xi.44
14 Mrs Sylvia Crabtree, 1970

CHAPTER 18

1 P.D., 4.vii.39
2 P.D., 8.ii.40
3 P.D., 20.viii.40
4 P.D., 11.vii.40
5 P.D., 18.ii.41
6 P.D., 26.xi.41
7 P.D., 1.xii.41
8 P.D., 22.i.42
9 P.D., 19.xi.42
10 P.D., 12.ii.42
11 P.D., 15.ii.42
12 P.D., 19.ii.42
13 T.T.A., 26.ii.42
14 P.D., 18.iii.42
15 P.D., 30.iii.42
16 P.D., 14.iv.42
17 T.T.A., 17.iv.42
18 T.T.A., 22.iv.42
19 P.D., 23.iv.42
20 P.D., 2.vii.42
21 P.D., 23.vii.42
22 P.D., 24.vii.42
23 P.D., 31.vii.42
24 P.D., 11.viii.42
25 P.D., 11.ix.42
26 P.D., 2.x.42
27 P.D., 2.x.42
28 P.D., 20.xi.42
29 P.D., 4.xi.42
30 P.D., 31.xii.42
31 P.D., 21.xii.43
32 P.D., 29.iii.43
33 P.D., 30.vi.43
34 P.D., 27.ix.43
35 P.D., 30.xi.43
36 P.D., 1.vii.45
37 P.D., 4.vii.45
38 P.D., 8.viii.45
39 P.D., 21.i.47
40 P.D., 4.xii.46
41 P.D., 13.xii.46

CHAPTER 19

1 T.T.A., 26.ii.37
2 P.D., 13.ii.40
3 P.D., 30.x.40
4 P.D., 25.vii.40

5 P.D., 31.vii.40
6 P.D., 13.ii.41
7 E. H. Carr to author, 1969
8 P.D., 18.iii.41
9 P.D., 4.vi.41
10 P.D., 29.vii.41
11 Douglas Woodruff to author, 1970

CHAPTER 20

1 P.D., 31.xii.37
2 P.D., 6.viii.28
3 P.D., 20.ix.38
4 P.D., 13.ii.30
5 P.D., 11.iv.46
6 P.D., 20.ii.46
7 P.D., 14.x.46
8 P.D., 18.vii.39
9 P.D., 23.vi.37
10 PD., 28.v.38
11 P.D., 2.ii.39
12 P.D., 16.ix.40
13 P.D., 16.v.36

CHAPTER 21

1 P.D., 5.v.41
2 B.W.L., May 1943
3 P.D., 1.i.45
4 P.D., 19.x.45
5 P.D., 7.viii.45
6 P.D., 30.iii.44
7 P.D., 20.iv.44
8 P.D., 31.v.44
9 P.D., 25.iv.46

10. P.D., 9.v.46
11 E. H. Carr to author, 1969
12 P.D., 23.v.46
13 P.D., 24.iv.46
14 P.D., 16.ii.45
15 P.D., 29.vii.46

CHAPTER 22

1 P.D., 18.i.45
2 T.T.A., 1.i.45
3 T.T.A., 1945
4 P.D., 22.xii.44
5 P.D., 6.ii.46

CHAPTER 23

1 P.D., 15.v.46
2 P.D., 4.ix.46
3 P.D., 5.vi.46
4 P.D., 28.v.46

CHAPTER 24

1 P.D., 6.v.47
2 P.D., 1.ix.47
3 T.T.A., 2.ix.47
4 P.D., 23.ii.47
5 B.W.L., March 1948
6 T.T. House Journal, April 1948

APPENDIX II

1 P.D., 11 March 1946

APPENDIX IV

Memorandum lent by E. H. Carr.

Index

Owing to limitations of space, it has not been possible to include all the indexable items.

The entry under **Barrington-Ward, Robert**, has been confined to those subheadings which cannot be readily found under other headings. Apart from that heading, his name is throughout the Index abbreviated to B-W. Similarly, Sir Winston Churchill is referred to as WSC, and Geoffrey Dawson as GD; *The Times* becomes *TT;* 'q.' stands for 'quoted', and 'n.' for 'footnote'.

Page reference numbers in **bold type** indicate that more than a line or two are devoted to the item in the text. Reference numbers in *italics* denote illustrations or their captions.

The alphabetical arrangement of headings is word-by-word. The subheadings are arranged mainly in chronological order.